GUNNAR
LANDTMAN
IN PAPUA

GUNNAR LANDTMAN

IN PAPUA

1910 to 1912

DAVID LAWRENCE
with assistance from Pirjo Varjola

ANU
THE AUSTRALIAN NATIONAL UNIVERSITY

E PRESS

ANU

E PRESS

Published by ANU E Press
The Australian National University
Canberra ACT 0200, Australia
Email: anuepress@anu.edu.au
This title is also available online at: http://epress.anu.edu.au/gunnar_citation.html

National Library of Australia
Cataloguing-in-Publication entry

Author:	Lawrence, David (David Russell)
Title:	Gunnar Landtman in Papua : 1910 to 1912 / David Lawrence.
ISBN:	9781921666124 (pbk.) 9781921666131 (pdf)
Notes:	Includes index. Bibliography.
Subjects:	Landtman, Gunnar, 1878-1940--Journeys--Papua New Guinea--Fly River Region. Landtman, Gunnar, 1878-1940--Journeys--Queensland--Torres Straits Islands. Kiwai (Papua New Guinea people)--Social life and customs.
Dewey Number:	572.9952

Cover design and layout by ANU E Press

Cover image: Gunnar Landtman interviewing Namai at Mawatta (VKK248_500)

Contents

Acknowledgements vii

Preface ix

Chapter 1: Papua: the 'unknown' 1

Chapter 2: Impressions and reflections 19

Chapter 3: Imaging the Kiwai 63

Chapter 4: Collecting and documenting the Kiwai 131

Conclusion: A witness to change 173

Bibliography of writings on the Kiwai by Gunnar Landtman 179

References 185

Index 201

Acknowledgements

I have been privileged to have been given an opportunity to work on the Gunnar Landtman collections in the National Museum of Finland and in the Museum of Cultures, Helsinki. My greatest thanks goes to Pirjo Varjola. Not only did she arrange from me to have a short-term scholarship over a freezing winter long ago in 1986–87 but she encouraged my ongoing research on the Kiwai people of Papua New Guinea. She also translated, from rather formal Swedish, an old copy of Landtman's travelogue, *Nya Guinea färden*, for this book.

The staff of the museum libraries, archives and collection storerooms in Finland have also been encouraging, supportive and interested in my work. I am more than grateful for the help given by Eija-Maija Kotilainen, Marja-Leena Hanninen and Heli Lahdentausta. I gratefully acknowledge the assistance of Sirkku Dölle and the staff of the Archives for Prints and Photographs of the National Board of Antiquities.

At the Australian National University, Dr Stewart Firth and the members of the Pacific History Board have been instrumental in having this work published. Dr Michael Young made many useful comments to early drafts and gave me much needed guidance. Financial assistance has also been received, with thanks, from Dr Colin Filer from the Resource Management in Asia Pacific program in the Research School of Pacific and Asian Studies of the College of Asia and the Pacific. This assistance made possible the publication of the numerous photographs that make Landtman's story so interesting.

My greatest thanks must go to the late Gunnar Landtman. He was a careful and meticulous collector, researcher and cataloguer. His photograph and artefact collections and his published and unpublished writings have made research into his expedition a fulfilling and challenging one. I only hope he would be pleased with the result.

My family has always encouraged my scholarship and sometimes wild adventures in the pursuit of research. They may not realise just how grateful I am for this support

This book is dedicated to the Kiwai people, especially those of Kadawa village near Daru who encouraged my work. We had many, many good times and only a very few difficult ones. To my Bala (brother) Nanu Mose and his wife Eleni: this is for you with my love.

David Lawrence

Preface

In his introduction to Gunnar Landtman's book *The Kiwai Papuans of British New Guinea* (Landtman 1927: ix), Alfred Cort Haddon wrote: 'Many years ago my friend, Dr Gunnar Landtman, came to see me at Cambridge, and as soon as we had greeted one another, he said, "I will go anywhere in the world you like to send me", which was rather a startling method of opening a discussion on a suitable field for ethnographical research'. Landtman's own perspective on this important meeting was a little more poetic when he wrote:

> One Sunday morning in January 1910 the many Gothic towers and tops of Cambridge offered an unusual sight by being covered with snow that had fallen during the night. This shining apparition disappeared during the day; the melting drops of snow were already glistening in the grass and the twitter of larks and chaffinches, the busying of the starlings conjured up the early feelings of spring, which in England can make itself known already during this early month. I shall remember this day particularly because it was then that, during a walk out from this venerable town of learning in the company of Doctor A.C. Haddon, the first plans were made for my exploration expedition to New Guinea (Landtman 1913b: 1. Translated from the Swedish by Pirjo Varjola).

These opening remarks, both poetic and prosaic, were to land Landtman on the southwest coast of Papua in 1910 where he was to remain, apart from various trips to the Torres Strait, until 1912.

This meeting was to be rewarding for both parties. Haddon would find Landtman a willing and productive researcher who would document the life and culture of the Kiwai of the southwest coast of Papua. This would fill in many gaps in Haddon's own work in the region. For Landtman, Haddon became a valuable mentor and guide who would introduce the young Finnish scholar into the wider world of British ethnology.

In those two years in Papua Landtman managed to cross the Torres Strait, visit many of the islands in the Fly estuary, travel overland and by canoe through the vast wetlands of the Aramia River floodplains and venture briefly as far as Goaribari Island in the Gulf District. In addition to his notes and manuscript that he eventually published, he recorded nearly 500 legends and stories, actually over 900 counting variants (Landtman 1917). This collection has been called 'probably the most extensive collection of Melanesian mythology ever published' (Wagner 1996: 288). Landtman also obtained a collection of over 1300 artefacts for the National Museum of Finland (*Suomen Kansallismuseo*) (NMF VK 4902)(Landtman 1933) and made a duplicate collection of nearly 700 objects for the then Cambridge Museum of Archaeology and Ethnology [now the Cambridge Museum of Archaeology and Anthropology] and took 572 photographs, also held by the National Museum of Finland (Landtman VKK 248). In addition, he made 38 phonograph recordings of Kiwai and Bine songs and dances (Landtman VK 4919). These rare photographs and phonograph recordings can now be seen to be objects of material culture in their own right.

Figure 1. Gunnar Landtman in Papua outfitted in style from the Army and Navy Stores, London, one of the main clothing suppliers to colonial officials and their families (VKK 248: 556)

While many of those photographs have been published in the more than 20 books and papers Landtman wrote on the Kiwai Papuans, the quality of the images has always been poor. Landtman used the same photographs in many of the publications. In his review of Landtman's catalogue of the artefacts now held in the National Museum of Finland, Albert Lewis of the Field Museum of Natural History in Chicago stated: 'Unfortunately, these so called plates [the half tone reproductions of the field photographs and the museum artefacts] are rather small. Two, and sometimes even three, may be placed on one page, making it impossible to see much detail'. Lewis complained that the photographs in the catalogue were the same as the ones in the main text published earlier (Landtman 1927) and: 'It is to be regretted that the illustrations, particularly the plates, could not have been reproduced on a larger scale' (Lewis 1934). These criticisms were rather churlish considering the limited resources available to Landtman to publish the catalogue at that time. Now, with digital technology and high resolution scanning, the images can be enhanced and reprinted.

But there are other reasons for re-printing the photographs. While much of the old way of life in the Fly estuary and the Daru coast has changed, cultural themes endure even in the face of modernisation. The past decades have seen enormous changes to lifestyles in the Fly River region. The last men's house (*darimo*) and the last communal longhouse (*moto*) are now only memories of the old people. Even the large double-outrigger canoe, the *motomoto*, is rapidly being replaced by fiberglass outboard motorboats (locally known as 'banana boats' by their shape). However, aspects of ritual, dance and ceremony do remain. While the old shark-mouthed, traditional drums (*warupa*) have been replaced by more cylindrical, overpainted wooden drums (*buruburu*), the dugong harpoon (*wapo*), dance headdresses (*dori*) and even old time dances and songs have not been replaced as there are no modern substitutes for these cultural identifiers. Women continue to make fine pandanus mats (*hawa*) for the floors and strong coconut leaf baskets (*sito*) for domestic use. Kiwai village houses are still made from mangrove timbers, black palm flooring and nipa palm walls and roofs. Iron sheeting may be a practical way of collecting much needed drinking water but the volatile nature of the wind and rain along the coast means that houses made from bush materials can be readily 'broken down' and rebuilt further inland on new sites. This is a process as old as the Kiwai stories of population movements and migrations.

Most Kiwai men are still predominantly subsistence fishermen but the overharvesting of dugong and turtle in the face of general rural poverty is a significant ecological and cultural problem. Dugong and turtle were formerly foods for celebrations and church festivals, now the meat is more often sold at the local markets. The seas and reefs off the southwestern coast of Papua are rich in marine life: along the coast fishermen can catch mullet, barramundi, prawns and crabs. On the coral reefs, rock lobsters, many pelagic fish and mackerel are common and in the rivers and swamps inland are crocodiles, wild pigs, Rusa deer and wallaby. Access to these resources requires permission from the landowners and money for motor fuel. While the rich sea life could provide work and incomes for coastal villagers, the lack of markets and poor transportation and infrastructure will always handicap the marginalised subsistence fishermen. Consequently, women must still labour in the swamps to extract the starch from the wild sago palms (*Metroxylon* sp).

Standards of health and education are low. In an attempt to find paid employment young men and women leave the region and move to the towns and cities. There is no welfare system in Papua New Guinea and often the urban poor are even more disenfranchised than the rural poor who still have access to some gardening land and fishing grounds. Crime and poverty are major social problems in Daru. The village was once safe from the problems facing urban life in Papua New Guinea but now even the villages are beset by alcohol, drugs and domestic violence. Change has come rapidly for the Kiwai. In the face of that upheaval it is good to reflect on the past.

In Landtman and Haddon's time, the life of coastal Papuan peoples was seen to be static and viewed in terms of the traditional past rather than the negotiated present. British ethnology, at the turn of the 20th Century, was strongly influenced by the scholarly, but largely theoretical, diachronic modes of analysis undertaken by E B. Tylor and J. G. Frazer. Although Tylor had formulated one of the most significant definitions of culture: the complex whole that includes beliefs, arts, morals, laws, customs and habits acquired by humankind as members of society, their ideas assumed a Victorian idea of linear progress from savagery to reason. The many small, fragmented Papuan societies were seen as culturally 'primitive' and most European settlers at that time had only superficial understanding of the peoples who lived around them. Even government patrol officers had a poor understanding of the complex social, cultural, spiritual and political environment of 'native' communities.

Papuan societies had never been the static backward groups that colonial officers, settlers, traders and missionaries liked to believe. They had always existed between the ebb and flow of population migrations and local movements, warfare, marriage and trade contacts and ceremonial exchange systems (Schieffelin and Crittenden 1991: 27). Local cultures grow, expand, contract, create and reinvent (Fitzpatrick 1991: 336). Melanesia is a diverse, exciting and often challenging part of the world: there are over 750 Papuan (non-Austronesian) languages and 400 Austronesian languages still spoken there. This constitutes about 25 per cent of the world's 4000 languages (Knauft 1999: 1). Haddon and Landtman would no doubt be surprised to see the resilience of Melanesian societies today.

Haddon's approach to ethnographic fieldwork was 'the saving of vanished knowledge' (Barham, Rowland and Hitchcock 2004: 59). Now this concept may be reinterpreted as the conservation and management of archaeological sites, ethnographic collections and historical photographs. Landtman's photographs may now be as strange and foreign to the Kiwai as they are to us. However, the Fly estuary and southwest coast of Papua is still full of legends and stories and many of the places depicted in Landtman's photographs continue to be the subjects of those stories that are told even today (Landtman 1917; Lawrence 1994).

The aims of this book are both personal and professional. Using the remaining correspondence to family, friends, colleagues and contacts it is possible to describe something of Landtman's personal journey of discovery in Papua. The Landtman collection of Kiwai material culture is the largest and best documented collection in the world. His collections are worthy of further study. By reproducing some of his photographs we can see the Kiwai as he saw them for the photographs are a reflection of the photographer's eye as much as the subject, and at a time of great change in the region, they show the natural grace and humanity of the people. This has not changed. The purpose of this book is to re-examine the diverse Landtman collections in light of broader research undertaken in the Torres Strait and south Fly in recent years. New approaches are needed that re-contextualise the Landtman and Haddon collections, perhaps the most innovative being the place of small-scale societies in the political ecology of borderlands (Hitchcock 2004).

The authors of this book have had a long history of contact with the Landtman collections. David Lawrence first began studying the Landtman material as a doctoral student researching customary exchange across the Torres Strait (Lawrence 1994). He was given a scholarship to study the Landtman collections by the Finnish Ministry of Education in 1986 and 1987. This enabled him to study the Kiwai collections in the National Museum of Finland. He was also fortunate to be able to spend two years of fieldwork in the Fly estuary region where he visited nearly all the communities described by Gunnar Landtman. Lawrence's family connections with Melanesia are strong for he grew up in Papua New Guinea and his great-grandfather was one of the main labour recruiters based in Daru at the time of Landtman's fieldwork. He continues to work in Melanesia. Piro Varjola was Senior Curator of the Foreign Ethnographic Collections at the National Museum of Finland and her team made the first, more comprehensive exhibition from the Landtman collection in 1987. This exhibition was then transferred to the Craft Museum of Finland (*Suomen kotiteollisuusmuseo*) in Jyväkylä where it was displayed between 1987 and 1988. It was then displayed in the Castle of Hämeenlinna until 1989. Pirjo Varjola was the Director of the Museum of Cultures (*Kulttuurien museo*) in Helsinki where a second, major exhibition of the Landtman material was created in 2001 (Lahdentausta, Parpola, Vainonen and Varjola 2001).

This book is designed to appeal to those who are keen to understand the dynamic nature of Kiwai culture. Despite poverty and neglect the Kiwai are a strong and vibrant people. They have a long tradition of work in the marine industries of the Torres Strait but their geographical position on the northern shores of Torres Strait mean that their health, welfare and standard of living are topics that should be better known and examined by the general Australian population. Regrettably their current social, economic and political problems are marginal to both Papua New Guinea and Australia. Landtman's research is still a foundation stone for understanding the position of the Kiwai today.

The Landtman collections may appear strange and exotic when viewed on display in the national museum of a prosperous Nordic society but for those Kiwai who have never seen the material, they can link the present with the past. This book seeks to be a bridge between these two worlds.

Chapter 1
Papua: the 'unknown'

Although the title of his landmark study was *The Kiwai Papuans of British New Guinea* (Landtman 1927), the southeastern part of the island of New Guinea officially became Papua in 1906 when administrative responsibility for the colony passed from the Colonial Office in London to the Commonwealth Government of the newly federated Australia. The Western Division of Papua where Landtman undertook his research between 1910 and 1912 was administrated from a small colonial outpost on the offshore island of Daru. Although the region is now the Western Province of Papua New Guinea, Daru remains the administrative centre for the vast, largely undeveloped tracts of savannah lowlands, riverine plains and mountains between the Torres Strait, in the south, to the Star Mountains at the western end of the New Guinea Highlands, in the north.

A geographical perspective

Geographically, the Torres Strait and Fly estuary region where Landtman chose to work is extremely varied. Papua New Guinea's longest river, the Fly River, and the largest lake, Lake Murray, are both in this province and the Fly River effectively divides the region in two. South of the Fly is the Oriomo Plateau, a generally featureless undulating ridge bordered in the north by the middle Fly and in the south by a narrow coastal plain. Soils on the coastal plain are poor, mostly clay, and easily become water-logged. This narrow coastal plain is often only three kilometers wide and three metres above mean sea level. The coast is fringed by mangroves and littoral woodlands but along the Oriomo ridge and inland away from the coastal swamps and rivers are some areas of good gardening land. To the local people this inland coastal plain and savannah country was known as Daudai.

In the Torres Strait there are more than 100 islands, islets, coral cays and reefs lying between 9°20′ and 10°45′S latitude and 141°15′ and 144°20′E longitude. However, only 16 are presently inhabited although use of the uninhabited islands, either permanently or temporarily, has occurred during recent times. The high, granitic islands in the west are an extension of the Cape York–Oriomo Ridge but the central islands are mostly low, sandy, coral cays. The eastern islands are fertile, basaltic islands of recent volcanic origin with patches of good vegetation. In the north, along the southwest coast of Papua are Saibai and Boigu Islands composed of low mangrove mud and peats overlying coralline platforms. Close to the western end of Saibai is another small granitic island, Dauan.

The only hill on the southwest coast of Papua, at Mabudawan (59 metres), is the highest point on the long exposed coast. For this reason, Mabudawan remains an important cultural site for coastal people of the region. This southwest, or Daru, coast extends from Parama Island in the east to the entrance of the Mai Kussa inlet, opposite Boigu Island. The wide triangular Fly estuary extends from Parama in the south to Dibiri Island in the northeast and to Sumogi Island at the entrance to the Fly River itself. In this swampy, very muddy and hot estuary there are about 40 islands and a number of tidal islets. The Fly estuary covers a vast area of 7100 square kilometres between 8° and 8°15′S latitude and between 143° and 143°45′E longitude. The entrance from Parama to Dibiri is 80 kilometres wide. The largest island in the estuary, Kiwai Island [Iasa Ura], is 60 kilometres in length and varies between five and 10 kilometres in width. However, the average water depth in the narrow channels of the estuary is only about eight metres and passages between islands are usually long and shallow with rapidly changing sandbanks. They can be very dangerous for at times of full moon a tidal bore can swamp small boats and inundate coastal villages.[

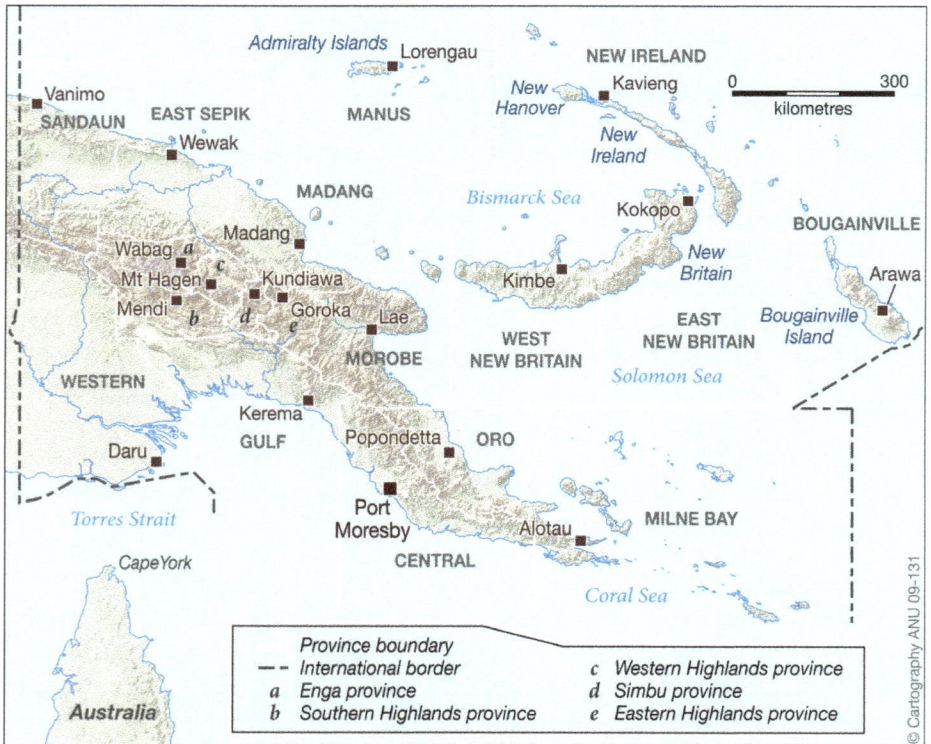

Map 1. Papua New Guinea

(Cartographic-GIS Services, College of Asia and the Pacific, ANU, 2009))

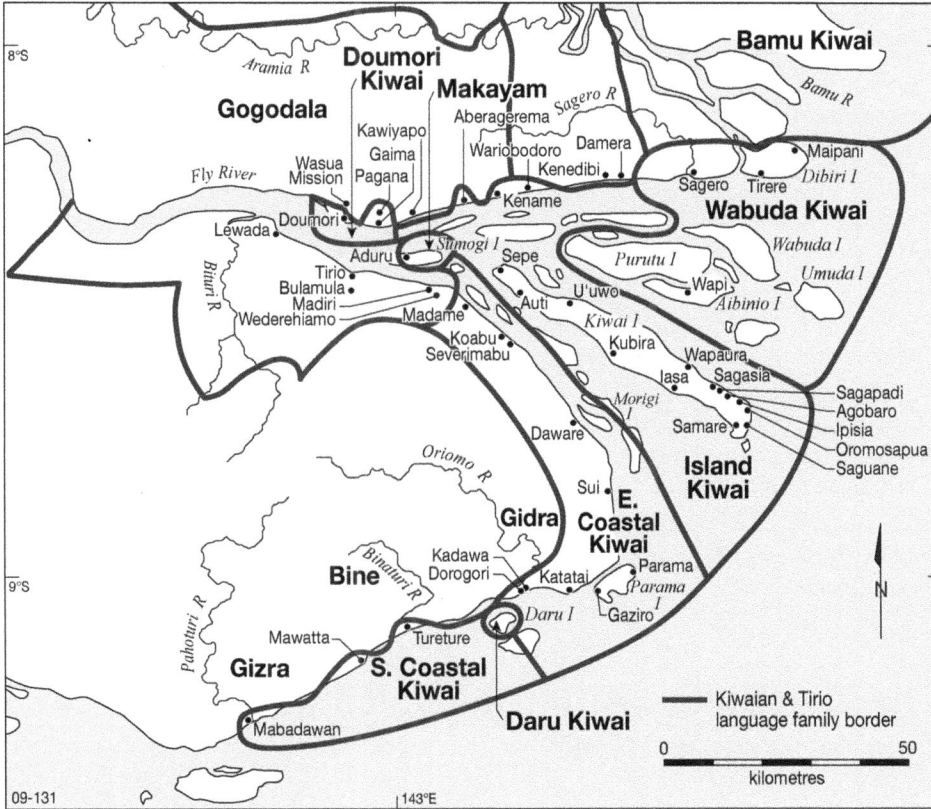

Map 2. Kiwai Area map (Burton and Lawrence 2009)

The People

Kiwai Island is the original home of the Kiwai-speaking people, some of whom have moved to live along the northern (Manowetti) bank and also on the western (Dudi) bank of the Fly estuary. The Kiwai who live along the southwest coast build their homes in a line along the narrow sandy foreshore between the sea and the coastal swamps and grasslands. From this coast they have unlimited access to the waters of the Torres Strait. In nearly all Kiwai communities the principal diet is fish, sago, bananas and some vegetables grown on the coastal strand. The coastal Kiwai are a sea people whose 'lands' are the offshore reefs and sand cays of the northern Torres Strait. They are the descendants of the island Kiwai who long ago moved out from their homelands on Kiwai Island.

Other inland people live along the narrow muddy rivers and creeks that intersect the coast and access to these widely spaced communities can only be affected by walking or by small canoe. The Gidra people, who speak Wipi language, live predominantly along the Oriomo River opposite Daru Island, west of Parama Island and behind the Kiwai communities of Katatai and Kadawa. Gidra is a Bine term for bush people. The Bine inhabit the coastal swamp and savannah country along the reaches of the Binaturi River and behind the Kiwai villages of Mawatta and Turituri. Further west the Gizra live along the Pahoturi River behind the Kiwai village of Mabudawan and west of the Pahotrui River are the lands of the Agob people. These inland people are primarily subsistence horticulturalists. Trade between coastal and inland villages continues to be important for access to resources, food and the maintenance of good relationships between small isolated communities. The Kiwai are marine hunters and their place, wedged between the sea and the coastal brackish swamps, is a tenuous one. Villages are largely self-sufficient for the Western Province remains one of the most underdeveloped regions of Papua New Guinea, itself a country struggling even now with social, economic and cultural problems in a politically turbulent part of the world.

The Cambridge Anthropological Expedition to Torres Straits 1898

In 1910, when Landtman went to study the social and cultural life of the Kiwai, the area was largely unknown to outsiders apart from a few missionaries who were mostly Samoan pastors, a few traders and labour recruiters, some plantation owners and the government officials stationed at Daru. At that time the social and cultural life of the Torres Strait Islanders was being compiled by Haddon and his associates, William H. R. Rivers, Charles Myers, Charles Seligman [originally Seligmann], Sidney Ray, Anthony Wilkin and William McDougall, who had comprised the members of the Cambridge Anthropological Expedition to Torres Straits in 1898 (Herle and Rouse 1998). Myers and McDougall were students of Rivers and Seligman was a colleague of Myers. This multi-disciplinary expedition has been considered a 'watershed' in British anthropology (Urry 1984: 98). During the Torres Strait expedition, Rivers formulated the principles behind the 'genealogical method' of cultural research. Rivers and the team found that in psychological tests the Torres Strait Islanders were equal to Cambridge undergraduates and in eyesight testing, they surpassed the students. Results which went against perceived wisdom of the time. In the Torres Strait, Rivers made an 'unprecedented scientific achievement: the creation of a psychological laboratory in the field' (Kuklick 1996: 620).

Even so, the team of Cambridge researchers only spent one year in Torres Strait, Papua and Borneo. In fact some members of the party only spent five weeks on the western islands of Mabuiag and Saibai and about four to five months on the eastern island of Mer. While the reports of the expedition remain a seminal work in Torres Strait studies, Haddon and his team did not make the break from the evolutionary methodology that dominated anthropology at that time (Mullins 1996: 349–50). Although the works are largely empirical the Cambridge Expedition is credited with establishing some of the philosophical bases for the ethnographic method (Herle and Rouse 1998). For Haddon, whose research background was in zoology, scientific analysis required direct observation. However, long-term fieldwork in a study area would be perfected by others, among them Gunnar Landtman.

The six volumes of the Reports of the Cambridge Expedition to Torres Strait were to be published over 35 years (Haddon 1901/03–1935). By 1910 four volumes, Volume II on physiology and psychology (1901–03), Volume V on the sociology, magic and religion of the Western Islanders (1904), Volume III by Sidney Ray on language (1907), and Volume VI on the sociology, magic and religion of the Eastern Islanders (1908) had been published. Landtman would have had access to these important sources before he sailed to Papua. His discussions with Haddon in Cambridge would certainly have given him a strong grounding in the social, cultural and religious aspects of Torres Strait Islander life. Volume IV on arts and crafts (1912) and the summary Volume I on general ethnography (1935) were yet to be published as Haddon was continually adding material to his original sources from correspondence that he maintained with many people resident in the region. Haddon had strong personal reasons for sending Landtman to Papua: he wanted more information on the cultures of the people of the northern coast of the Torres Strait, areas that he had only briefly visited. Haddon needed more information on his significant discovery that small isolated communities did not contain an undifferentiated mass of unthinking conservatives but that society was highly complex, people differed widely from each other in character and temperament and exhibited considerable differences of opinion (Kuklick 1996: 620).

Haddon's unpublished journals of his two trips to Torres Strait, the first in 1888 and the second with the Cambridge Expedition (Haddon 1888 and 1898) record his growing interest in Melanesia and his disappointment that the affinities of cultures across the Torres Strait remained largely unknown despite European contact. Haddon, like his contemporaries, was drawn to ethnology by a belief that cultures had to be studied and documented before 'all traces of their primitive ways of life were lost' (Quiggin and Fegan 1940: 98). The Cambridge expedition was planned along the lines of earlier natural history expedition although Haddon, Seligman and Rivers brought a new sense of importance to

5

the collection of data and an emphasis on methodology and research (Urry 1972: 50). It also became apparent that traditional societies defied analysis by large survey teams. It was Rivers who later developed the methodology that a lone, generalist ethnologist should live for a year or more among a community of perhaps 400–500 people marked off from surrounding peoples. This ethnologist should ideally learn the vernacular language and develop close relationships with the community in order to gain access to every feature of social and cultural life (Kuklick 1996: 623). However the communities and cultures of the Torres Strait and south Fly region did not live in isolation from each other. Here the local people were the inheritors and elaborators of a similar Melanesian maritime culture that included clan and totemic allegiance, long-distance trading, warfare and marriage alliances, a common technology, a complex web of magic and stories with adapted social and cultural solutions to the problems of a comparatively resource-poor terrestrial environment and a resource-rich marine one (Shnukal 2004: 327).

In addition to the reports of the expedition of 1898, Haddon had written papers on the ethnography of the Western Torres Strait Islanders (Haddon 1890a), legends of the Torres Strait Islanders (1890b and c), the decorative art of the Papuans (Haddon 1894), the classification of stone clubs (Haddon 1900a) and a study in the anthropogeography of British New Guinea (Haddon 1900b and c). Haddon's expedition to the Torres Strait marked a break between the amateur and the antiquarian interests in exotic cultures and the development of professional anthropology. But Haddon also stressed the importance of museums, arranged on scientific lines, to illustrate and supplement anthropological teaching, and he acted as Deputy Curator of the Cambridge Museum many times and later donated over 10,000 photographs and his personal papers to the collection. Haddon was concerned with the lack of interest in the ethnology of the Torres Strait Islanders at a time when communicable diseases like influenza and the measles were having a devastating impact on small communities in the region (Haddon 1890a). He wrote a more popular account of the expedition to the Torres Strait, Papua and Borneo and titled it: *Headhunters: black, white and brown* (Haddon 1901).

Haddon was making his life's work the study of Melanesian anthropology. He was well aware that his observations in the Torres Strait had been made 30 to 40 years after major demographic and social impacts had taken place (Barham, Rowland and Hitchcock 2004: 3) and was keen that the Kiwai coast should be comprehensively surveyed for he wrote: 'when we turn to the western division of British New Guinea we find quite a different state of affairs [from understanding cultures and customs of the peoples]: nothing, however, is known of the greater part of the district' (Haddon 1900b: 269). For Landtman, Haddon was an important professional contact and mentor. Haddon no doubt saw in Landtman a keen, able and enthusiastic candidate for testing newly developed theories on the nature of cultural contact and social change along the Daru coast. However, Haddon's scientific studies of art, artefacts and cultures remained grounded in his intellectual models of comparison based on natural science. Local meanings and ethnographic context were of little value to him (Busse 2005: 447). While Landtman's ethnography may seem old-fashioned today, his grounding was in a different intellectual tradition: the folkloric, linguistic and ethnic heritage of the pre-Christian Swedish and Finno–Ugric (Uralic) peoples of the Scandinavian and Nordic countries. Still, it is little wonder that someone as open and eager as Landtman should soon find himself on a boat to Papua for, as he wrote: 'My field of research linked up with that of the Cambridge Anthropological Expedition to Torres Straits of 1898, as it was Dr A. C. Haddon who suggested it [studying the Kiwai] to me' (Landtman 1927: v).

Edvard Westermarck and ethnological traditions in Finland

Landtman was introduced to Haddon through a mutual association with the sociologist Edvard Westermarck who made several study tours to Morocco from 1897 and spent two years there from 1900 to 1902. Long term fieldwork was already part of intellectual tradition in Finland. Westermarck had been appointed to the chair of Professor of Practical Philosophy at the University of Helsinki in 1906 [then still officially known as the Imperial Aleksander University] and was also Professor of Sociology at the University of London from 1907. Unlike many of his fellow academicians who studied in Germany, Westermarck studied in England and was attracted by the empiricism of the British sociologists as opposed to the idealism of the German Rationalists (Vuorela 1977: 60). His methodological basis for research focused on experience and the comparative approach in which social phenomena were examined from many elements collected from primary research among 'primitive' peoples.

Westermarck was essentially an evolutionist and his philosophy following on from the theories of Herbert Spencer that dealt with the evolution of language, literature, science, art and forms of government. Spencer had an assistant search travel literature of the period for evidence of the customs of primitive, uncivilised peoples that he tabulated in a series of volumes called *Descriptive Sociology* (Spencer 1873–81) to provide him with data to support the theory that all human history was a history of social progress. This Victorian idea of the unilineal progress of human kind meant also that British empiricism was not far removed from positivism that said that all proper knowledge was derived from and supported by the scientific method: ideas that were germinated in the natural sciences. It was this empiricism that attracted Haddon and he continued to use data supplied by correspondents in the compilation of the Reports of the Cambridge Anthropological Expedition to Torres Straits (Haddon 1901–35). However, Westermarck found that data collected by amateur travelers, colonial officials and missionaries were unsatisfactory and so his long career in Morocco was spent personally studying the religious and moral concepts of the local Arab and Berber peoples.

Westermarck actively promoted this model of long term fieldwork in small communities to his students. He also introduced British evolutional anthropology and sociology into Finnish academic circles and sponsored the study of non-European cultures to his students like Landtman. Westermarck, and his students like Karsten and Landtman, were from a core group of Swedish-speaking liberal academics in Finland active at a time when a national revival era was encouraging the collection and study of oral traditions. The absorption of Finland into the Russian empire following the Napoleonic Wars stimulated the development of a strong nationalist identity grounded in the Finnish language. Folklore was to be the basis of this national patriotism and the native language the 'only true organ of expression of the national culture' (Vuorela 1977: 16). Centuries of Swedish rule had also influenced Finnish identity. At the beginning of the 20th Century, about 12 per cent of the population of Finland spoke Swedish as their mother tongue and even under Russian rule this minority continued to hold important political and economic roles. Swedish was the language used by the government, most civil servants and the clergy. Finnish-speaking country folk often had no surname but were given one, in Swedish, when they were sent to school or joined the army. The Swedish-speaking minority varied from being coastal fishers to factory owners, from civil servants to high ranked nobility and since the early 1880s had their own political party, the *Svenska folkpartiet i Finland* (The Swedish People's Party). Their driving force in society later guaranteed them linguistic rights after Finland was declared a bilingual state in 1919.

The national epic, the *Kalevala*, had been first published by the physician Elias Lönnrot in 1835 who had undertaken extensive fieldwork in Karelia collecting folk poetry and songs. Lönnrot later became professor of Finnish language at the University of Helsinki (Salminen and Landtman 1930: 359). The publication of the epic poems stimulated great interest in establishing the cultural origins of the Finnish people and their own cultural traditions. The origin of the *Kalevala* poems became the subject of much intellectual research and discussion especially following the work of the scholars Julius Krohn and his son Kaarle Krohn (Wilson 1976: 241–49). The *Kalevala* became a sacred symbol and a strong nationalist icon that set Finno–Ugric peoples apart from their Swedish and Russian neighbours. Linguistics, ethnology, history and comparative religions became distinctive academic fields within both the Swedish-speaking minority and the Finnish-speaking majority. There are still separate Swedish-speaking,

Professorial Chairs at the University of Helsinki, notably in history, law and medicine. Separate Finnish and Swedish language and literature societies were established that sponsored and funded research into the ethnology of the minority and majority cultures. The most important societies continue to operate in Finland today. By 1906 Finland had established a central museum in Helsinki to being together the disparate collections of ethnology scattered around the city and university. Sensitivity to Russian rule meant that the State Museum of History and Ethnology could not be renamed the National Museum of Finland until after Independence. The establishment of the museum further encouraged researchers and Westermarck, Landtman and his colleague Karsten made substantial collections of material culture now housed in Helsinki.

In its older Finnish usage, ethnography meant the study of the material culture of a people and ethnology was understood to be the branch of learning dealing with a traditional culture, more specifically the material, economic and social aspects of a people. Thus the concept of ethnology covered the study of non-European societies, ancient civilisations and, within modern European societies, the traditional elements of rural and peasant culture that remained juxtaposed against an urban, industrialised society. There were solid grounds for the establishment of this branch of learning. The study of comparative religion had been introduced into Finnish academic circles in the late 19th Century as an ethnological and folkloristic field of study. However it was not concerned with studies of the major world religions but with the evolution of beliefs and practices among the Finno–Ugric peoples, and this later spread to studies among various cultural groups in North Africa (Edvard Westermarck), Papua (Gunnar Landtman), South America (Rafael Karsten) and Palestine (Hilma Granqvist) (see Isotalo 1995 and Suolinna 2000). Westermarck broadened anthropological research in Finland and although he remained interested in comparative religion he extended this to the evolutionary study of the fundamental social institutions of marriage and moral ideas.

From 1918 Westermarck served as Professor of Philosophy and Rector of the Swedish-speaking, Åbo Academi in Turku. The mood of academic inquiry in early 20th Century Finland was liberal, dynamic and open to new philosophical ideas (Attonen 2007). Finnish academic circles were strongly influenced by the German Enlightenment and Landtman had also studied for a time in Germany. However, Finnish scholars, like Landtman, also benefited from the impetus of research on religious traditions of the indigenous Finnish people for these pioneers were 'doing excellent fieldwork at the time when the first functionalists of the French and English schools were still in their cradles. First-hand observation and the mass of notes and texts provided by them constituted the basis of scholarly work for many generations to come' (Honko quoted in Anttonen 2007). Certainly Landtman's research in Papua was based on the universalist, *Människan som kulturvarelse* (man as a cultural being) type of research favoured in Finland at that time. So, with a solid grounding in sociology, oral history and ethnology Landtman was an ideal candidate for research into the culture and history of the Kiwai.

Landtman's contacts in England and Papua: entry into the Haddon network

As soon as the travel plans were made, Landtman sought to purchase the necessary equipment for his long stay. He later wrote: 'Mr C.G. Wheeler [from the London School of Economics] was of great help when choosing all kinds of necessities. He had recently returned home from an expedition to the Solomon Islands and helped me with good advice. Together we bought my equipment in the Army and Navy Stores in London. I was excited with the various objects, as they were particularly nice and practical.' (Landtman 1913b: 3). Indeed, Gerald Wheeler would have been a reliable source of information. On the Percy Sladen Trust Expedition to Melanesia in 1908, accompanied by W. H. R. Rivers and A. M. Hocart, he travelled to the Solomon Islands and undertook research on the folklore of the Mono-Alu people of the Shortland Islands off the southern coast of Bougainville in what was formerly German New Guinea (Wheeler 1926). The Shortland Islands are now part of the Solomon Islands. No doubt Wheeler would have been another of Haddon's colleagues whose network of associates was wide. Haddon had fortunately also established a good personal relationship with the Lieutenant-Governor and Chief Judicial Officer of Papua, Judge (later Sir) J. P. Hubert Murray, a formidable figure in the history of colonial administration in Papua.

Murray took an active interest in ethnology and encouraged his patrol officers to report on social and cultural practices of the Papuan people. These reports and maps were regularly published in the annual reports of the colonial administration (Annual Reports on British New Guinea 1886/87–1905/06 and Annual Reports on Papua 1906/07–1919/20). Artefacts obtained from patrol visits and confiscated during police intervention, especially during tribal fights, were incorporated into a museum in Port Moresby. Some of this material later found its way into major state collections in Australia. Murray also assisted in the collection of artefacts for Haddon especially when Haddon and Hornell began writing the monumental book on the canoes of Oceania (Haddon and Hornell 1936–38). In return for Haddon's encouragement and assistance, Landtman was to present the Cambridge University Museum of Archaeology and Ethnology with a duplicate collection of artefacts (CUMAE E1912.79) from the Western Division (Landtman 1927: ix). In return Landtman was to win high praise from Haddon who later wrote: 'The book [*The Kiwai Papuans of British*

New Guinea] is so packed with interesting information that it will always form an indispensable handbook for ethnologists' (Landtman 1927: xvii). Indeed, Landtman's work continues to be a primary source of information on the coastal Kiwai of Papua New Guinea.

Landtman was again fortunate in that he arrived in Papua before Murray had chosen an official Government Anthropologist and before Murray's opinions of anthropology had changed. Murray became annoyed by Bronislaw Malinowski when he worked in the Trobriand Islands from 1915 to 1918 (Malinowski 1935 and 1953 [c. 1922]) and although he was keen to appoint a Government Anthropologist it was not until 1921 that he was able to appoint W. E. Armstrong, one of Haddon's former students, as assistant Government Anthropologist in Papua. Armstrong worked only briefly in the Southeast Division and then returned to Cambridge after a year. The Chief Medical Officer, W. Mersh Strong, was then appointed to the post and while Strong wrote on medical conditions for native labourers and on the Roro and Mekeo languages it was not until 1922 that F. E. Williams was employed, first as assistant Government Anthropologist, but then promoted to Government Anthropologist in 1928. Over the next 20 years Williams was to produce some of the finest writing on Papuan ethnology available to us today (Williams see especially 1928, 1930, 1936, 1976). However, Murray and Williams effectively isolated Papua from outside anthropological activity following this appointment. Under Williams, Papua virtually became a closed field of research that he alone surveyed.

Landtman's personality and his productivity established his good reputation in the eyes of Murray for later the Papuan administration even contributed financially to the publication of the English language volume on the Kiwai (Landtman 1927). Murray held little respect for any anthropologist who attempted to advise him on 'native' administration. Lewis Lett (1944: 108) in a largely hagiographic tribute to Murray's rule was direct and scathing in his opinion of anthropology and anthropologists when he wrote that 'anthropologists [were] those strangely unscientific scientists' whose practice of 'Anthropology varies in its aims and in its principles according to the predilections of its innumerable prophets, and differs so widely that it is impossible to class them together as representing definitely established theories or opinions'. While these opinions were largely directed at Malinowski and the theory of functionalism developed in a later period, the underlying tension between the Papuan model of colonial administration and criticism of it in operation were fermenting slowly. Landtman wisely refrained from expressing any public opinions. He also refrained from open criticism of the Christian missions and their work in Papua.

Landtman's contacts with the local missions: again the Haddon connection

With a formal letter of introduction signed in London by the Rev. Wardlaw Thompson, the Foreign Secretary of the London Missionary Society (LMS), and addressed to the Rev. Ben Butcher and the Rev. Edward Baxter-Riley, Landtman sailed to Papua (Landtman 1910–21: Thompson 9 February 1910). Again, Landtman was fortunate with his contacts. The LMS, a Congregationalist Protestant mission society, had commenced pastoral work in the Western Division in 1872 when the Rev. Samuel MacFarlane and the Rev. A. W. Murray landed at Mawatta, a Kiwai village located at the mouth of the Binaturi River, with a small group of Loyalty Islander [Lifu Islanders] and Rarotongan [Cook Islander] pastors and built a mission there. Later a trading station was established nearby. Association with the LMS was more than just coincidence for Haddon regularly gave lectures to the students of the LMS in London and to intending missionaries studying at Cambridge.

The presence of Papua and its seemingly unknown peoples and potentialities, so close to the open frontier of north Australia, stimulated tentative exploration of the Fly River before effective government control of the vast region (MacFarlane and Rawlinson 1875–76, D'Albertis 1881, Everill 1885–86, Stone 1880, Strachan 1888, Macgregor 1888–89). In 1890, the Administrator of British New Guinea, Sir William Macgregor, had given the LMS a vast sphere of influence from Milne Bay to the Torres Strait. The only exception was at Yule Island north of Port Moresby where the Congregation of the Sacred Heart established a Catholic mission in 1885. The LMS maintained a presence in the Torres Strait until its churches were handed to the Anglicans in 1914 but in the Western Division of Papua the LMS remained active until the 1930s.

The first government outpost was established near Mabudawan at the mouth of the Pahoturi River in 1891, largely to pacify the internecine fighting along the coast. Despite the belief that the area was the best and healthiest location along the coast for a government station, the site was poorly chosen. Daru with its ridge of volcanic soil, its safer harbour and its more fertile gardening land was the home to a few local families, some of whom were descendants of original inhabitants previously driven off by the Kiwai. Cedar cutters and the crews of pearling and bêche-de-mer boats also used the island as anchorage and as a place to cut firewood and buy food (Annual Report on British New Guinea 1889–90: 66). By 1895, Daru became the principal government station, a water and fuel depot and the base for missionaries, traders and the exploration of the Fly River region. Later the traditional inhabitants of Daru gave up rights of occupation to the colonial government (Beaver 1920: 49).

Despite the ambitions of MacFarlane and Murray, the missions on the Daru coast did not prosper until the Rev. James Chalmers assumed responsibility for the LMS in the Western Division after the retirement of Samuel MacFarlane in 1886 (Chalmers 1887, Wetherell 1993). Chalmers established a base at Saguane on Kiwai Island but, after the death of his wife there, he relocated the mission to Daru in 1900. James Chalmers published useful material on the Kiwai (Chalmers 1903) and he was the first missionary to make contact with the Gogodala, north of the Fly River, in 1898. The vast network of channels and rivers along the coast of Papua stimulated interest in exploration and even in 1892 J. P. Thomson was writing that detailed anthropological investigations into the cultures of the peoples of the Fly River were needed by the colonial administration (Thomson 1892: 118). However, after Chalmers and his assistant Tomkins, together with a party of local missionaries, were killed at Dopima village on Goaribari Island near the Omati River in 1901, Edward Baxter-Riley had to completely re-establish the Fly River Mission (Annual Report on British New Guinea 1900/01 Appendix D and E: 25–37). In retaliation, all the men's houses in Dopima and nearby villages were burnt by the colonial police in an action that further alienated both the administration and the mission. Samoan pastors (*Faifeau Samoa*) formed much of the second generation of missionaries and these Pacific Islander pastors in both the Torres Strait and on the Papuan mainland influenced social life in the small communities: much of the pre-contact ritual life was forbidden, music styles were changed with the introduction of Samoan polyphony and new dances like the Samoan sitting down dances and Rotuman '*Taibobo*', a formation dance, were introduced (Neuenfeldt and Costigan 2004: 116).

Missionary activity, although highly significant, was not the primary catalyst for social change among the coastal Kiwai and the inland tribes of the Daru coast. The main impact came from wage labour on the fishing and pearling boats in the Torres Strait that commenced as early as the late 1860s when floating stations and permanent shore stations were established by entrepreneurs eager to access the pearl shell and marine produce of the Torres Strait. Recruiting also served to partly pacify tribal fighting along the coast. Conditions on the boats were hard with men, usually the young men from the communities, working for long hours and for many months at sea before being paid off in Daru. The time at sea became a new initiation period with its seclusion from women, a struggle for status and a return, laden with goods, being substituted for the traditional rites of passage (Beaver 1920: 295 and Lawrence 1991: 375). Papuan labour was so valuable that even the Australian Immigration Restriction Act of 1901, the so-called White Australia policy, introduced after Federation in 1901 that precluded the importation of Pacific and Asian labour, was structured to allow for contracted labour from Papua to work in Torres Strait (Schug 1995: 157–58).

The economic and political situation in the Torres Strait

The economy of the Torres Strait was based on bêche-de-mer fishing and pearling, volatile industries subject to periods of boom and bust. Maritime exploitation had commenced in the Torres Strait as early as 1869 when a bêche-de-mer and then a pearl shelling station was built on Tudu Island near the Warrior Reefs by Captain William Banner (Chester 1870) who employed 70 South Sea Islanders [mostly Polynesians] and some of the remaining Tudu Islander families. By 1872, over 500 Pacific Islander labourers had been brought in to work the permanent and floating pearling and bêche-de-mer stations (Mullins 1997). Pearl shelling activities expanded rapidly but the growth of lawlessness in the region prompted the establishment of Thursday Island in 1877, the main town on the Queensland side of the border. By 1883 over 200 boats employing 1500 men harvested the pearling fields of the Torres Strait with Thursday Island the only real port of any importance in the region. At the turn of the 20th Century, the Torres Strait and the pearling field off Broome in Western Australia accounted for over half the world's mother-of-pearl shell (*Pinctada maxima*) supplied to the button and ornament markets of Europe and America. Secondary marine produce came from trochus and bêche-de-mer, items that could also be collected by surface divers operating on a variety of small and large vessels such as brigs, barques and schooners (Schug 1995: 46 and McPhee 2004).

Only later did the common form of pearling lugger become introduced into the Torres Strait. This vessel was a standardised clinker-built, double-ended vessel with two masts each supported by a dipping lug rig, hence the term lugger. They were generally 5-8 tons measurement rigged for three sails and partly decked over. They only contained a small cabin aft with a bunk and lockers for the crew of up to 10 men. Conditions were not comfortable and Landtman and the local missionaries found these work boats unpleasant means of transport for long trips across the often rough waters of the Torres Strait. Thursday Island become a major shipbuilding and trading centre but the small island close to the tip of Cape York was inhabited by a mixture of whites, Polynesian labourers, Japanese pearlers and shipwrights, indigenous Torres Strait Islanders, Papuans and Malay marine workers. Thursday Island was the commercial heart of a rich marine resource region. It was Landtman's first port of entry. It was a typical north Australian town: hot and dusty, built of timber and iron, with little architectural appeal.

Figure 2. Thursday Island. The Burns Philp wharf and the Federal Hotel (VKK 248: 566)

Landtman described his first impressions of the wood and iron buildings, the palm trees, the dusty streets and the salty sea air:

> We arrived at Thursday Island in the middle of the night but could not go ashore as it was dark. At six [in the morning] we landed. It was April 12 when I ended my trip on the steam boat. From then on I had to get along as well as the circumstances granted. I walked up and down the deck impatiently not knowing how things would develop. I knew, nevertheless, that the first few hours after coming ashore would clarify the situation in many respects. I looked at the area with the greatest curiosity and tried to figure out the islands with the high dry hills wooded with bushy forest, with strips of beach here and there, and the open sea glittering in the Sound, on the whole a right idyllic landscape.

> Finally we pulled up at the long pier and I went ashore leaving my belongings onboard for the time being. Thursday Island looked almost like a small town with two long streets running parallel to the shallow beach — but there was little else. However the beach was magnificent with its fine sand. Most of the small buildings had both walls and roof of corrugated iron and on the garden side there were whole lines of closed

cisterns [galvanised iron water tanks] for collecting rainwater. The town had a hotel, shops and a couple of bank offices. The population seemed to be the most variegated set I had ever seen, a product of almost all of the most eastern and oceanic peoples with the whites forming the smallest group. The more or less mixed Papuans, the Chinese and the Japanese were the largest groups.

Almost immediately, I had the good luck to meet the person whom I had been advised to turn to: Mr. Walker, the director of a combined business and mission company called The Papuan Industries. With religious management, the company tries to bring productive activity among the Papuans and develop the natural resources of these regions. This meeting was the first of the favorable circumstances at my arrival. It was most important time to begin for the dry season had just arrived and I would have time until December when the rainy season would start.

My money arrangements were in good order at the bank but the post let me down even though I should have been prepared. I had been cut off from all information from home and I was thirsty to know what had happened there but the mail had not arrived as quickly as I had so I only received a few newspapers and a couple of letters. They had been sent about the same time I left home and contained no news.

During my stay at Thursday Island I visited the sympathetic Mr. [Hugh] Milman, the Resident Magistrate to whom I had a letter of introduction. He died later. He was very friendly and hospitable and I decided never to neglect visiting him when I came to Thursday Island.

Our hotel [The Federal Hotel] lay right on the beach and we could hear the waves breaking in all night. I listened to the rattle of the crowns of the palm trees during the quiet hours, and it was pacifying like a mild rain.

Often during the next two years would I remembered with pleasure my stay in this peaceful town, free from household troubles, with a verandah containing easy chairs inviting one to study the fresh newspapers, and also, where one could walk back and forth on the wide solid surface of the floor instead of along the springy pliant bark planks with holes ready to trap your foot — as in Papuan huts (Landtman 1913b: 25 to 28. Translated from the Swedish by Pirjo Varjola).

Landtman's stay on Thursday Island would be short for Walker was keen to return to his mission on Badu Island. The combination of missionisation, commercial activity and government control gradually stopped the lawlessness and raiding conducted by the men based in the pearl shelling stations of

Torres Strait and assisted in suppressing inter-tribal warfare between coastal village groups as well. When Landtman arrived the Papuan coast was relatively peaceful although sporadic tribal fighting continued especially near the former Dutch New Guinea [now West Papua] border and along the middle Fly. Letters of introduction facilitated Landtman's work. Baxter-Riley on Daru and Butcher at Aird Hills in the Gulf District to the north were both men of substance who would not only work for many years in the region but would become to be known as authorities on the language, social and cultural life of the peoples they converted to Christianity (Baxter-Riley 1925, Butcher 1963). Their local assistants, the Samoan pastors, were figures of power and authority in their small communities and being the only representatives of the LMS, demanded obedience and respect (Wetherell 1996: 79).

Using his letter of introduction from Thompson, Landtman was able to base himself in mission and trading outposts along the coast and into the Fly estuary and so avoid, unnecessarily, the small European enclave in Daru. Daru was still accessible from the coastal communities where Landtman worked and by 1910 the government offices had records of nearly 15 years of contact with local people. Many of the Resident Magistrates were men of wide experience in Papua and well educated. They too would be useful points of reference for Landtman's work (see Jiear 1904–05; Beaver 1920; Annual Reports on British New Guinea 1886/87–1905/06 and Annual Reports on Papua 1906/07–1919/20; Austin 1925). In all, apart from the climate, Landtman had an ideal study area for his research.

Chapter 2
Impressions and reflections

Gunnar Landtman was particularly concerned with his personal correspondence while in Papua and made many references to the delays in receiving and sending mail from the isolated outposts along the Kiwai coast. The Landtman collection in the Museum of Cultures in Helsinki contains three folders of correspondence filed by Landtman himself. One folder (VKKA Landtman 1910–21) contains all the letters and postcards in English received from missionaries and trader contacts in the Torres Strait. Two other folders contain the correspondence in Swedish that Landtman sent to his father, his sisters Irene and Louisa and his aunt.

Landtman's family correspondence reflects his conservative Swedish heritage. His father Ivar Alfred was on the board of the Bank of Finland. The family was urban middle-class and Swedish speaking who lived in Malmi outside Helsinki and maintained a country villa at Sipoo (Sibbo) east of the city. Landtman was educated at a Swedish-speaking boys' school and studied the classical program of that time: Mathematics, Languages (Swedish, Finnish, German, Latin, Russian and possibly French), History, Natural History, Religion, Psychology, Literature, Art, Music and Gymnastics. He then studied Sociology and Practical Philosophy at the University of Helsinki. For his PhD on the Origin of Priesthood he accessed some material found at the British Museum and completed his doctorate in 1905. Before his Papuan adventure Landtman worked as a teacher at a private school for girls (*Svenska Privata Läroverk för Flickor*) in Helsinki. During this time Landtman was competing for a tenured position at the University of Helsinki with Rafael Karsten, his colleague and rival, and while he was in Papua he corresponded with his aunt who had financially supported his excursion and with his sister Irene, who was particularly important for she reported on his progress for appointment in the sociology department. Landtman's social and cultural background was very different from that of his hosts, white or black.

The Torres Strait: the stepping stone into Papua

Badu, one of the largest islands in the western group was the centre of Papuan Industries Ltd, the mission and trading enterprise established by the Rev. F. W. Walker. Walker, described as 'calm, earnest and plodding' (Wetherell 1996: 8) had been a LMS missionary in Papua where, with Charles Abel, he helped found the Kwato Mission in 1891. At Kwato students were taught elementary subjects and technical education along with Bible studies. The boys learnt manual skills like carpentry and the girls, sewing and lace making. The Kwato industrial mission model formed the basis for the Papuan Industries enterprise. This combination of commerce and Christianity was an attempt to develop local education and trade skills, within a solid Protestant ethos, that would enable both Torres Strait Islanders and Papuans to acquire European skills (Austin 1972; Haddon 1935, 1: 17–18). Or, as Walker wrote, it was formed from a 'need for properly organized Industrial Missions to add "Works" to "Faith" and to teach the savages how to beat their swords into ploughshares, and their spears into pruning hooks' (Walker quoted in Fife 2001: 261).

Figure 3. Badu Industries store and house on Badu Island, Torres Strait (VKK 248: 565)

The combination of commercialism and conversion was not fully supported by the LMS hierarchy largely because they were concerned that it would alienate potential supporters especially those from the business community. Walker was not popular as he had commissioned the construction of a mission yacht, the 'Olive Branch', whose extravagant cost at £1800 lost him his position with the LMS (Austin 1972: 44; Wetherell 1996: 48). Walker was forced to resign in 1896 by the same Rev. Thompson who gave Landtman his letter of recommendation to Butcher and Baxter-Riley (Wetherell 1996: 98). Walker then engaged in island trading and evangelising with his brother Charlie although he re-joined the mission in 1901. In 1904 Papuan Industries Ltd, with its motto 'Faith and Works', was incorporated in Queensland. Walker's idea was that a Christian trading company could engage in commercial activities, like pearling, bêche-de-mer fishing and plantation development, while providing technical assistance to local people in order to protect indigenous rights to land by creating independent 'native enterprise and the creation of innumerable small peasant proprietors all along the coast' (Walker quoted in Ganter 1994: 69 and Austin 1972: 47).

Landtman's first contacts in the Torres Strait were with the members of the Papuan Industries and their associates along the southwestern coast of Papua. Landtman was wise to take their advice and assistance for later he wrote in *Nya Guinea färden*, his book of reminiscences of his travel to Papua, that:

> Mr. and Mrs. Walker had recently returned from a trip to Sydney and I now had the chance to follow them to Badu Island in Torres Strait where the headquarters of the company were situated. Actually, the company boat, the "Goodwill" lay by the same pier as the Dutch steam boat I had arrived with.

> The "Goodwill" was a combined sailing boat and a steam boat, and half a freight ship, half a pleasure boat. I only needed to transfer my belongings over to her (Landtman 1913b: 27. Translated from the Swedish by Pirjo Varjola).

While economic and social programs were being formulated, political changes were coming to the region. In 1911 the Aboriginal Protector on Thursday Island, W. Lee-Bryce, instructed white teachers on the islands to replace the Pacific Islander missionary teachers and permitted the teachers to supervise the island councils and courts (Mullins 1997: 9).

The 1897 Aboriginal Protection Act was widened to include Torres Strait Islanders and part of this effective government control of Islander employment came to be known as the 'company boat' system (Schug 1997). By 1912, Papuan Industries had 10 pearling and bêche-de-mer boats working in the Torres Strait and the government controlled the 10 boats that were in reality owned by Islander clans. By comparison, there were approximately 260 'wages' boats owned by pearl-shellers operating in the Torres Strait at that time (Ganter 1994: 67). The protector of Aborigines in effect had control over both fleets when Papuan Industries were forced to sell their pearl-shell through the government offices. Money earned by Islanders was held partly in trust and partly deposited with Papuan Industries. Workers and their families had to 'buy' goods from the stores: this was then credited against their account in the passbook system. This paternalistic control was greatly resented by Islanders.

The white teachers watched how the island pearling boat crews worked. An adverse report from them could result in boats being taken away from one community and given to another. The local protector relied on the advice of the expatriate teachers and controlled the labourers' savings bank passbooks. In 1912 the main inhabited islands of the Torres Strait were declared native reserves: access to the reserves was strictly controlled and local people were restricted in their movements off the islands. Papuan workers recruited from the Kiwai villages were also subjected to the permit system and the labour recruiting was closely monitored and supervised by government officials on Daru. Papuan Industries was even able to issue its own bank notes that local people could use only in the company tradestores.

It was on Badu that Landtman had his first meeting with the daily life of Torres Strait Islanders. The kindness and graciousness of the people seemed to surprise him at first. His impressions were expressed in a language typical for that period though considered racist today:

> When some men from the "Goodwill" came to take us to the ship I felt I shook hands with the very first genuine inhabitants of Torres Strait. They all spoke in a broken so-called Pidgin English. They were well fed strong men with woolly hair and very dark skin. Their faces expressed the most sincere goodwill at the meeting.

> The "Goodwill" took a rather high speed with the help of both sail and steam, and we were further assisted by the tide. It is particularly difficult to navigate in the Torres Strait because of coral reefs and sand bank with which a large part of the Strait is filled ... It would have been out of question to sail against tidewater.

> On the Badu station we were met by a large group of native women and children. They had come from a nearby village to greet Mrs. Walker. They had a variety of faces, shining with delight. One by one the women came to shake hands, clucking their tongue with pleasure. Their clothes looked grotesque as well, sack like cotton garments in bright colors, hanging down from shoulders to the ankles [mu-mu or Mother Hubbards: a long cotton dress with sleeves instituted by the missionaries in the name of modesty. Now adapted into various forms as part of national dress in the Pacific]. It was a pity that missionaries and contact with Europeans had brought along such a change in dress. When the women came they carried the small naked children on the back, and when the mothers arrived they pushed a hip out so the children could sit like on horseback.

Filled with curiosity I took the first opportunity to go to the village of the natives for a meeting and to get acquainted. About 300 blacks lived there in huts mainly lifted on poles and with the roof and walls made of palm leaves. I walked to the village quite slowly in order to be able to look around without stopping. The buildings looked most primitive with a mat for a door and the majority of them without window openings, there were no chimneys either. I tried to speak to some of the men and was glad to notice that they seemed to have nothing against a discussion, on the contrary. Everyone gave a benevolent grin showing a considerable row of teeth and offered a hand with the similar delighted clucking as the women. We could understand each other somehow although it was necessary to get accustomed to the Pidgin-English of the blacks. It was impossible to understand the old ones. The voices of the children were the same shrieks and cries as in Europe (Landtman 1913b: 28 and 29. Translated from the Swedish by Pirjo Varjola). [Note: Landtman used the terms *svarta*, the blacks, and *svartingar*, the blackies, as well as a more general term, *infödd* (sing) *infödda* (pl) and *inföding* (sing), *infödingar* (pl), the natives, in his books. At the time these terms were in common use.]

Papuan Industries had established two trading and plantation centres on the Papuan mainland, one at Dirimu [Dirimo] near Mawatta, and the other at Madiri at the top of the Fly estuary. The resident managers, G. H. Murray at Dirimu and J. B. Freshwater at Madiri, began clearing the bush and planting coconuts and rubber in a potential commercial operation (Austin 1972: 52). Both these ventures would have only a limited life. However, they were both places that Landtman could use in his intensive fieldwork in the region.

Landtman's work with the Kiwai clearly interested the LMS missionaries and he appears to have been a popular and personable guest for Walker wrote to him to say that he had a place at Badu whenever he need it (VKKA Landtman 1910–21: Walker 19 July 1910). Landtman would indeed need to revisit Badu and convalesce following an attack of malaria. Badu Island, in the western Torres Strait, is part of the high dry outcrops of the Oriomo Plateau. For Landtman, no doubt expecting a tropical rainforest surrounded by coral reefs, the image of the high dry island was at first confusing:

The vegetation on the dry and sandy Badu was actually quite poor, but I thought it wonderful. In vain I was looking for plants that I might recognize. Never before had I felt so completely ignorant of nature. In places the grass was man high and inside the forest there were very dense thickets. I was absolutely unfamiliar with this kind of surrounding and moved hesitantly amidst the tangle with the feeling that I might be met by some supernatural being any time. Knowing that there were lots of snakes, it was nerve wracking to hear the rustling of the grass every so often, although the noise was mostly made by lizards [goannas] hurrying away, some of them of considerable dimensions. Everywhere there were gray ants' [termite] nests made of clay ... some of them a metre high. The forest trees were decorated with flowers, particularly orchids ... Blotchy and dripping of sweat I returned from each climb between the hills and from the bush where I had to cut my way with a big knife [machete/bush knife] (Landtman 1913b: 30. Translated from the Swedish by Pirjo Varjola).

A small private commercial plantation had also been established on Mibu Island in the Fly estuary by J. Cowling who was to be one of Landtman's hosts. Mibu, a low sandy island off the Dudi coast, was land owned by the Sumai village on Kiwai Island. However, the plantation economy, so much a part of southeastern, central and northern Papua, was not successful in the Western District and commercial developments have never prospered. Mibu Plantation lasted longer than the others but it too failed to thrive. Daru remained the only centre of commerce in the vast lower Fly region.

The LMS mission at Saguane was a centre of mission activity on the heavily populated southeastern end of Kiwai Island that provided opportunities for Landtman in his travels. A small mission remained there after Chalmers moved south to Daru. Butcher and Baxter-Riley also gave Landtman letters of introduction in Kiwai for him to use in his travels between mission stations (VKKA Landtman 1910–21: Baxter-Riley 1 July 1910). Landtman would have found personal relationships between missionaries confusing for while Baxter-Riley on Daru was a supporter of F. W. Walker and the Papuan Industries model, Ben Butcher was a long-time critic who accused Walker of deceiving his supporters about the PI prospects (Austin 1972: 57). In his private letters home Landtman was to express similar doubts about the viability and operations of the commercial mission.

While on Badu, and later on other mission stations, Landtman was obliged to attend Sunday services. The style of service, the length of time spent at church on Sunday and the form of hymn singing were all noted in his travelogue:

On Badu and other mission stations all Sundays were spent almost completely at religious exercise with bible class and the singing of psalms. This all happened between the actual services, three altogether. The morning and evening prayers — also on weekdays — were conducted on the knees. This was expected of everyone present. The services were held in a church in the village and Mr. Walker was giving a sermon in Pidgin-English. The London Missionary Society, the only mission society active in Torres Strait and the western district of British New

Guinea, and the Papuan Industries function in the spirit of the English Free Church, that is the so-called Congregationalist Church. We white ones sat during the services on a platform in front of the congregation. … Inside the church one was hit with the sight of the unattractive bright dresses of the women and the European trousers of the men! I had never heard the likes of the bizarre loud singing performed by the natives modifying European psalm melodies in their original way. … Holy Communion was executed once a month on all stations, using ordinary bread (once I was there when the bread was replaced with potato), and cocoa milk [coconut milk], and every white was expected to take part in the communion (Landtman 1913b: 30 and 31. Translated form the Swedish by Pirjo Varjola).

Again, the stay on Badu provided other opportunities to learn local customs. Landtman spent some time out on the work boats with the local Torres Strait Islanders and was especially interested in marine hunting of dugong (*Dugong dugon*) and sea turtles (especially *Chelonia mydas*: the green sea turtle). The techniques described by Landtman have not changed to this day:

One morning I went along to hunt sea turtles together with five natives of Badu. Canoes, the vessels of old time, have been abandoned in this part of Torres Strait and the natives go about in sailing boats with one or two masts. These boats they rent from the whites. The Company [Papuan Industries] is pleased to hire out boats as it is well paid and the natives then leave the fish, turtles, mother of pearl shells and pearls for the Company to sell. Our boat, the "Argan", was the kind of boat described above, it was as big as a smaller archipelago yacht back home, strongly built, completely decked and covered with copper. It was steered with two ropes attached to the sides of the boat and running through a block to the rudder. Almost all sailing vessels were of this kind, they were also used by missionaries and other whites. How many days did I later spend on these "luggers" and "cutters" during slow sailing trips?

As soon as I had come onboard a dinghy was lifted on the deck and the "Argan" that had been sailing back and forth while waiting, set sail towards the sound between the islands of Badu and Moa. I noticed two or three huge harpoon shafts on the deck, about three fathoms [about three metres] long and made of very heavy wood [*wap* or *wapo*]. They were very beautifully carved and painted. The shafts are thick and heavy at the end where the harpoon head is attached while the thin end is usually decorated with a tuft of [cassowary] feathers. The harpoon head is of iron, and with barbs, it is stuck in a hole in the end of the shaft, it is surprisingly short, not longer than two or three inches. A long and rough rope is attached to the harpoon head, it lies folded in a circle on the deck so as to run out easily. The same harpoon was used to hunt turtles as well as "dugongs" or sea cows, immense grass-eating sea mammals with a fish-like tail like that of the porpoise (Landtman 1913b: 32: Translated from the Swedish by Pirjo Varjola).

Landtman later collected a fine example of a hunting harpoon that he gave to the National Museum of Finland. However, to send it home he had to cut off the head and the end of the shaft. It now rests in three pieces in the museum storerooms. On that day sailing with the Islanders Landtman was more interested in the technique of hunting than in collecting artefacts:

The wind was strong and we made good speed. The sea did not particularly matter as we were protected by some low reefs. As soon as we had reached open water the harpoon was put in order and the man who was to throw it also took his place in front of the boat. He was naked with only a cloth around the hips [lava-lava]. After sailing a few minutes we saw a dugong lifting his head. Even though it was too far to throw the harpoon, it was considered a good sign. We sailed on without changing direction because after a dugong or a turtle has dived again, it is useless to try to follow. Out on the open water a man climbed up to the top of the mast to have a look and also the other men, except the one steering, stood looking around with interest. The harpooner went out to stand on the bowsprit checking the sharp harpoon head which was sitting in the end of the shaft; he also made sure that the line would be able to roll out. The man held the shaft in his hand and kept a sharp eye on the water in front of the boat. At times when the weapon felt too heavy and there was no immediate use for it he laid it down for a moment.

A few times we saw swimming turtles. They looked like a collection of sea grass so that it would have been easy to mistake them for it. They were shining gold just below the surface and if you looked carefully you could see the neck and the head stick out of the water. Before we were close enough, they nevertheless dived and disappeared. The only possibility to get at them was to come straight close without alarming them or if the harpooner standing in the bow happened to see one underwater. The men communicated with each other only by whispers and signs, now and then one could see them make a gesture one way or another where an animal had shown himself and disappeared. Sometimes the helmsman had to change course according to their signs. A couple of times the harpooner seemed to aim his weapon towards something we could not see but the distance was obviously too long since nothing happened and the harpoon shaft was again lowered.

When we came to the other end of a long reef the sail was dropped and we sailed with the bare rig along the shallow coral structures shining through the water. This place was well liked by sea animals finding food in the abundant seagrass. We saw a couple of brown creatures disappear in the water, the men gesticulated heatedly to each other and from time to time we expected the harpooner to throw his weapon. Unfortunately we did not get near enough to any of our prey and we started to tack back.

Then, suddenly, we saw the harpooner aim his weapon at something in the water, crouch and throw himself with the harpoon in the water, adding to the strength of the thrust with his own weight. In the same instant the line started to run out. The man had disappeared underwater but dived up at once, grabbed the loose harpoon shaft and swam to the boat where he and the shaft were helped onboard. The dinghy was dropped into the water and the line, now straight, was unfastened from the "Argan" while the harpooner and another man quickly took to the little boat, the harpooner taking charge of the line and the other man at the oars. We others were tacking in the vicinity.

We saw the harpooner slowly collect the line although at times he had to loosen it during the fight with the turtle. I was wondering how the short harpoon head would keep in the animal but the men were convinced of their success. When most of the line had been rolled back in the boat the harpooner suddenly threw himself in the water again and disappeared for a long while. The companions of the man drew in the rope which had been tied around the arm of the diver, finally the man appeared together with the turtle fighting fiercely, the turtle was wildly throwing his free limbs, the four fins, head and tail. The diver had grabbed the animal from the neck with one hand and from the opposite side of the shell with the other. He could not move in this position but was hauled in by his companions. He was only able to hold on to the shell of the turtle. The animal, too, despite being in his own element, seemed completely helpless in the grip of the hunter. We could see the harpoon head sitting deep in the back of the animal (Landtman 1913b: 32–35. Translated from the Swedish by Pirjo Varjola).

This is one of the most accurate and sympathetic descriptions of a dugong and turtle hunt that one can find in the early ethnographic literature from the Torres Strait. Slowly Gunnar Landtman was starting to find his way into the life of the peoples of the Torres Strait and Kiwai coast.

The mission networks along the Kiwai coast

In the meantime, Ben Butcher had been brief in his letter of introduction issued to Landtman. In his undated note written from Damera Point on Wabuda Island in the Fly estuary he instructed his pastors and the villagers to see to the needs of Dr Landtman: *nou awo wade dubu* [He is a good and important man]. The pastors were requested to make the people available for him so that he could write of their customs. Butcher wrote that they were to give him all their assistance for *nou moro namira* [He is my friend].

Baxter-Riley was more fluent in coastal Kiwai, or at least an abbreviated mission version, and wrote on 1 July 1901 from Daru to the Samoan *Faifeau didiri* [Dear Pastors] that Landtman was a man of importance from London [*Londidini*] and a friend of Rev. Thompson [*Misi Tomasoni*]. Baxter-Riley wrote that Landtman was a great teacher and all the village people were to be available for his work. Landtman was to be allowed to rest in their mission houses and they, the mission staff, were to see to his needs and cares. If he became ill they were ordered to look after him [*Nou temeteme nigo aepuai wade*]. His name is Dr Landtman [Dr *Lanedetemani*]. The mission staff was instructed to cook for Landtman but just in case the burden would be too great Baxter-Riley informed the pastors that he had his own food [*Nou irisinimabu naito* [*nanito*] *wagati* [*owagati*]. Landtman was always careful with his food especially the dozens and dozens of canned foods ordered from Morton's Foods through the Army and Navy Stores in London (Landtman 1913b: 44).

The small mission launch that had to supply the outposts and plantations was sometimes able to take travellers and became a convenient means of transportation for Landtman. However he had to wait for the availability of the boat which, from the correspondence, had persistent engine trouble (VKKA Landtman 1910–21: Butcher 29 August 1910). Certainly, Landtman made a long visit to Kiwai Island between June and December 1910 but he had to land at Ipisia and walk to Samare due to the strong southeasterly winds that made sea travel impossible (Landtman 1927: 9 and VKKA Landtman 1910–21: Walker 8 September 1910).

> In the beginning of May Mr. Walker and Mr. Freshwater, another member of the Papuan Industries staff, left for a three weeks trip on the "Goodwill". They would be going to certain areas in New Guinea where the Company had bought land for plantations, and I went along. During the trip I had a good opportunity to cast an overview of a good part of the area I had chosen for my study. We visited Thursday Island before leaving and I remember that just as we were getting into a boat to be rowed to the "Goodwill" a messenger came with a telegram informing me that I had received one of the big Rosenberg grants. This news made

the trip all the more pleasing and interesting as I now could plan my work with a much better [financial] security than before (Landtman 1913b: 36. Translated from the Swedish by Pirjo Varjola).

The research funds from the foundation were an important link between Landtman and the developing National Museum of Finland. Dr Herman Fritiof Antell (1847–93), himself a wealthy collector, stipulated that the interest from one million gold marks bequeathed to the Finnish people should be used for acquisitions for a National Museum: it also provided assistance to several important explorers at that time among them Gunnar Landtman. Antell was the illegitimate son of Petter Herman Rosenberg, a wealthy currency speculator of Vaasa, who in turn was the illegitimate son of Colonel P. H. Rosén von Rosenstein of Upsala (Talvio 1993: 12–15). Landtman's catalogue of artefacts was subsequently published with assistance from the Antell Commission.

Landtman's tour of inspection first took him to Mawatta at the mouth of the Binaturi and then to Dirimu where Papuan Industries had established a plantation. Both would be important places for Landtman's research:

> I was having the most curious feeling of expectation when I headed towards the village of Mawatá [Mawatta] a few days later, taken there in a boat by a few men from the Goodwill. Mawatá is situated on the main land of New Guinea in the mouth of the Binatúri river. It later became my best working area in New Guinea. The ship lay in anchor a few kilometers behind us on the shallow coast. Mr. Walker and Mr. Freshwater had stayed onboard. The landscape opening in front of me lay flat such as were the areas in all of this part of New Guinea. The outline of the forest formed an endless even line without the smallest hill. The coast was solely made of swamp and mangrove trees.

> When we went ashore the natives collected around us helping us willingly to draw the boat on dry land. The grown men generally understood Pidgin English. I was stared at with great curiosity and the smallest of the children did as is usual: they looked shrieking and crying for shelter from their mothers. The natives made a friendly impression on me and I immediately found the village very promising for future studies. How strange and curious were the people and their houses then which later became so common..

> The "Goodwill" sailed over the shallow bank during the tide in the evening [the entrance to the Binaturi is only accessible at high tide] and dropped anchor a bit up the river. At that time the water reached as high as the bushes on the beach. We got up early the next morning in order to take a rowboat to the village of Dírimo about 20 km from

the river mouth. It was just before sunrise, only the slightest stream of light was seen in the east. The river lay calm and black. One could hear the murmur of the sea at the river mouth and imagine how the waves rushed in one after the other in the dark. Soon a cheerful melody like a morning tattoo sounded on one side of the river, six tones staccato as clear as if they had been played by a flute. The same signal was heard immediately from the other strand [river bank] and an alternating music started crossing over the river, now quite near, and then repeated as an echo from far in the forest. The invisible morning watch of the forest was a modest swamp bird [most probably the Pied or Torresian pigeon, *Ducula bicolor*, found throughout the lowland swamps and on the Torres Strait islands. The black and white feathers were prized in the making of *dari* headdresses and it makes a distinctive cry, especially in groups]. No matter how exciting its wake up sounded in this daybreak, the happy sound made me anxious each grey morning I heard it later because when you hear this sound [you know] there is the terrifying mangrove swamp [near], the dark side of the paradise of New Guinea.

[Later] We visited Mibu island in the delta of the great Fly River. One white man [J. Cowling] was living there alone with a few natives, growing cocoa-nuts [coconuts for copra]. In order to come to his place we had to row about one kilometer up a saltwater creek lined with nipa palms ... It was ebb time and terribly muddy. The palms stretched over the water and it was quite dark beneath the leaves. At the landing we had to be dragged through the mud in a small dinghy towards the only solid ground there was. Never before had I seen a white man live in such an isolated place.

We took the "Goodwill" a half day's distance up the Fly to Madiri on the right bank of the [mouth of the] river. Papuan Industries possessed land there just like in Dirimo. I observed the landscape around this majestic river from the deck of the ship. Also here the land was completely flat. We passed some of these unbelievably long houses built on poles. A whole tribe or clan lives in one. The natives gathered on the strand to look at us and through my binoculars, and to my pleasure, I saw completely naked people among them. At any rate, rather original subjects for study. Canoes came to meet us and the oarsmen looked at us from a respectful distance resting their paddles. ... One day a big canoe arrived from a village up the river full with men in arms and ornaments, it was the wildest company we had met so far on the "Goodwill". With the help of a translator we were able to carry on a good conversation mostly concerning the objects they brought along and we wanted to see. As usual, they found it very funny when we handled their things and tried to figure out how they were used. … A lively barter was soon going on and natives kept coming from all directions to the "Goodwill" bringing artifacts. Once a man came with a finely worked stone axe and as he was well paid, I found myself soon the owner of five others (Landtman 1913b: 37–42. Translated from the Swedish by Pirjo Varjola).

Refining the research area

However, Landtman also began to realise that the research area first envisaged was too large and that the scope of his research needed to be refined:

> I began to understand with rising eagerness what enormous research material there was available in these villages and it was almost painful to realize that the time available was not going to be long enough to see and do practically anything else.

Subsequently, he settled on Ipisia village on Kiwai Island as the first location for his field work and returned there on the 'Pearl', Ben Butcher's mission boat:

> From Dáru we took course towards the village of Ipisía situated on the northeast coast of Kiwai Island in the delta of the Fly River. This was the place I had chosen for my first headquarters. We arrived on June 30 [1910] and were met by the Samoan missionary Tovía stationed in the village. The mission house, built from the same material as those of the natives [mangrove timber posts and frame, nipa palm wall and roof] had been taken down in order to be rebuilt. It was not finished yet but a small hut nearby was given to me for the time being. A grown boy whose name turned out to be Ápau [Daniel] was hired as my servant. He was given [by Landtman] a mosquito net, a blanket, soap, towel, a knitted blouse, a loin cloth [*lap-lap* in Papua] and a knife and he was beside himself with these presents. In the beginning we were not able to talk with each other and I almost might have taught him Swedish just as well as English but he spoke an intelligible Pidgin-English much sooner than I learned to speak Kiwai.

> I stayed in Ipisia for almost six months. When Butcher sailed away I was left on my own with my task. I felt again as I had felt a couple of times before, when leaving England and when arriving on Thursday Island, that I was facing an important decision. It was time to find out what the conditions for my work were and for me to show what I could achieve. There was no one else I could put the blame on, not even the blacks, if I

failed. I would stay here until I had finished my work, only then I would leave the post. No later, but no sooner either (Landtman 1913: 45–46. Translated from the Swedish by Pirjo Varjola).

Searching for excitement: the journey to the Aramia wetlands

It appears that curiosity got the better of him for while Ipisia seemed a perfect starting point Landtman also joined with Ben Butcher on an exploration of the Aramia wetlands north of the Fly River. In his first letter home to his family in Finland, dated 25 October 1910, Landtman described, only briefly, the trip that he knew was to an area of marginal significance and so he wrote mostly of its geographical interest. He did say that he was hoping to see some tribal fighting, or be near to some, and that it looked 'promising at one occasion only'. He felt that it was a good test of planning abilities and was pleased that the amount of food and trade tobacco had been carefully calculated. However, the visit to the Gogodala area north of the Fly estuary was a near disaster when the canoes were swamped by a tidal bore that came up the Bamu River (Butcher 1963). The expedition had started well but it was to be a near disaster and Landtman only later wrote:

> One day in October [1910] Mr. Butcher arrived in Ipisia on his boat the "Pearl" to fetch me for a planned excursion together to the inland. It was our intention to try to go from Gaima on the western bank of the Fly River to the Bamu River on the east and beyond; a stretch a white man had never gone — to the best of our knowledge. Gaima is the only mission station on the left side of the Fly and its inhabitants belong to a completely different tribe than those of Kiwai [the Gogodala], and are much more original. After a day's visit in Gaima we sailed over the Fly to Madiri on the opposite bank. A new member on the Papuan Industries staff, Mr. Murray, a very sympathetic Scotsman, had been stationed there just recently and we found that he had been sick with malaria for a few days already. We tried to take care of him and luckily his fever went down the following day (Landtman 1913b: 130. Translated from the Swedish by Pirjo Varjola).

During the trip to the Aramia wetlands, Landtman encountered the dangers of travel overland across open grasslands, through the numerous swamps and along muddy rivers. It probably helped to confirm his ideas that he needed to restrict his work to the southwestern coast, closer to the Torres Strait and to Daru:

One swamp followed the other and later during the day we arrived to a wide swamp land or preferably a grassy lake that took us well over an hour and a half to cross. The water reached to over our knees all the time. Now and then we sank with a splash up to our stomachs and had to remove all things from trouser pockets to keep the possessions dry. The sun was scorching hot right above us, the water felt cooked and we kept panting and grunting; the wandering was going to be difficult. The humid air was steaming like in a hothouse; it was full of swamp smells and heat. The mud was stinking and our brown khakis turned gray.

Finally we approached the village called Nída or Kúbu, where we were to spend the night. The village consisted of a huge long house in which all of the inhabitants of the village lived. We took the last steps feeling utterly tired and Butcher said he had been about to "fall down". That was the case with me, too. We were hardly curious of how we would be met in the village and I thought to myself that if we had been suddenly attacked and there had been scuffle we would not have been able to put up much resistance in the condition we were in. But some words of explanation by our interpreter were enough; the men gathered around us, took our things and brought us in the house. The long house was raised on poles just the way buildings generally are in this country. We went up a broad ladder to a widening on one of the short sides of the house, on the same level with the floor. The small rounded entrance situated at a short distance allowed just one man in at a time; this obviously served some defensive purpose.

The interior of the house was almost dark. It differed from the Kiwai houses by having spaces separated by poles on both sides of the long central hall going from one end to the other of the building. The women, who were not allowed to the inner part of the house, lived in the narrow triangle formed sections along the long walls of the house. We immediately paid attention to the variety of household utensils, many of which were quite different from those used by the inhabitants of the mouth of the Fly. They were also generally much more ornate. Most of the men wore no clothing whatsoever, careless as in paradise for their nakedness, and the women had a narrow, insignificant grass cover only.

The journey across the vast Aramia floodplains continued the next day but the travel was punishing:

Our hands and arms down from rolled shirt sleeves were cut by the sharp grass, and our companions had bleeding marks on their bare feet, due to the leeches. At places there were flocks of birds, and the man who was leading had the opportunity to shoot. We slept that night in the village of Bárimu [now Balimo] in one of the best built houses we had seen in New Guinea; it was about 125 meters long. Many of the inhabitants had never seen a white man before, and their surprise and curiosity was immense.

We had come to the banks of a shallow lake filled with isles and capes and this waterway was said to be connected with the Bámu River and thus our tour could be continued along the lake. We bought a big canoe hollowed out of a tree trunk and decorated much more richly then the canoes on the coast. There was no outrigger. The bow was ornamented with a head half reminiscent of a boar and half of a crocodile. The length of the vessel, the carvings at both ends counted in, was 69 feet. The price consisted of a few pounds of tobacco, a few axes and two smallish packs of cloth. Some of our men went on foot back to Gáima and we engaged a few new men for the oars, a couple of whom did not wear as much as a thread. In order to be of help both Butcher and I grabbed a paddle each and so we were on our way. We were all standing in the canoe [the Bamu Kiwai and the Gogodala people still paddle this way] and paddling simultaneously while one of the men was steering. We first thought that our vessel was terribly heavy but got slowly accustomed to it. This way of traveling was far quicker than the troublesome walking. There were fluffy blue and white water-lilies blossoming on the water. We came from the lake into a small river [the Aramia] where the water was flowing slowly (Landtman 1913b: 132–34. Translated from the Swedish by Pirjo Varjola).

Even during the difficult travel along the Aramia waterways Landtman could see some of the majesty of the vast wetlands:

We saw an unforgettable sunset during which a glowing dust blanketed the gold and the green of it all. Big blossoming trees spread their fragrance around. The river stretch seemed to be longer than we had thought and we had to hurry in order to be in time for the meeting [with the "Pearl"] in the mouth of the river.

Near disaster occurred as they party on the single canoe approached the junction of the Aramia and the Bamu when the tidal bore hit:

Towards the morning, when the comparatively short high tide was over, we again started to move our paddles. The flood got wider and wider, appearing remarkable and majestic. Now, during the low tide, we saw numerous crocodiles. They floated along the stream and could only be spotted on surface by a sly shadow, or they had crept up in the mud of the shore, and hurried back in the water at our approach.

We had been wondering several times how it would be to meet the dangerous tidal wave [tidal bore] that sweeps in from the mouth of the river during full moon, and changes instantly the direction of the river from going out to going against the natural flow. This "bore" that is said to be quite incalculable is also very frightening. It reached us during the fore noon. The ebb was at its lowest when we heard a strong rush from a distance, approaching us. Our native oarsmen were instantly alarmed. They turned the bow [of the canoe] immediately towards the land shouting and with disorder, lashed the water with their paddles. ... We were stopped by the mud and had all to get out to haul the canoe by wading in the soft mass. At the same instant an enormous wave appeared in the bend of the river, the top breaking in froth.

Like a high wall, gray as lead, the mass of water rolled on, flushing both shores of the river at a considerable height. We were half way to solid ground when the wave was quite near, the natives left the canoe and made an escape to the shore at full speed. Butcher, Báidam [the Torres Strait Islander mission pastor and teacher at Gaima] and I stayed on the land side of the canoe in order to keep hold of our vessel if possible. The canoe was sideways against the stream. The masses of water were upon us with a roar, and instead of being able to hold the canoe in its place, the heavy vessel was lifted up on top of us, and we three found ourselves under it, clutching to it reeling. The canoe was flushed far towards land and we followed it as if ploughing through the mud. It all happened with a swooning speed, we were afraid every second that we would be stuck under the canoe or to feel a trunk of a tree or a fallen tree to hit our back, and we were not even able to shout to each other. When I saw Butcher let go and a tree trunk sweep over the spot where his head had been, I thought, "This is the way a man perishes", and facing the horror of this sight, I thought, "This cannot be real". I myself was close to being unable to breathe because of the amount of mud and water, and was pressed deeper down, but when I was almost forced to give up, the canoe stopped against something, I was not crushed and I was able to creep forward.

To my great joy I saw over the water Butcher, too, working his way towards land. He, as well as we others, had pulled through the adventure, unharmed. We all had eyes, nose, mouth and pockets full of mud and looked 'beautiful'. Báidam, who had been at one end of the canoe, had been saved the simplest way. The surface of the river rose with the tidal wave several feet at once and continued to rise rapidly well over its earlier level. Water was wallowing deep in the spot where the canoe had been stuck in mud a moment earlier. Many of our belongings were lost, I lost my cork helmet and rifle, the Browning [pistol] attached to my belt, the cartridges in my pocket and my hunting knife, and I felt totally disarmed.

We used the incoming tide for resting and for bringing ourselves, our things and the canoe together. Then we had to continue to paddle industriously under almost constant rain. The river was well over half a kilometer wide, but this remarkable water way was not marked in the maps. At each turn we expected to arrive at the place where it joins the proper Bámu, but it was only in the late afternoon that we reached where two rivers come together. We still had over 40 kilometers to get to the coast, and to reach the "Pearl" before dawn (Landtman 1913b: 136–39. Translated from the Swedish by Pirjo Varjola).

The survival of the party was remarkable considering the remoteness of the region, the lack of reliable communications and the uncertain nature of the response of the local people to the sudden arrival of strangers. Landtman was always careful in his letters home although he did mention that he would have to find a replacement Browning pistol lost on the boating accident there. He was more pleased with his abilities to undercut the going price for trade tobacco. The local white traders only gave the local people five sticks of tobacco for one shilling but Landtman always paid six sticks for one shilling and so was considered a more promising employer.

Return to Kiwai Island

The volatile nature of the wind and waves of the Fly estuary was a learning experience for Landtman. On the return to Ipisia, Butcher and Landtman were carefully watching out for one of the main long houses of the village when they realised in their absence it had been swept away by the same bore that had caused such destruction on the Aramia River. The inhabitants of the long house were able to salvage their belongings as the damage occurred during the daytime. The people presumably built a series of temporary small houses although later, in December 1911, when Landtman returned to Ipisia he found, to his surprise, that the 17 small 'modern' village houses had been pulled down and five new longhouses rebuilt in their place.

Ipisia was also a centre for the local recruitment of workers for the Torres Strait pearling fleets and in his letter home of 9 November 1910 Landtman reported on the lack of success that the recruiters were having that season. Ceremonial life still played a big part in the regulation of villager movements and the fact that Landtman reported on the concentrated efforts spent on gathering food to feed the dancers and onlookers of a 'big dance' are some indication that men would not have been able to go away at that time. He tasted *gamoda* (kava) and found it unpleasant but found the behaviour of the missions just as unpleasant. In Landtman's opinion the missions should concentrate on efforts to clean up the communities and introduce order and hygiene rather than try to change all that was original. In this letter he informed his father that he was beginning to find photography interesting and to be more content with the results of his early work. Landtman wrote that he was especially pleased with the results of interior photographs taken in darkened longhouses that lacked internal light and windows. He wrote that he had received some phonographic apparatus from the Psychological Institute in Berlin but was only able to experiment with it. However, by October 1910, he was able to report that he had already commenced writing down his 200th folktale.

In the meantime, Ethel Zahel, the head teacher at the Badu Native School, took the opportunity of regular correspondence between Badu and the mainland plantations to ask Landtman to obtain some artefacts for her sister in Europe. It would appear that Landtman complied with this request (VKKA Landtman 1910–21: Zahel nd). The traders and plantation owners were both keen hosts and sources of useful information on the people in the region. At this time, Landtman had made the acquaintance of William (Fred) Hodel, a trader who had business interests on Thursday Island and in Cairns (VKKA Landtman 1910–21: Hodel 10 October 1910 and nd). Hodel had other connections too: he started a short-lived newspaper on Thursday Island called *The Pearler* and he was a supporter of small-scale pearl-shelling operations, particularly the ones employing white labour. Hodel was a political supporter of the left-leaning Labour platform and against Papuan Industries and government assisted 'company boats' practice. He supported the growing Aboriginal protectionist policies of the State Government that were being implemented from Brisbane by Walter Roth, the Chief Protector of Aboriginals (Mullins 1997: 6 see also Mullins 1995).

Despite his opposition to the mission it appears Hodel joined Papuan Industries in 1912 and ran the company-operated shipyards on Badu and Thursday Island. Hodel and Walker saw commercialism from two very different perspectives: Walker, the evangelist, saw his goal the creation of a 'yeomanry of producers' (Ganter 1994: 96). Hodel, the trader and pearler, saw Islanders and Papuans as a labour resource to be exploited under the strict paternalistic guidelines of a settler society. Islander communities became Reserves, segregated from contact with white Australia, where every activity was regulated by the local Protector under a policy of paternalist exclusion. Hodel supported the Protector's objectives and his presence in Papuan Industries eased the friction between the Queensland government and the mission no doubt at a cost to the Islanders and Papuans employed in the maritime industries (Ganter 1994: 86). Creating a working class rural peasantry in Melanesia was doomed to failure.

Figure 5. Pearling boats careened at Thursday Island (National Library of Australia an23358066-v)

In a letter to his father from Ipisia dated 14 November 1910, Landtman told of how pleased he had been with his early work on Kiwai Island. Landtman was coming to terms with the internal dynamics of village life. An old man, Gabia, one of his most important informants and one keen to discuss everything even the most secret information, would only come to talk at a time and a place to suit the old man (Landtman 1913b: 118). Gabia feared he would be killed by sorcery if he were overheard and he sat with Landtman far from other people in a corner of the verandah that surrounded the mission house. The fear of sorcery was real especially in the estuary. By this time Landtman had begun to understand some basic Kiwai especially the stories told by an old man, perhaps his other informant Kaku, who had been a language teacher to the missionary James Chalmers. By 11 December 1910 his initial work at Ipisia was finishing and even though he planned to return in a year or two (around 1911) Landtman was pleased with the quality and quantity of his work in the region. According to other letters he had a difficult time with his health at Ipisia and had to go to Badu to recover from malaria over Christmas of 1910 (VKKA Landtman 1910–21: Ethel Zahel and C. H. Walker 26 January 1911; Haddon 1916; Landtman 1913b: 122). Only later did he write of the terrible fevers, pains and sense of hopelessness that malaria brings:

After a short stay in Ipisía I had my first meeting with malaria, and it happened quite suddenly. The quickly rising fever lasted five days without a break and my temperature rose as high as to 40o and a little over. I was feeling awful and vomited strongly. I had lively and beautiful dreams but waking up was terrible. The first grey dawn that strained in through the door brought along confusion and a painful feeling of an early winter morning at home. In the hopelessness that seems to be so typical of malaria it was my hope just to die a bit nicer than be sunk in the swamps of New Guinea. So this was what it all had come to after all the plans I had made for my trip. During daytime I dragged myself to the verandah for a while forgetting each time the low ceiling against which I hit my head. This happened when I was still living in the small hut. Although I made notes in my diary about my experiences each day I lost a day probably as the result of delirium and when I then was well again the missionary Tovia and I did not agree what week day and date it was. I insisted that he held his Sunday services on Monday. It took three weeks until we could set upon the correct date with the help of a white man who came sailing to Ipisia.

The fever stopped as soon as it had come [this is characteristic of malaria]. On morning I woke up with normal temperature and not even having a headache and when the fever did not return during the next days I knew I had won this time although for a time felt quite weak. After this I stopped being afraid of malaria particularly since it seemed that an attack could be won [caught] on the spot. During the fever I took 1,8 grams of quinine daily according to the advice of the doctor's book and I had to continue with rather large doses for some time. The permanent cure that is recommended for healthy people as a rather effective protection against malaria is to take regularly 0,9 grams of quinine each on two immediate weekdays for example on Sundays and Mondays (Landtman 1913b: 122–23. Translated from the Swedish by Pirjo Varjola).

Despite his physical trials, his work continued. Haddon's special task for Landtman was the collection of genealogical tables [släkttabellerna] along the lines of the methodology pioneered by W. H. R. Rivers, the acquisition of material culture and the recording of 36 Kiwai songs on the phonograph for the Berlin Institute (VK 4919 Nos 1–3; 6–14; 17–39 and 45–46). Landtman's attempts at collecting genealogical tables from the various Kiwai and bushman groups that he visited were not particularly successful, likewise the recording of songs and dance music was only moderately productive. However, these are the first recordings of Kiwai music and include examples of the introduced 'Taibobo' dance and some traditional songs. By the time Landtman commenced his work with the Kiwai the mass-produced hard celluloid cylinders had mostly replaced the fragile wax cylinders that were the first mass-marketed sound recordings. Although the hard plastic cylinders could not be shaved for re-use, they were practically indestructible and were a near permanent recording. The disadvantage of the cylinder was the quality of the recording and playing equipment: the phonograph used a belt to turn the mandrel and a slippage could result in pitch fluctuations. Consequently, the recordings made by Landtman are often uneven in quality. He was dealing with heavy equipment, a difficult physical environment, songs and dances that were performed outdoors often in a windy area and a lack of familiarity with the technology itself.

The Kiwai language recordings were made between 10 November and 9 December 1910 at Ipisia village. In a letter home dated 13 December 1910 Landtman reported that he had to travel from Daru to Thursday Island to pack and send material by ship to Haddon in Cambridge. His servant Apau left, having been contracted by a labour recruiter for work in the Torres Strait pearling fleets, and Landtman hired Ganame, another young man from Ipisia who had experience working for one of the Resident Magistrates in Daru and was familiar with European cooking. Landtman began to warm to the local people and found to his amusement that he was probably the first scholarship recipient of the Antell Commission to have been required to establish a tobacco and calico trading business to finance his local artifact collecting. In this respect he was following the path of his mentor, Haddon, who had commenced his ethnology work in the Torres Strait in 1888 with the collection of material culture to support his work as a zoologist. Fortunately Landtman's efforts at collecting Kiwai material culture did produce results and by the end of his stay in Ipisia, Landtman had also recorded 250 oral accounts that he classified into legends (*saga*, pl *sagor*) and stories (*sägen* pl *sägner*) (Landtman 1913b: 141).

Christmas on Badu

Landtman left Ipisia on 18 December in the mission launch, the 'Louisa' although he had to chase the recalcitrant postman to Iasa to retrieve his badly missed mail from Helsinki. On the way to Daru the launch ran aground in Toro Passage, a treacherous narrow boat way between Parama Island and the mainland that still causes trouble for people entering and leaving the wide Fly estuary. On Daru he paid the customary courtesies and visited the officials in charge of custom's declarations before sailing to Badu. On his first Christmas Eve in the tropics, Landtman experienced the dramatic differences between the frosty Nordic season and high summer in the Torres Strait:

On Christmas Eve we were approaching Bádu Island, more than uncertain that we would arrive there for the evening, and when the tide turned against us between Moa and Bádu we knew that we had to spend the night onboard. It was a Christmas night full of feeling. We lay at anchor in the middle of the sound and saw the hills on the both sides reflecting in the water, a strange sight to us, accustomed to the flatness of New Guinea. A light was flickering in a distance on the Badu station like a Christmas star. I gave the men some extra provisions and meditated for a while on the deck before retreating to the mosquito net hung up in the cabin. But once, waking up during the night, I went up to the deck in the beautiful full calm Christmas night. A decreasing moon illuminated the wonderful view getting paler, and big sea animals were splashing and breathing invisibly around us in the completely calm sound. Early in the morning of Christmas Day we dropped anchor outside the Papuan Industries station on Badu where I was warmly welcomed by the Walker family. A Christmas party was held in the afternoon in the village church, along with a Father Christmas and a tree with full foliage instead of a Christmas tree as there are no conifers in New Guinea. Here, amidst full summer, there was not much that could make one feel like the European mid-winter festival (Landtman 1913b: 145–46. Translated from the Swedish by Pirjo Varjola).

Return to the Kiwai coast

Landtman spent that Christmas, 1910, at Badu in the company of the Walker family for he wrote to his sisters Louisa (22 December 1910) and Irene (31 December 1910) that his letters were accompanied by nine large boxes and three bundles of artefacts for Cambridge and a smaller parcel for his family in Finland with instructions that they were to give the Samoan mats to their Aunt if they decided to keep the feather decorations for themselves. Landtman returned to the southwest coast of Papua in early 1911 readily believing that he could survive a wet season on the Daru coast although another attack of malaria at Christmas should have made him more aware. He also obtained his replacement rifle and Browning pistol on Thursday Island before heading to his second study site at Mawatta (Landtman 1913b: 147). He arrived back in Mawatta in February 1911 and although he delighted in the situation of the village at the mouth of the wide Binaturi river and surrounded by large coconut groves he was aware of the large swampy areas behind for access to any inland villages required days of trekking through these swamps particularly during the wet season. Even Masingara, the closest Bine speaking village, that was only a couple of kilometres along a solid path during the dry season was a difficult wet slog otherwise. In a letter of 2 February he again wrote to Irene to say:

I am greatly satisfied to be back in my own district [among the Kiwai]. This is where I enjoy myself best. This letter will probably be picked up by Walker who drops by on his way to Badu. The Freshwaters [managers of the Madiri Plantation] will be coming along and probably Murray [from Dirimu Plantation] and thus I may be the only other white person on the mainland from the Dutch border in the west to the Fly River in the east. I am living here in the mission house which is quite like the one in Ipisia except that it has been divided into three compartments, one of which is occupied by the Samoan missionary family (away at the time being) … The inhabitants [here] speak a dialect of the Kiwai language. People are falling ill with dysentery — many people particularly children are dying.

The Samoan pastor at Ipisia lost a child to dysentery and Apineru, the pastor at Mawatta, moved his family to Daru after two members of his family had died. In order to keep the spread of dysentery away Landtman was forced to stick to a diet of porridge, two baths a day and coconut milk. When the supply of coconuts dwindled he remained on powered milk and so was relieved when he would write that the coconut supply had improved. In the same letter, continued on 5 February 1911, Landtman wrote that the people of the Mawatta district were easier to approach than those of Kiwai Island and he decided to allow people to tell him the stories that they chose to commence with rather than the more delicate topics he would have like to discuss. The people of Mawatta had much more regular contact with labour recruiters, white missionaries, traders and government officers and so would have understood quickly Landtman's role as a researcher and collector especially one who paid good prices. He noted that they rapidly organised themselves into some order and many people have been to talk with him.

Again in 18 February 1911 he wrote to his father in Helsinki that the people of Mawatta were much nicer than 'my dear and difficult people of Ipisia' and that they appear to be a bottomless well of tales and stories of magic. By now Landtman had 20 informants, all of a good age, a bit on the older side and 'they wait their turn to be heard'. Landtman wrote that by now he had collected 325 stories and folktales and that 'their number rises slower as the stories are so much longer and therefore also better'. He revised his research techniques for he noted 'I have not started using the systematic questionnaires, I am merely skimming the overflow that comes unasked'. He also remarked that he was leading a very regular life: the same program every day followed by a walk in the evening come rain or shine. This pattern of regular habits would have eased his approach into the community of Mawatta as every move would have been noted and discussed. His predictability would have calmed the fears of having a strange white man living within the local area. He would have been the subject of much discussion and amusement.

He still delighted in the strange, fierce beauty of the land and the good advice of settlers and administrators about not returning to the coast during the wet season gradually became understood:

> It was now raining heavily every day, although almost never all day for at least part of the time, at regular hours, the sun burnt intensely in between. One was astounded by the high blue skies in the evening with sulfur-yellow clouds here and there predicting the bad weather that broke with frightening thunder, during which the rain was pounding so heavily that you could not hear your own speech. Along with the rain, and the wind from inland, there appeared myriads of mosquitoes, a most painful discomfort. During these days I was not able to stay in my room where the dark corners were filled with mosquitoes, and when I did venture in, I stood in a buzzing cloud of flying enemies looking for a spot where to get you - unless they had already found one. Also on the verandah I was, regardless of the breeze, a target of constant torture and was not able to stay in the same place for any long period. It might happen that in my desperation I crept in the middle of the day into my bed to find peace at least for a while inside the net, and in the evenings I had to dress myself in two layers of clothes (Landtman 1913b: 150–51. Translated form the Swedish by Pirjo Varjola).

Comments on the Staniforth Smith Expedition to the Strickland River

Again on 5 March 1911, Landtman wrote to his father that it was Sunday and therefore a day for letters. He commented on the controversial expedition mounted by the Acting Lieutenant Governor of Papua, Miles Staniforth Smith (1912) who attempted to travel between the Aird River in the Gulf District to the Strickland River in the Western District on a rather wild adventure. Staniforth Smith only took along provisions for 30 days and when the expedition was reported lost a rescue expedition 'the size of a small army' according to Landtman was sent to find it (see also Schieffelin and Crittenden 1991: 33–40). One of the leaders of this rescue team was Wilfred Beaver, a Resident Magistrate from Daru and by now a friend of Landtman. Landtman expressed a wish to be part of the rescue mission but no doubt good sense prevailed for he did not go. In the meantime, he described his regular hunting parties searching for crocodiles and birds. The large hornbills and cassowaries were a particular hunting favourite as they are easy to spot. The country behind Mawatta is full of wild pigs, Rusa deer and wallabies and it appears that Landtman enjoyed hunting with the local men but found the countryside both beautiful and deadly. One time hunting boars, while he shot at flying foxes nesting in the swamp trees he was standing only a few metres from a large crocodile (Landtman 1913b: 162–63) and although he appears to have enjoyed the exercise he found that even in the tropics one can be quickly chilled by the strong wind and sudden rain that blows across the Torres Strait.

Life at Mawatta and Dirimu

The particular problem was, and continues to be, mosquitoes. Landtman noted that 'their number if absolutely phenomenal' and in times of desperation he went to his room, and pulled down his mosquito net that covered the table and chair as well as the bed, in order to have peace. In this 'room' he 'takes private lessons in superstition'. He also saw himself from the local people's view for Landtman lived in the mission area but brought seemingly vast amounts of money, tobacco and cargo [goods] with him. His presence was a valuable status symbol. In return not only was he presented with valuable legends and stories but supplied with fruit, vegetables as well as dugong and turtle meat and fish, at high cost. One hand of large bananas cost two sticks of tobacco. His young servant Gename took charge of the cooking and no doubt both sides were pleased with the arrangements:

> Ganáme took care of the kitchen most satisfactorily and our household was organized in the simplest way. I got up at about six thirty and had my breakfast of porridge, cacao and fruit as always with my meals. For lunch about 12 o'clock usually one or two cans of conserves were heated up in hot water, and rice was cooked most of the times to be mixed with it. The second course consisted of a little more rice mixed with jam, marmalade or cooked fruit. Instead of afternoon tea I had fruit and cocoa milk [coconut milk], and the supper before sunset varied according to circumstances. In the mission stations rainwater was collected in cisterns, but I hardly ever drank this water other than in the form of tea or cocoa, together with condensed milk, because the cocoa nuts were so much nicer for drinking. My only bread consisted of biscuits kept in hermetically closed cans, apart from the occasional baking of Ganáme who now and then made some kind of bread [damper] in a frying pan. What remained from our meals he divided between his friends amongst the villagers who were competing for friendship. Opened conserve cans and the like could not be kept from one meal to another. We were infuriated by the ants if sugar or something else tempting had been left in a a place

where they could get access to it. Ganame who enjoyed displaying his skills made at times all kinds of New Guinea extravagances, chocolate blancmanges, fruit omelets or pancake. And I thought sometimes that with a work that mainly consisted of writing down stories, in a village with obedient blacks, with flowers, fruit and pancake, my existence could be compared with a life in a fairytale (Landtman 1913b: 154–55. Translated form the Swedish by Pirjo Varjola).

Life in the community was not all Paradise or a fairytale existence for sharks often came up the mouth of the Binaturi looking for food scraps thrown into the river and crocodiles crept under houses at night hunting the village dogs or the remains of turtles left on the river banks. Crocodiles also took people from the village, particularly women and children washing in the river or the sea. Only small crocodiles were caught for food that reminded Landtman of lobster: only the tail can be eaten. While he was staying in Mawatta village he went on a number of dugong hunting trips and on one trip as many as eight canoes from Mawatta were joined by three from a neighbouring communities, possibly Tureture close by. Landtman thought that the group of canoes reminded him of a Viking fleet and remarked, with some perception, that 'perhaps some similarities could have been pointed out in this respect' (Landtman 1913b: 166). The reputation of the Kiwai as marine hunters and raiders was still strong. The use of the *narato*, the dugong hunting platform, was still evident along the Papuan coast at this time but declined due to safety:

Hunting platforms were erected on the reefs, one for each canoe, and when the high tide came at sunset, one of the men stepped on the platform while we others were waiting in the canoe anchored nearby. We knew that the man on the platform was busy calling in the dugongs with all kinds of magic and tricks of which we nevertheless could not see or hear. A little distance away were the other platforms with the figure of a man on top and the black shadow of the canoe nearby till the dark became too dense for us to see any of the others. We waited excitedly for the man to give a sign of catch, but our harpoon man kept standing although we were able to tell by his movements that he was following with his eyes a dugong swimming outside a throwing distance (Landtman 1913b: 167. Translated form the Swedish by Pirjo Varjola).

While the work was interesting and Landtman was pleased and proud with his efforts at Mawatta, he was often homesick and waited impatiently for mail from Finland and news of the daily life of his family far away. Contact with Murray from Dirimu was one source of comfort for the Papuan Industries plantation and store was only a short distance up the Binaturi river. It appears from correspondence dated 15 April 1911 that the Papuan Industries mission was building Landtman a house at Dirimu where he could base himself in the region. Actually Landtman financed the building of the house himself:

> Since my first visit in the place, I had had a house built at my expense in the part of Dírimo that belonged to Papuan Industries. At that time I had planned to make the village as my headquarters. This house that I planned to leave as a gift and small compensation for the Company was now very useful and allowed us each an airy room and a dining room to be shared, as well as the obligatory verandah round the house. Building with native labor and from native materials is cheap in New Guinea, and the rather large house cost me only about 250 Finnish mark. In this distant place, just about two days' journey from the nearest white people in Dáru, Murray and I led an ideal life. Murray was a keen naturalist and collector although his work on the plantations did not leave him much leisurely time. We had each our servant taking care of us, and the only trouble was caused by the numerous mosquitoes, existing inland even during the south east monsoon. They even disturbed our meals (Landtman 1913b: 171. Translated form the Swedish by Pirjo Varjola).

From Dirimu Murray and Landtman made the long journey inland to Jibu village near the headwaters of the Binaturi that was located on undulating, long, low, grassy hills covered in eucalypts and pandanus trees (VKKA Landtman 1910– 21: Murray 15 June 1911). In early June 1911, Landtman planned to make a trip along the coast to Mabudawan and Marukawa: 'a small island 12 hours from here [Mawatta], this island is a source of many stories. I am planning to shoot a bit too. … An old man by the name of Namai, the best of my teachers, follows me step by step almost'. Namai was to be one of Landtman's most important informants and the subject of some of his best photographs. Landtman also wrote that 'It is just Namai to whom I owe so much about my understanding of the Kiwai people' (Landtman 1913b: 152). Namai also turned down a worthwhile job with a Resident Magistrate on Daru to work and travel with Landtman along the coast. On 15 June 1911, Landtman was able to describe the success of his trip to the west. He never ceased to be enamored of the scenery and the wildlife for he wrote:

> We crossed the Mai-kasa river [Mai-kussa: actually a large tidal inlet] about two kilometers wide at its mouth, and visited an inland village on the other bank. The scenery at the estuary was one of the most beautiful I have seen in the country. A school of perhaps thirty porpoises were dancing around in the glimmering water, swimming a bit up the river, and here and there I saw the spiky elongated contour of a crocodile floating just below the surface. Besides crocodiles I kept observing sharks with a particular interest during this trip, to my mind they were

an object of legendary shimmer from the exciting books for boys. The elegant and suggestive back fin was cutting the surface of the water nervously swimming in circles around our vessel. Once I saw a long fight for life or death between two huge sea animals. They made the water splash high, but I was not able to make out which animals they were. I often had the feeling that these tropical depths were hiding secret and terrible monsters of an unthinkable kind (Landtman 1913b: 177. Translated from the Swedish by Pirjo Varjola).

He reported on the journey to Mabudawan that every place near there has a history of some legendary ancestor. The coastal Kiwai told Landtman the stories of the travels of the souls on the way to Adiri the land of the dead in the west and of other legends that he recorded for his collection:

From my travels I particularly remember those made by canoe to Mabudavane [Madudawan] in the west on the coast, where the people had their gardens and a number of houses. A little distance away from the beach there was a single huge boulder, where the mythical being Wáwa lived. He was at times seen by the natives, grinding his stone axe against a cliff nearby, as you could see from some longish marks in the stone. On Páho island nearby I saw the place where the spirits of the dead cry under the dáni tree, and the lumps of clay they throw at the branches of the tree. Also the spring out of which the dead people drink, the place where they dance and the foot prints of the mythical Sidó in the hill just as the natives had described. A small creek [Pahoturi] was running into the sound between Paho [Island] and the main land (Landtman 1913b: 160. Translated from the Swedish by Pirjo Varjola).

By 20 June 1911 Landtman was again happily residing in his own house back near the Dirimu Plantation for he wrote: *'Egen härd är guld värd'* [Your own fireplace is worth gold]. He reported to his family that Mawatta had been a goldmine of information and G. H. Murray, the manager of the Dirimu plantation, sent his whaleboat to collect Landtman from Mawatta so that he could study the inland people along the Binaturi River. The 20 kilometre journey by boat from Mawatta to Dirimu had taken a crew of six plus two in reserve, including his new servant Ganame and 'uncle' Namai. In Dirimu, slightly outside the area of the coastal Kiwai and located on Bine people's land, Landtman was able to concentrate on revising and ordering his notes. He used Dirimu as a base for his photographic expeditions in the hinterland although these were not to be a great success. Landtman then made two recordings of Bine songs on 12 June 1911 at Mawatta. However, these would be the last recordings he was able to make (VK 4919 nos. 40 and 41).

Figure 6. G. Murray and G. Landtman at Jibu (VKK 248: 549)

Change came rapidly to the area Landtman was studying. Another correspondent of that time, J. Cowling of Mibu Plantation, reported that when he first came to the Daru coast in 1896, Mawatta was a trading centre and that the Kiwai sailed canoes into the Torres Strait and sold them there. Now [in 1911], he wrote: 'the Kiwai and the Islanders owned whaleboats and the trade has declined but the people at the "fountainhead" cannot understand the decline'. This canoe traffic, according to Cowling, commenced at the Bamu River and the canoes were sold on to Wabuda Island, then to Kiwai Island and on to Mawatta (VKKA Landtman 1910–21: Cowling 27 June 1911). Cowling was correct in his general assessment but the patterns of customary exchange continued despite the introduction of the cash economy (Lawrence 1994).

Mail to and from the isolated plantation at Dirimu was irregular: 'I have been without mail for a record time recently. Latest letter from home had a date over 13 weeks old and it is now four weeks since it arrived. Both Murray and I are expecting to receive a fat mail bag each'. However, Landtman was dismayed by his trips into the interior: 'I have made several excursions here [Dirimu] but with negative results for me, the surroundings seem to be uninhabited. A hut here and there and you meet almost the same people everywhere as these people move about constantly' (VKKA Landtman to his father dated 9 July 1911). He found the inland people shy and difficult and it made him eager to 'remember the dear Ipisia people'. Landtman politely turned down a wish by F. W. Walker that he should take up trading on behalf of Papuan Industries. While he often publicly and politely expressed his trust in the work of the commercial mission, in private he had doubts about its viability.

His work was proceeding rapidly however for he wrote to his father: 'I have now been through my manuscript from Mawatta and I am still as content with it as before. The Ipisia manuscript seems insignificant in comparison even though I was quite happy with it at the time'. No doubt his faith in the Kiwai Island work was responsible for his decision to return there later in the year. Boredom as well as the need for change drove him to row the mission dinghy down the Binaturi River to Mawatta where he was well received by the locals eager for tobacco. Landtman miscalculated the current and the rapid darkness and the row back upstream took seven hours. Not only was he frequently tangled on underwater branches and logs but the crocodiles scared him more than once. The local people however had other explanations: 'For the crocodile or whatever animal it may have been the people immediately had an explanation: it had not been a crocodile but the malevolent spirit of a woman who had recently been taken by a crocodile there' (VKKA Landtman 1910–21 Letter to his father 9 July 1911).

However, not all his work produced positive results for, as he wrote to his father, certain ceremonies and rituals were still conducted away from the sight of traders and missionaries and especially visiting ethnologists:

During the night some time ago a ceremony was held in the forest a distance from the village. It went on the next day; we could hear the singing and the drums. I went there in the morning putting the Browning [pistol] in my pocket for the sake of romance because the blacks can be a little difficult concerning secret rituals. I do not know how they found out about my approach but when I arrived on the spot everything had been put aside and I was allowed to sniff around with my suspicions. But when you are with them alone, just the two of you, they tell you much more than they allow you to see (Letter dated 9 July 1911).

Malaria was a constant threat for all who lived in the region. Murray was found seriously ill on Landtman's return from Mawatta and exhibited that standard pattern of symptoms: a proper fever for five days and then the patient feels immediately well again. However, if untreated, the bouts recur again and again. The only relief from work was hunting in the bush with Murray and local men. The water fowls in particular were curried by Landtman's servant Gename. It appears that Landtman had not eaten curry before although he reported that he enjoyed the taste. He would have been unimpressed to learn that food was curried to disguise poor quality meat. He continued this letter on 17 July 1911 and was pleased to report that the Psychological Institute in Berlin had sent a praising letter about the collection of recorded songs sent off in December 1910. Landtman had not been especially happy with the results but was cheered by the letter of congratulations especially in contrast to a letter received from Haddon who: 'had squeaked that the packing of the boxes was to be criticized even though the objects had luckily arrived in better shape than he [Landtman] deserved'. Landtman wrote of Haddon's apparently difficult and demanding nature: *'Hoppas linnet lägger sig till härnäst'* [I hope his indignation will disappear [at least] until next time].

By this time Landtman had perfected the techniques of collecting both artefacts and oral histories and was becoming better skilled with the use of the photographic equipment. On 8 August 1911 he wrote to his father: 'how pleased I am with these masses of notes even if I cannot make a general overview and evaluate everything now — but if I had calculated my best possibilities for doing the job at 100 at home, I can now consider having achieved it all at a level of 1000 or a million .... The number of fairytales, adventure stories, dreams etc is now over 500'. While Landtman's intellectual success was being quickly achieved in the wilds of Papua, the expansion of the missions was slow and tedious. The manager of the Madiri plantation, J. B. Freshwater, not only had to construct a house and store at the plantation, and single-handedly supervise the planting of the coconut and rubber trees, but he had to cross to Kiwai Island and supervise the construction of the new church at Sumai built in the standard prefabricated style of North Queensland Protestant chapels.

Figure 7. The new mission church at Sumai (VKK 248: 537)

In August 1911, Landtman was able to visit Buji in the far west close to the Mai Kussa and Cowling in a long letter informed Landtman of the history of the settlement at Buji, the raids by the 'Tugeri' and the efforts of the government to establish a permanent police post on the coast (VKKA Landtman 1910–21: Cowling 13 August 1911). Landtman was again able to visit Marukawa Island near Mabudawan and he crossed to Boigu and Dauan in the Torres Strait where he photographed important story sites. He felt well and happy in a letter to his sister Irene and wrote: 'I think I have never been in a better [physical] shape and form than here. I made recently a rather difficult march to a village inland [from Buji]. Old Namai was so stiff legged on return that he had someone let blood from them, the universal cup'.

His 'teachers', the local people, were bottomless: 'like the oil pot of the widow'. However, the time at Mawatta was starting to pall: 'The next places I shall visit for shorter periods of time, [I] shall try to leave for the really wild [areas] in order to take photos and get ethnological artefacts' (Letter to his aunt 3 September 1911). Despite the lack of adventure, Mawatta was a valuable field site and Landtman proposed sending his Mawatta manuscript to his father at the earliest opportunity. In the meantime he made up for the problem of European influence by 'having had the natives dress themselves for an old ceremony and perform some parts with dances and gestures, the missionaries did not particularly like it, I think but the whole thing was quite impressive and colourful, and identical with the descriptions I had before' (VKKA Landtman 1910–21 Letter to his father 11 September 1911).

However, while the spectacle was impressive the phonograph failed to operate and the songs and dances could not be recorded on the cylinder. He continued to travel along the coast as far west as possible and on 1 November 1911 he again reported to the family on the successful journey to Buji, on the Mai Kussa, and other places and islands on the way. This trip appealed to the call of the wild for he wrote: 'I went a bit inland [from Buji] and came to a village where I had a chance to take photographs of the people, stark naked, and obtained a collection of objects, some of them quite beautiful. My own wares intended for trade were finished (too soon) and finally I had to give away in exchange some of my own things, a shirt, a knife, soap, biscuits and other food'. By 6 November 1911 he wrote to his sister Irene that he was ready to return to the Fly estuary but had to make the journey by canoe as the mission boat was unavailable. He was nervous at having to get his precious photographic equipment, watch and gun 'bound to the canoe as things are known to fall over the side from time to time' but in fact in the Fly estuary the large *motomoto*, canoes with double outriggers, are more stable and comfortable than any European boat.

Return to the Fly estuary

Landtman meanwhile made a complete inventory of his artefacts, notes and supplies and left them in the care of Murray at Dirimu. After eight months in the Mawatta area he once again he set out for the mouth of the Fly and another trip to Gaima. By 13 November 1911 he was writing to his father from the home of the Freshwaters at Madiri Plantation and again planning to cross to Gaima on the other side of the Fly River. Gaima, a Gogodala community, had recently been the scene of the murder of nine men who had returned from the pearling fields in the Torres Strait. They had been robbed and murdered by their own villagers and Landtman was advised by the civil administration not to travel to the community until it had been secured by the police from Daru. However, accompanied by the local Samoan pastor and his own boat crew he travelled over to the village and found it peaceful. While his own men did not want to stay overnight in the longhouse, Landtman and Ganame remained on shore for two nights. He wrote to his father: 'I am particularly content with this trip. I got a good deal of photographs and also objects, among them a number of them deriving from the excursion [made previously] with Butcher and myself. We brought them in but had not been able to take them along and had sent them back to Gaima where they were well cared for'.

Landtman voiced some general criticisms of the nature of colonial pacification of the middle Fly region and, while the Papuan government of the day could be described as little more than benevolent, well-regulated police rule, someone so strange and foreign to the local people as Landtman would not have been seen as a threat. The fact that he was accompanied by a pastor and carried valuable tradestore goods would also mean that he was unlikely to be a victim of communal violence.

Again, luck was with him. From Madiri, Landtman reported that he had gathered large numbers of artefacts and made many good photographs: 'the several dozen that I have taken here leave all the others far behind in all respects, the topics too are absolutely better, the people are so original and naked that the pictures cannot be looked at by gentlemen and ladies simultaneously'. From Madiri, Landtman planned his circumnavigation of Kiwai Island. He started in Sumai (Paara) village and wrote (24 November 1911) that he had arrived on the mission boat the 'Goodwill' and paid Walker for the transportation. Life was a mixture of adventure and work but he wrote to his father that he could feel the final four months of his stay in Papua coming to a close. His perceptive criticism of the role and operation of the Papuan Industries mission would not have pleased his kind and generous hosts, the Walkers, Murray or the Freshwaters:

> The whole of the Walker family is leaving for England in February [1912] in order to stay for one year. So we will probably meet there. The intention of Walker is to get more capital for his Christian industrial mission company. The original share capital of £31,000 plus income from seven years is almost gone and he hopes to get support by appealing to the religious souls in England. If Walker were not obviously an honourable man this would all be a pretty swindle because Papuan Industries has been a pure business company with God's name put between the numbers and calculations, not one pound has been given by the company for mission purposes. ... The prices of the company [stores] are the same as those of their competitors as "it is not good at all for the natives to be sold products too cheap."

In all he found the people of Sumai stiff and unwilling to communicate unlike the open people of Mawatta. Still, the Kiwai Islanders had not been influenced to the same extent by European influences and the information gained was rich and important. Again, the success with the photographic equipment was a source of pride and in particular a series of photographs of the inside and outside of long houses, possibly at Auti, was the topic of a letter to his sister on 6 December 1911.

By the end of December 1911, Landtman was in the large village of Iasa on Kiwai Island. He planned to continue his journey around the island by canoe and was preparing for a special trip, once again with Ben Butcher, to the Gulf District. The plan this time was to go in a new motor boat the 'Tamate' [named after the missionary James Chalmers] along the coast of the Gulf of Papua where Landtman hoped to meet real 'cannibals'. Indeed the 'Tamate' was the envy of government offers and traders. Landtman was well aware of this and wrote:

> The meeting of Butcher and I was very hearty, and he was extremely happy with his boat that offered him a most comfortable place to stay and that reached a speed of 11 knots making him independent of all flows of tidewater. The "Támate" had a beautiful salon furnished with wood, a room for the men plus a kitchen, bathroom and illumination with acetylene, it had cost 50,000 marks although not directly paid for by the London Missionary Society but paid by separately collected funds for this particular purpose. Due to his new boat Butcher was now the foremost person in the area, leaving the government officials far behind. Generally, there prevailed an ambitious jealousy between "the government" and "the mission" and both wanted to, although for different purposes, be seen as the real protectors of the natives. Without taking so much the side of the government, all traders were against the mission, and on the whole the general behaviour between the few white people in the area left much to be desired. The atmosphere was so irritating that people often did not even want to tolerate other people's opinions. Perhaps this worked in analogy with experiences of other circumstances like those on sailing ships, polar expeditions etc. Butcher and I agreed that he should come to fetch me in Ipisia on about the 15th of January for a joint expedition east along the coast to the wild areas around the Aird or Kikori Rivers, where we would be meeting cannibalistic tribes. I went with him to Iasa where we parted from each other for the moment (Landtman 1913b: 180. Translated from the Swedish by Pirjo Varjola).

From Iasa, Landtman sailed by canoe to Ipisia. He was comfortable on the 'rather spacey platform [deck] in the middle' of the *motomoto* but the tides and currents of the Fly estuary conspired against him. The tide had gone out and the large, heavy canoe had to be poled across the mud of the Iasaoromo channel that divided the districts of Samari from Iasa and Wiorubi. This took hours and by the time the tide had turned, the canoe had only just reached the other side of the island. Here the exhausted travellers slept on the beach. As there was no wind in the early morning, Landtman walked the long beach to Ipisia: a route that he knew well. Now, instead of imagining a difficult time ahead he was pleased to be welcomed as a returnee: *'jag överslätades'* [I was overwhelmed with hugs].

Gename's village wedding

Landtman returned easily to the established life of the village. Gename, his servant, married amid feasting, dancing and fighting when one village argued that their dancers were better than those of another community. The fight, with fire brands being thrown, coconuts and sticks raining on the crowd, women and children shouting and screaming, appealed to the sense of adventure in Landtman. The tumult was carefully documented, photographed and recorded:

> Ganáme got married a couple of days after my arrival — I had the honor of donating the wedding dress to his bride. There was a big dance during the night, and later an infernal fight broke out. I was told it started because of a quarrel between the people of our village and those of another, about who were the best dancers. I was developing photographs when the "spectacle" broke out. The racket grew louder with miraculous speed until it all exploded in a wild tumult. You could hear feet stamping as if there were a herd of horses, smashing with poles that were breaking, shouts and thuds. I hurried out. I have seen many fights before but this one was the prettiest. The village was illuminated like in daylight, full of flaming torches lit in haste by the women. People rushed back and forth like blind men, hitting around with stakes and throwing cocoa nuts, pieces of wood and firebrands at each other. It was no play; there was savagery in their gestures. You could hardly see who belonged to which side. The firebrands flying about made a magnificent sight, and seeing the sparking lights it felt at first that the house was on fire. The women were screaming loud when one of them was hit. The missionary Tovia and I up on the verandah shouted to a man running past asking what the fight was all about, and he stopped for some blinks of an eye gesticulating, when he was hit in the back by a projectile that was too much for him and he sprang off again. The grand gesticulations and the excitement of the man were worth seeing, and almost all of the people were still wearing their full dancing outfits. We had to press ourselves against the wall because of the projectiles coming towards our roof. ... In about a half an hour the tumult began to quiet down, changing more into shouting and lesser handling, and I returned to my plates. The next day a great number of men showed marks of the fight, some of them of rather serious kind. One man came to me with a wound by an arrow in his foot (Landtman 1913b: 181–82. Translated from the Swedish by Pirjo Varjola).

When the village returned to normal, and he had finished treating the injured he and his crew continued their travels around the island. The strength of the tide in the estuary can be daunting when sailing on a canoe without motor power and Landtman later wrote to his family that: 'we reached strong tides in the Fly, many times it was completely calm. It was tearing hot in the middle of the day, you could not read because looking at the paper blinded your eyes, nor could you lie outstretched, it was just possible to sit straight and a banana leaf inside the [sun] helmet was welcome'.

Landtman's program was essentially determined by external forces. He wrote to his aunt on 3 February 1912 that he was forced to remain in Ipisia longer than expected while waiting for Ben Butcher who had made an agreement to take Landtman on the trip to the Gulf District. Butcher had not shown up and consequently Landtman was running out of supplies in the middle of a heavy wet season when there was little garden food available. He wrote: 'The worst difficulty in this country [Papua] is the impossible situation of communication'. In the Fly estuary this remains a problem even today. Landtman was concerned that he had to return to many places in the district where he had left his collections, photographs and notes and that time was running out before he was expected to leave for England. During the enforced stay he made short expeditions to the eastern bank of the Fly where he participated in some of the unplanned and unexpected drama of village life:

> … just before daybreak. All the young men had quietly gone out the house, taking their weapons and dressing themselves up. They made a mock attack on the house at the early hour. It immediately led into a terrible commotion, with the men surrounding the house running, and screaming and banging the ground with their clubs and poles. It all was arranged to frighten and wake up the people inside, particularly the women and the children, and it served as an introduction to the ordinary dance to follow. I was awakened and told about the plan just before it began, because the men wanted me to fire a few shots to add to the enjoyment. I did so, but kept a number of shots at hand for certainty's sake, just in case the gentlemen should be tempted to go further, now that they had started the fun (Landtman 1913b: 184. Translated from the Swedish by Pirjo Varjola).

Journey to the Gulf District

Landtman again returned to Ipisia and finally, just when he was about to give up hope, on 3 February 1912 Butcher sent a short note to shore telling Landtman that the 'Tamate' was sailing for Wabuda Island, the Bamu and the Gulf District with a brief stop at Goaribari Island and that if he wished to go he must pack immediately. The region around Goaribari Island and the Purari delta was one of the least explored areas of Papua and Landtman's excursion, like his trips to Gaima and the Aramia region, were mostly made out of curiosity. They lay outside his field of research but he wrote in his travelogue:

> We then spent some ten days in the delta area and a bit up the Aird. The delta was unbelievably large and offered the strangest landscape I had seen. The land was completely low and wet with vegetation of nipa palms and mangrove trees, and between them was a network of canals that transformed the delta into a hopelessly confusing labyrinth. We went in a wrong direction many times, for a couple of hours, at times, the "Tamate's" speed was necessary to save us from being completely lost (Landtman 1913b: 190. Translated from the Swedish by Pirjo Varjola).

The region had strong memories for the people of the London Missionary Society for Ben Butcher was seeking a place to establish a new mission and a chance to convert the killers of the missionary martyrs:

> One day we visited the village of Dopíma on the island of Goaribári, where the missionaries Chalmers and Tomkins from the London Missionary Society had been killed and eaten in 1901, along with their party of eleven natives from Kiwai. How it happened is and will stay unsolved, because no actual facts are known, and the punishing party that was sent to the spot some time afterwards only found some traces showing what had happened, but no witnesses existed of how it had happened. Chalmers and his party had arrived with the mission ship "Niúe" presumably at a moment when one of the ceremonies of the natives was going on, and the presence of strangers could not be tolerated. Chalmers and his party went ashore despite warnings, and they were not to be seen again after the moment they vanished from the sight of the people remaining onboard. Even the "Niúe" was attacked but escaped (Landtman 1913b: 190–91. Translated from the Swedish by Pirjo Varjola).

Landtman and Butcher spent about 10 days in the Gulf District in search of a location for Butcher's new mission. Despite the dangers and the discomforts Butcher and his family finally settled at Aird Hills on the Kikori River, a place discovered by Butcher and Landtman on this trip:

> We spent the nights always onboard the "Tamate", and when we stayed outside certain villages, it regularly happened that after nightfall men came paddling in their canoes, offering us the company of one or another female relative. There might be half a dozen canoes and more floating around the "Tamate", each with a man and a woman or two couples. We gathered that this habit offered to strangers and especially the whites

did not solely have with hospitality to do but also was connected with certain magic beliefs [This was a custom in certain groups especially from the Bamu River region. It was a sign of friendship and establishment of fictive kinship relationships which prevented the stranger from attacking his host. There were no magic beliefs attached to the custom].

Sighing at the sinfulness of the world Butcher went around with his lantern, illuminating the canoes, perhaps to see what the girls looked like and giving them each a piece of tobacco. The quiet nights on the river were divine, and sitting in our deck chairs we listened to Butcher's gramophone that brought back memories of forgotten melodies.

It was Butcher's intention to find a place in the area for the main station for a new mission district they planned. Finally he found one on an island on the upper part of the delta at the foot of a group of rather high mountain peaks which, seen from a distance, melted together into one considerable elevation called Aird Hill. It was an isolated hill in the flattest of lowlands. The mountain formations in the middle of the island were surrounded by swamp on all sides but one, where Butcher found a piece of solid land high enough and safe from the reach of any kind of high tide. We spent a couple of days in the neighborhood trying, unsuccessfully, to make contact with the natives who from time to time cautiously showed themselves in their canoes from a distance (Landtman 1913b: 194–95. Translated from the Swedish by Pirjo Varjola).

The successful mission and trade school established by Butcher was instrumental in the conversion of many of the local communities (Butcher 1963). Landtman wrote to his father on 16 February 1912 from Daru that he had only time, during the rapid travelling, to take some photographs and make notes but that despite the speed of the trip he was pleased to have made the journey.

Meeting with Sir Hubert Murray

Again, Landtman's good luck favoured him for on the trip with Butcher he met Sir Hubert Murray, the Lieutenant Governor of Papua also on an exploration trip to the Kikori and Daru, and so was able to return to Daru on the government steamboat the 'Merrie England'. However he was mindful of the state of his equipment and clothing after two years in the villages of Papua for he later wrote:

I spent then four days onboard the "Merrie England". At the time of leaving my headquarters in Mawata I had not planned for a journey with Butcher and still less prepared to meet with his Excellency, and that is why the clothing I had with me, worn through two years of hard conditions was somewhat slight. Luckily I had a small reserve so that I was able to join in at the dinner table with some decency.

This journey would have consolidated his association with Murray who as a man was careful with his friendships. Murray would have admired Landtman's courage and dedication. Back in Mawatta Landtman wrote to his sister on 18 February 1912 that he was pleased to find his manuscript and collections safe but still distributed in three places and he had to make arrangements for the consolidation of the material before his imminent departure. After two years in the field Landtman was well travelled and had amassed a fine collection of folk-lore, artefacts and photographs. It appears he had also written a draft of his final manuscript and he later wrote in his travelogue:

How satisfied I was for the completeness of my notes; the pages of the manuscript that was kept in a large iron box had grown in numbers so much that counted them now by the weight, and I felt a certain satisfaction each time I lifted the heavy box. The number of fairytales, stories etc alone were over 800, variations included (Landtman 1913b: 196. Translated form the Swedish by Pirjo Varjola).

In his last letter from the field addressed to his aunt written on 18 March 1912 Landtman wrote to say that: 'To my great pleasure I have just received all boxes and sacks full of objects, my manuscript and the photographs I was forced to leave behind on various mission stations in the area'. His packing more or less completed he managed to have a local merchant construct wooden crates and he filled them with coconut husk as packing material.

Return to England and then to Finland

Landtman returned to Europe by way of Cambridge in April 1912 where he stayed for a few months unpacking and sorting his artifact collection. At Cambridge he wrote the first of his many papers on the Kiwai (Landtman 1912b). Landtman made an early visit to Finland to see his family before returning once again to Cambridge. It was on the second trip home that he had a near disastrous experience when his ship sank in the Kattegat strait off Denmark and the manuscript of his main book on the Kiwai went down with his belongings. Letters from his friends record the distress felt at such a loss (VKKA Landtman 1910–21: Rosalie Walker 17 February 1913 and F. W. Walker 17 February 1913). Landtman was not to be dismayed for long by this accident for he hired a diver to retrieve his material and, after drying the manuscript, only a few pages were found to be damaged (VKKA Landtman 1910–21: 24 May 1913). Fortunately his artefact collections and photographs had been shipped to Finland earlier.

Post-script: further letters to and from the field

Correspondence with missionary and trading friends in Papua continued after Landtman returned to Helsinki. In a letter to Landtman, G. H. Murray complained of the long and heavy wet season of 1913 that caused serious flooding to the Dirimu plantation. Murray condemned the narrow parochial attitudes of the European settlement in Daru and wrote of the small-mindedness of colonial officers in their dealings with each other (VKKA Landtman 1910–21: Murray 15 May 1913). In the letter, Murray re-introduced Wilfred Beaver, the particular subject of some of these petty jealousies and someone Landtman had befriended in Daru.

Wilfred Beaver was an experienced government officer who later wrote requesting assistance with a monograph that he was preparing on the people of the Western District (VKKA Landtman 1910–21: Beaver 24 July 1913 and 14 November 1913). Beaver had served in a number of areas in Papua and led the overland team to find Staniforth Smith and his expedition party in the Gulf District. After his year long leave in Britain, Beaver returned to Papua and was posted to the Buna and the Orokaiva Districts where he had previously served. He asked if Landtman would contribute a chapter to his book on the Kiwai and hoped to have the final manuscript ready by 1915 (VKKA Landtman 1910–21: 29 December 1913). He asked for permission to use eight of Landtman's plates in his book although the published edition contains only a few of Landtman's prints together with the photographs from other sources (Beaver 1920). In his final letter Beaver offers his gratitude to Landtman for sending the chapter on religious beliefs and practices to the publishers in London and comments, now that the First World War has commenced in Europe: 'I have been trying to get away but can't manage it just now' (VKKA Landtman 1910–21: Beaver 25 May 1915). Wilfred Beaver, a keen observer of Papuan social life and customs who had been educated at the University of Melbourne and in Brussels, was killed at the Polygon Wood in Belgium in 1917. His book was later published posthumously (Beaver 1920). It remains an interesting and useful descriptive account the Kiwai people and colonial attitudes during that period.

In March 1914 the Lieutenant Governor wrote to Landtman acknowledging the receipt of the travelogue, *Nya Guinea färden* (Landtman 1913b), a paper on the poetry of the Kiwai (Landtman 1913c) and the study of two Kiwai legends, *Två Papuanska sagor* (Landtman 1913d). Leonard Murray, the Official Secretary, later wrote from Government House in Port Moresby to acknowledge with thanks the receipt of Landtman's substantial book on the folk-tales of the Kiwai Papuans (Landtman 1917) (VKKA Landtman 1919–21: Leonard Murray 26 August 1919).

The last letter in the correspondence file to Landtman, from Ethel Zahel (VKKA Landtman 1910–21: Zahel 3 November 1921) reports that the Madiri plantation is doing better than the Dirimu one and she has returned to the islands to teach in the Badu Native School as she felt lost in England and more at home in the Torres Strait. It is of little wonder that she felt at home on Badu for Ethel Zahel was an interesting figure in the history of education and administration in the Torres Strait. She was born in Mackay in Queensland but moved to Thursday Island with her solicitor husband in 1905 (Lawrie 1990). When her husband died there Zahel became a temporary teacher on Yam Island. Her only daughter died of malaria and so Zahel moved to Badu and opened the Badu Native School in 1909. She lived with F. W. Walker and his family for many years.

In addition to her duties as teacher she was also the clerk and treasurer of the Badu court, the registrar of birth, deaths and marriages and in 1915 was given administrative control over the 'company boats'. Zahel was one of the white teachers appointed to sign authorisations for the provisioning of vessels and determining advance payments for pearl-shell and bêche-de-mer brought to Badu for sale at Papuan Industries store. Zahel supervised the court on neighbouring Moa Island. She was praised for her work as she was considered bright, vigorous, intelligent and forceful. Together with Walker and his family, she would no doubt have been interesting company for Gunnar Landtman during his enforced stays on Badu. But perhaps unwittingly, she was part of the system of restrictive control over the very people she had come to love.

Papuan Industries Ltd failed to thrive financially despite the long years of work and Walker was continually forced to make representation to the LMS authorities and the Queensland Government for assistance. Walker and his family lived and worked in the Torres Strait until his retirement in 1922 when he briefly returned to the mission at Kwato (Wetherell 1996: 129; Ganter 1994: 86). The company continued under the direction of J. B. Freshwater, formerly of the Madiri plantation, who was the impetus behind the sale of the Papuan Industries properties to other agencies. Madiri was sold to the Unevangelised Field Mission (UFM) an evangelical religious society that relied more on 'muscular' Christianity but one that was ultimately more successful than the LMS. The presence of the missionaries did little to resolve endemic warfare in the lower Fly River. Following sale of the Madiri mission activity at the mouth of the Fly was disrupted in the 1930s by threats of attack from the Suki Lakes people to the west. The Suki were much feared and the UFM missionaries had to move to the relative safety of the Manowetti banks where the land was more productive and the population greater (Lawrence 1995: 62–63). For safety, the local people moved further inland to Balamula or southeast along the coast to Madame.

Despite the inherent paternalism of the mission Papuan Industries did increase Islander involvement with the Australian cash economy and some of the essential commercial foundations of F. W. Walker's enterprise remain. Papuan

Industries became Aboriginal Industries when it was bought out by the Queensland Government in 1929 and in 1939 it became the Island Industries Board (IIB) (Beckett 1987: 49–50). Since a change in constitution in 1984 the IIB trades as the Islander Board of Industry and Service (IBIS) with stores on all inhabited Torres Strait islands and a local staff of 200. Papuan villagers along the southwestern coast, with permission to cross into Australian territory under the Torres Strait Treaty, continue to shop at these island stores. Papuans no longer work in the marine industries of the Torres Strait.

Chapter 3
Imaging the Kiwai

Gunnar Landtman was an avid photographer as well as artefact collector and folklorist. By 1911 he had made a sufficient collection of glass-plate negatives to send back to his father in Helsinki. These plates were sent through his missionary friends at Badu from where Rosalie Walker, the wife of Rev. F. W. Walker, wrote thanking him for allowing them the opportunity of seeing the negatives and for giving the missionaries the chance to make prints if they wished (Landtman 1910–21: R. Walker 19 October 1911). In all, Landtman took over 500 photographs while in the field. During his expeditions not only did he travel with his personal effects, his own food, a growing artefact collection and phonograph recording equipment but he also took along his photographic equipment and special photographic papers brought from Finland. When this ran out he was forced to use lesser quality material from Australia. He regularly complained of this to his family.

Ethnographic photography at the turn of the 20th Century

Ethnographic photography was a developing field technique. It had a long tradition in colonial India where Lord Canning, the first Viceroy after 1858 and a keen photographer, requested civil and military field officers to make collections of the different tribal groups for his personal interest. Much of this material was subsequently published in the eight volume work, *The People of India* (Watson and Kaye 1868–75) which contained 480 photographic portraits of various races, castes and tribes in India together with descriptive and historical information (Falconer 2002: 52). This form of field photography was mobilised as a means for having knowledge about subject peoples and from its earliest days photography became a tool of ethnography in the service of colonialism and imperialist expansion. This invested photography with a power greater than just mere technology. The photographs are stylised, composed images that are certainly impressive but lack any feeling for the humanity of the subject. Along with comprehensive data obtained from topographical mapping, revenue surveys and detailed archaeological surveying, ethnographic photography became part of the imperial ideology to tabulate, systematise, catalogue and ultimately control the natural and human resources of the Indian subcontinent (Falconer 2002: 55).

In Papua photography had been used extensively by the members of the Cambridge Anthropological Expedition in 1898 and the Haddon collection at Cambridge holds around 300 photographs of the Torres Strait and 300 of Papua taken by Anthony Wilkin, the junior member of the expedition (Edwards 2000: 123 note 9). Many photographs from these collections were published in the reports of the expedition (Haddon 1901–35). The members of the London Missionary Society were also keen recorders of local scenes and customs and Ben Butcher and the Rev. W. G. Lawes, among others, took many images now held in the Council for World Mission Archives at the University of London, School of Oriental and African Studies (www.cwmission.org.uk). Photographs by Charles Abel from the Kwato mission are held at the University of Papua New Guinea in Port Moresby (University of Papua New Guinea NG collection ALX-1)(Pacific Manuscripts Bureau 2006). Most of these images were originally collected to be used in talks and lectures on the success of the missionary enterprise in Papua.

At the same time, photography was being used in the Australian colonies as an exercise in attracting settlers and securing ownership of the vast alien continent. Between 1886 and 1888 an outstanding collection of engravings, and some photographs, was published by Andrew Garran in subscription format under the title, *The Picturesque Atlas of Australasia*. It also played a significant role in developing a sense of nationalism in late 19th Century in colonial Australia (Garran 1886–88; Hughes-d'Aeth 2001). J. W. Lindt, one of the most important figures in early colonial photography, also published a series of illustrations titled *PicturesqueNew Guinea* that was part of a group of photographic studies of Pacific island communities that supported Australian sub-colonial expansionism in the Pacific (Lindt 1887). The use of the term 'picturesque' in the titles gives some indication of the style, and orientation of these publications. Photography, for ethnographic study and research, was not part of the early scene.

In Finland many linguists, ethnographers and travellers at that time used photography during their excursions and adventures in Karelia, Siberia, North Russia and Central Asia. Marshal Carl Gustaf Mannerheim, on an early intelligence gathering mission from Moscow to Beijing between 1906 and 1908 took over 1500 photographs and even developed a celluloid film in his tent. Mannerheim also returned with over 1000 artefacts collected with money from the Antell legacy (Mannerheim and Hilden 1969). Photography has a rich history in Finnish ethnology (Varjola 1982).

Techniques and technology

The political and social power of the image was beginning to be recognised early in the life of ethnographic photography. Everard im Thurn, the botanist and museum curator who later became High Commissioner of the Western Pacific and Governor of Fiji between 1904 and 1911, was very influential in anthropological circles in England and published an important paper on the anthropological use of the camera in 1893 (im Thurn 1893: 184–203). im Thurn was also to become President of the Royal Anthropological Institute of Great Britain and Ireland from 1911–20 and he lectured on the intrinsic, aesthetic and humanising use of photography, though largely in terminology that would be considered patronising and derogatory today. He supported naturalistic photography of 'native' peoples that removed the posed arrangements commonly affected at that time.

Everard im Thurn was one of the first to actually describe and recommend photographic material to travellers and ethnologists. For his earlier work in British Guiana [Guyana] he used both a smaller hand-held camera for immediate photographs and a larger fixed view camera. However he wrote that the small hand cameras of that time 'are an abomination and are really much more difficult to work with [for] satisfactory results than are fixed cameras' (im Thurn 1893: 201). The large view camera of the period consisted of a front standard that held the lens plate, the shutter and the lens. This was joined to a back standard by means of a bellows, a flexible, accordion-pleated box that had the ability to accommodate the movement of the two standards. The rear standard held the film plate. This rear standard was a frame that held a ground glass used for focusing and composing the image before exposure. The whole apparatus could be collapsed for transportation but required the solid support of a fixed base.

im Thurn also recommended the use of tele-photographic, concentric lens, and although film substitutes based on xylonite [celluloid] were becoming available, he preferred the use of the heavy glass-plate mainly because the lighter films of that time did not keep their condition in tropical regions. His recommendation, and this would have still been relevant to Landtman in 1910, was 'On the whole it seems best at present to take a certain number of good glass plates for the special work' (im Thurn 1893: 201). It was then necessary for the ethnologist to have a dark room or darkened tent and a changing bag to keep the plates after exposure. Dry developing chemicals, such as amidol, a colourless crystalline compound, were also available but in addition to this cumbersome equipment, clean water and chemicals, it was essential to have good ventilation to counter the effects of heat, damp and insects.

All would be handicaps to Landtman's work in Papua. The field photographer then had to store the plate in dry, preferable black, velvet bags and the bellows of the camera had to be kept supple with vaseline. This would certainly have been very attractive to bush insects and cockroaches. The glass plates had to be packed carefully in air tight, lockable containers with naphthalene and then transported with waterproof coverings (im Thurn 1893: 203). All this equipment would have be beyond the ability of one lone field researcher to manage: it was still a time when an ethnologist could be sure that he could employ a number of local porters to assist in his work. Landtman wrote regularly of his servants' capabilities and even later people like Malinowski employed a servant in the field. The fact that Landtman managed to compose over 500 images in a difficult and unpleasant physical environment was indeed impressive. As Michael Young noted in his excellent study of the Trobriand field photographs of Bronislaw Malinowski, anthropology and photography have 'parallel historical trajectories' (Young 1998: 4). However, Malinowski, working in Papua from 1915 to 1918, was a much more successful photographer despite his claims to the contrary and his dislike of the art. He produced a collection of about 800 images (Young 1998: 21). Perhaps one can mildly disagree with the statement that 'No other anthropologist of Malinowski's generation made photographs work so hard in the service of ethnographic narrative' (Young 1998: 5). Landtman was not a 'militant' self-promoter, nor a 'Socratic teacher' skilled at out-manoeuvring his rivals (Young 1998: 3). Regrettably, Landtman was also not such a creative writer in English and Kiwai culture, unlike that of the Trobriands, had little power to attract following generations of students.

The search for objectivity

Whether posed or naturalistic, photography as a field research tool was also a technology that allowed for objectivity combined with commonly held evolutionist values. 'Native' or 'primitive' peoples were photographed in various performances, actions, dances or rituals to illustrate the hierarchy of human evolution. The positivist assumption was that if culture could be seen to be happening it would be embedded in observable gestures, ceremonies and artefacts. These photographs could then act as an aide-mémoire for the researcher or as a 'transparent method of visual note-taking' (Young 1998: 4). However, the idea that photographs could form neutral, transparent and objective data ignored the social role of the subject and the inherent power of the ethnocentrism of the photographer (Ruby 1996; Quanchi 2007: 11). What the camera sees depends on who is using it. Early ethnologists sought out subjects that followed a taxonomic classification inherited from the natural sciences. Images of physical types and facial structures of local people were keenly sought, social customs, rituals and performances were important subjects that were recorded either as they happened or were ordered to be performed for the photographer's benefit. The other major subject was material culture of all types such as clothing, body decoration, house and building styles, weaponry and means of transport. Certainly early photographs by colonial officials, explorers, missionaries and ethnologists were part of a process that alienated and objectified Papuan peoples and cultures.

Landtman undoubtedly gained from association with W. H. R. Rivers and C. G. Seligman [Seligmann] who had accompanied Haddon on the Cambridge Torres Strait expedition of 1898. According to Edwards (2000: 105) a clear distinction can be made with ethnographic images of this period. Some are of a naturalistic, non-interventionist style representing observational photography of the style encouraged by Everard im Thurn. Others show a more controlled interventionist mode: a scientific photography designed to illustrate facts. For Haddon, both styles were important for they were strongly influenced by his romantic primitivist subjectivities that existed alongside systematic scientific intention (Edwards 2000: 112). In 1902 Rivers worked with the Todas tribes of the Nilgiri hills in southern India (Rivers 1906). Although he employed two professional photographers to take his field photographs he actively supervised their work. Rivers's study of the Todas became an immediate classic and a major influence on ethnological fieldwork at the turn of the 20th Century (Hockings 1992: 179–86). Seligman and his wife worked with the Veddas [Wanniyala-Aetto] people of Ceylon [Sri Lanka] in 1907 and 1908 and they too used photography in the field (Seligmann C. G. and B. Z. 1911)(Poignant 1992: 64). Both Seligman and Rivers continued to publish well-regarded, influential material on Melanesian cultures. Seligman's publication on the Melanesians of British New Guinea would have provided substantial background information for Landtman's work with the Kiwai (Seligman 1910) and Rivers was also working on a major two volume study into regional cultural history at the time of Landtman's Cambridge visit (Rivers 1914).

In Papua perhaps the earliest use of the camera for ethnology was made by R. M. Williamson who photographed the Mekeo and Goilala people in 1910 using the grand vista imagery that was undoubtedly creative and inventive but retained a sense of cultural and physical distance (Williamson 1912; Macintyre and MacKenzie 1992: 158–64). The technique of the day emphasised the use of diffused lighting on the subject of anthropological photography. High art photography on the other hand called for the use of side lighting and the removal of extraneous elements like buildings and scenery. This approach placed the subject in a Romanised, Arcadian setting and examples can be found in the popular Pacific travel books produced at that time. Typical of this sort of material is Burnett's photographic travelogue of Polynesia and Papua that included images of undressed women posed for visual effect in exotic scenery. Many of these images were taken by professional studio photographers although Burnett also photographed local people and scenery in places like the Solomon Islands where Melanesian women were not considered a 'woodland nymph' or a 'Tahitian beauty'. (Burnett 1911 and Thomas 1992: 369). These photographs were used as picturesque illustrations to add local colour to the text. Photography was developing both a professional and a popular use. On one hand 'native' people were the subject of racist misogyny that supported sexual stereotyping and on the other hand ethnologists were only beginning to understand the documentary significance of field photographs.

In another excellent study of the photographs of F. E. Williams, the Government Anthropologist of Papua from 1922 to 1939, Michael Young and Julia Clark (2001: 56) wrote that Williams would have accepted photography as a tool of his trade, used unreflectively and taken for granted as a medium of ethnographic recording. These photographs, held by the National Archives of Australia in Canberra, capture the immediacy of life of the ordinary villager. There is a tendency in Landtman's photographs, like those of Williams, to position the subject in the middle distance in order to record the place of people within their natural environment. This positioning in the optimal distance meant that the image contained both the subject and enough situational background for the observer to read the social and cultural context of the subject. This was also a technique later favoured by Malinowski: it was in effect a 'methodologically driven style' rather than a sign of reticence or modesty (Young 1998: 17). In Landtman's work there are few single portrait photographs but these are named and described. Landtman was not as skilled with his photography as Williams but then again Williams had the advantage of one decade of technological improvements, better local knowledge, a staff of carriers and as a government official was able to command the use of boats and equipment that were beyond the reach of a sole ethnographer like Landtman.

In a recent study of early photographs of Papua and Papuans, Quanchi (2007: 21 and 85), basing his interpretation of historical photographs on the theory developed by Roland Barthes (1993), states that images from the 1880 to 1930 period contain two essential elements: the 'studium', the coded, obvious and mostly singular reading, and the 'punctum', the divided and mostly multiple meanings. More simply the images contain both an intended meaning, established by the subject matter, composition or framing at the site of taking the photograph, and an unintended meaning, the one discerned by the reader at the site of use or exhibition. In other words, the scholarly versus the personal interpretation. According to Quanchi (2007: 86) photography undertaken by colonial officials, missionaries and early anthropologists serves as a metaphor for colonialism in that both are predatory, acquisitive, presumptuous and objectify the subject. However while Quanchi's work contains a detailed, valuable list of references and substantial bibliography, the interesting hypothesis is marred by his numerous and unacceptable errors of fact: 'Guntar Landtmann' (Quanchi 2007: 290 footnote 12) being only one of them. There is no detailed analysis of Landtman's substantial collection of photographic work.

The privileged position of the photographer

However, photographs do expose the anthropologist's privileged field of view (Poignant 1992: 65). It is obvious that Landtman took his photographs from a position of power, he was a white man working in a colonial society where his subjects, both black men and women, were not in a position to challenge his privileged place and purpose in their communities. This is not to deny Landtman his sense of humanity for his photographs, notes and letters show that he was a man of perception, humour and decency. Some images may be posed but they are not contrived. Landtman's photography was experimental: there are landscapes, vertical as well as horizontally framed images, a number of portraits, some stilted posed groups of dancers that lack colour but also some dramatic, powerful images, no sequences of images as can be found in Malinowski's collection but like Malinowski the height of the camera is generally commensurate with the height of the subject (see especially Young 1998: 16–17).

Landtman's photographs are socially constructed artefacts that tell us not only about Kiwai society and culture between 1910 and 1912, but also tell us much about the society and culture of the photographer. The meaning of these images can now be comprehended as something negotiated between subject and maker rather than fixed ethnocentric products of early 20th Century romanticism. There is a great deal of information on the subjects of the images that can only now be discerned with better access to sites, our greater ease and ability to communicate with people in the region and with over a century of documented history. Landtman photographed and recorded all his visits to story sites and villages and took numerous photographs of scenery, ceremonies, people and material culture. They document his personal journey along the Daru coast and into the Fly estuary. Apart from longhouses at Gaima, no photographs were taken on the near disastrous trip to the Aramia and the later journey to the Gulf. It is possible to follow this path commencing at Buji in the west.

Daudai

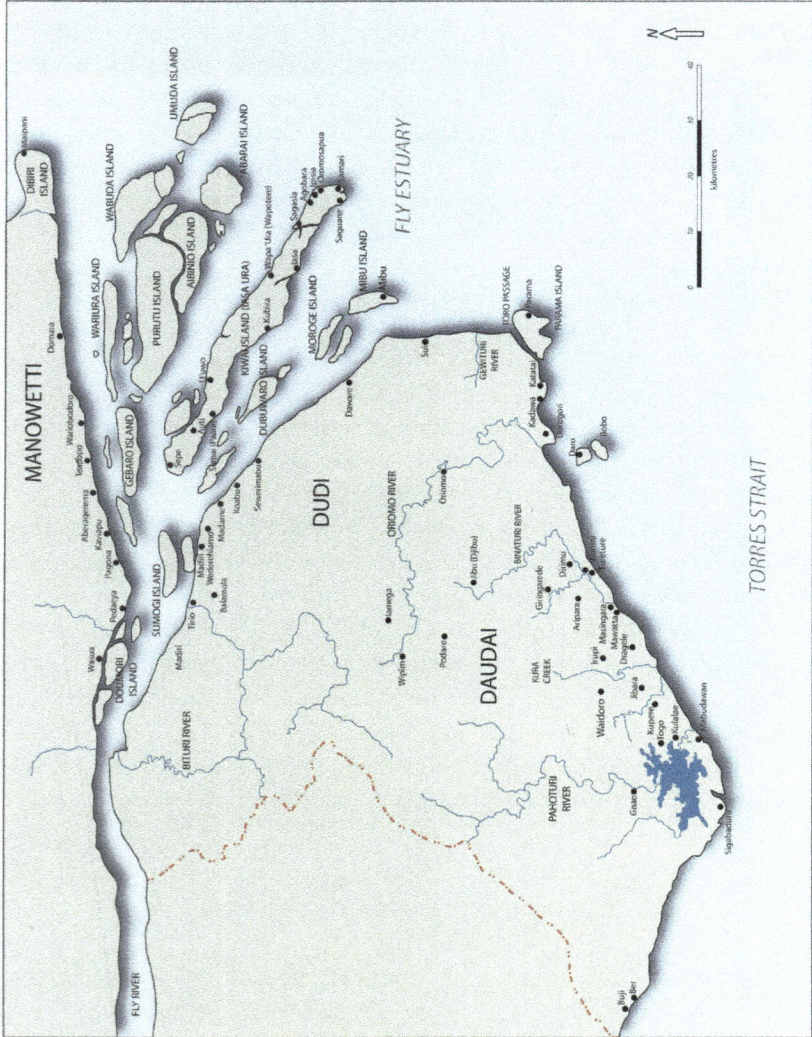

Map 3. Daudai, Dudi and Manowetti (Cartographic-GIS Services, College of Asia and the Pacific, ANU, 2009)

Buji

Buji was established in 1897 with the remnants of the Agob-speaking people from the Mai and Wassi Kussa estuaries who had been decimated by raids from the Marind-amin or 'Tugeri' from the Merauke area of Dutch New Guinea. In 1898 the whole Agob population was reported to be only 250. Raids by the 'Tugeri' were common in the 1870s at Boigu and recorded on Saibai in 1882. Even in 1895 Boigu was a miserable collection of huts and a half roofed church and most of the population consisted of people from the Papuan coast seeking refuge from the raiders. Sir William Macgregor, with an armed patrol, made contact with 'Tugeri' invaders off the Wassi Kussa inlet in 1895 and captured and destroyed a number of canoes. Some were given to Boigu Islanders and some to coastal Papuans in compensation for damage done during raids. However despite acknowledging the need to repel the 'Tugeri' Macgregor was sorry that they were not inhabitants of British New Guinea as he called them 'active, powerful, daring, enterprising spirits' (Annual Report on British New Guinea 1889/90: 75).

The raids only stopped along the Daru coast with the death of the last war chief, Para, and a European trader named Martin near Mawatta around 1888 (Lawrence 1994: 412). This story is still told by the people of Mawatta and Mabudawan. Once the raiding stopped the scatted Agob-speaking people were able to move to the coast and re-establish traditional contacts with the Western Islanders of the Torres Strait. Life near the Dutch New Guinea border however was still precarious for the Marind-amin continued to raid the communities of the Morehead River as late as 1902. A report on the settlement of Daru by the Acting Administrator of British New Guinea in 1903 continued to refer to the trouble posed by the 'Tugeri'. Only after the establishment of the permanent Dutch police post at Merauke was the raiding finally contained. The Dutch colonial government was then required to pay compensation to coastal villagers for loss of life and property (Beaver 1920: 11). Buji men continued to dress as warriors at the time of Landtman's visit. Even today the Agob people supply cassowary feather headdresses, drums, bow and arrows to the Boigu and Saibai Islanders for their use in ceremonial dances for which they are renowned.

According to oral accounts, the people of Buji formerly lived in small bush camps where they slept on the ground. They had no permanent houses and moved according to the season between their hunting and fishing camps. The legend of Ubrikubri tells of their long connections with the Torres Strait Islands of Badu and Moa [Mua]: a man, named Ubrikubri, and his daughter lived near the site of Buji village. The girl had no children to care for and so she asked her father to find her a piglet that she could raise. This was an old custom that trained girls for marriage. The father brought her various animals but the daughter was not satisfied and eventually the father found a small crocodile that he gave her. She lovingly raised this animal on yams and taro and fed it by hand. One day she told her father to care for the animal as she was going to the bush. The father reached in through the fence surrounding the crocodile but the animal grabbed him and dragged the father along the beach and into the water. It took the man to Boigu, nearby, and then back to Buji thereby creating the channel between the two communities. In the meantime the girl was searching for her father and eventually found his body near some rocks on the mainland. The girl left that camping place and moved along the coast. The crocodile meanwhile moved to Buru Reef, a story site for Mabuiag people, and to Moa [Mua] and then to Badu. It can still be seen in the channel between the two islands. In the story both the father and the crocodile are named Ubrikubri and the legend links the Agob people with the Western Islanders of the Torres Strait. It explains the wanderings of the Buji people (Lawrence 1994: 405–06; Schug 1995: 79).

Figure 8. Man from Buji village dressed as warrior with feather headdress, pubic shell cover, wallaby teeth necklace and hunting bow and arrows. The man is also carrying a hooped pig catcher mistakenly called a man catcher (VKK 248: 137)

Currently the Agob-speaking people continue to live in the small isolated and impoverished coastal communities of Buji, Ber and Sigabarduru between the Mai Kussa and the Pahoturi Rivers. They maintain close contacts with the Torres Strait Islander communities of Boigu, Dauan and Saibai and cross to these communities for fuel, food and medical attention.

Mabudawan, Marukawa and Dauan

The islands of Paho and Marukawa, and the hill at Mabudawan on the mainland, are particularly important being associated with the myths and legends of heroes such as Sido, Kuiam and Wawa. Mabudawan was the site chosen by Resident Magistrate J. B. Cameron for a police post in 1891 but this was moved to Daru by the R. M. Bingham Hely (Lawrence 1994: 300; Annual Report on British New Guinea 1897/98: xxiv).

Figure 9. Marukawa Island off Mabudawan. Mabudawan and the small offshore islands are the only rocky outcrops along the southwest coast (VKK 248: 2)

Cameron's first problem was to determine the owners of Mabudawan and the offshore islands. The government finally accepted the Agob people's rights of ownership of this area they called Mabunardi. However, by this time the

Kiwai who had come as police with the administration had occupied the coastal areas near the mouth of the Pahoturi (Lawrence 1994: 407). Mabudawan, the Agob people say, is a corruption of the real name for the hill that the Kiwai could not pronounce. Mabudawan is also culturally important for the Gizra-speaking people of the eastern bank of the Pahoturi. The legend of Geadap (Giadap) and Muiam, the most important origin story of the Gizra, tells how the two brothers came into being at Basipuk, also known as Basir Puerk (Laba 1996: 302), an area at the foot of Normandor (the Gizra name for Mabudawan) (Numandorr according to Laba 1996: 302). The important cultural sites at Dabu and Normandor are now too close to the Kiwai village for the bush people to visit (Lawrence 1994: 300 and 423–24).

The Agob people of the scattered coastal and bush villages still tell of how the Kiwai came to occupy Madudawan and this is verified in colonial records. A Kiwai man from Kadawa [Mawatta] named Kesave came to Mabudawan with the government patrol officers and when he returned to Mawatta he told his people that Mabudawan was a good place to settle. When Kesave returned the Sigabarduru people gave him a woman called Makar, the widow of Kowdi. She had many children from Kowdi but Kesave and Makar did not have children together. Kesave also had a wife, Kutai, at Mawatta and sometimes he lived at Mabudawan and sometimes at Mawatta (Lawrence 1994: 408). Kesave [also spelt Kesawe] was often wounded during his long police service and acted as sergeant to Wilfred Beaver when on patrol around 1910 (Beaver (1920: 79–80; Annual Report on British New Guinea 1891/92: 48). Kiwai occupation of Mabudawan was only very recent when Landtman visited the site.

There are many story sites in and around Mabudawan on the offshore islands and reefs. Many of these sites are contested by inland, coastal and island people all along the southwest coast (Lawrence 2004). A complex network of social ties connects the people of the widely-spaced coastal communities of the northern Torres Strait. A geographical and social web fosters a feeling of identity strengthened by centuries of ritual, exchange, intermarriage and the shared use of land and sea (Schug 1995: 233). This fragile network is now being challenged by the imposition of international laws and treaties that prohibit and control movement across the open sea.

Legends of Wawa, Sido and Kuiam

The Legend of Wawa

Figure 10. The house of Wawa in the rock that opens and closes (VKK 248: 478)

According to legend, Wawa is a short, thick man who lives in the large rock at Mabudawan. When he wants to go to sleep he goes into the stone that closes over him and when he wants to make a garden, the stone opens up again. He carries a large bundle of arrows and a basket in one hand and a bow in the other. On his arm he wears an arm bracer and in it a cassowary feather decoration. On his head he wears bushes and flowers that he takes off when he works in his gardens. The taro that he plants grows overnight and so he has plenty of food. He can see both Saibai and Mawatta from his beach. One day on the beach, when the water had risen high, he saw two turtles: one male and one female. As he could not carry them himself, he called a bush man, Jabi, to help him. Jabi said that in return he should have one turtle. However, they argued over which turtle: the female turtle is better meat and so both wanted the 'fat' turtle. In the end, Wawa fell asleep and while he was asleep, Jabi picked off the lice in his hair and put them in a bowl. Jabi stole the female turtle and ran back into the bush. Because he was afraid of Wawa, he took his family further inland and built a hut high on poles away from the ground. He took with him animals from the bush like the dog, the wallaby, the cuscus, the pig and the cassowary. Wawa's lice meanwhile had turned to crabs on the beach. Wawa went in search of Jabi and his family and wanted to kill them all. He asked other bushmen to help him. When Jabi threw out the cuscus, the bushmen killed it, when he threw out the wallaby, they did the same, and the same with the cassowary and the pig. In the end Jabi and his wife threw out their small daughter and they killed her too. The fight then stopped and Wawa, satisfied with his victory, went back to the beach and returned to his stone home. The bush people moved away from the coast and went inland. On the beach is a place where Wawa sharpened his stone axe. The area near the rock is well known for its mud crabs which are said to be the lice from Wawa's hair. (Landtman 1917). This is also the story that accounts for the reasons why the coastal people and the bush people have to live apart from each other and why there is also no intermarriage between them.

The Legend of Sido

The most important ancestor legend of the Kiwai is the story of Sido. The legend of Sido links the islands of the Fly estuary to the southwest coast and the northern Torres Strait. It may be seen not only as a descriptive account of how the area became inhabited but as a political document. The movements of Sido are mirrored in the migrations out of Kiwai Island and along the southwest coast by the Kiwai people themselves. The image of the wandering culture hero is a common one. This hero, known by various names such as Muiam, Geadap, Kuiam, Sido, Hido, Iko or Souw, is part of a series of linked myths that serve to unite different cultures right across the south Fly, the Torres Strait and even as far as Cape York. The hero myth also serves as a metaphor for the supreme being capable of creating and improving people, giving them their social organisation and customs as well as revealing matters of human sexuality, reproduction and mortality (Busse 2005: 463; Wagner 1996: 287; Laba 1996: 300).

The following is a very brief account of a long and complex story of which a number of similar versions exist. Sido was created at Dibiri, but was chased away because he was making magic and went to U'uwo on Kiwai Island. There he met two women joined together at the waist. By magic one of the women gave birth to Sido [his rebirth] and after he grew they taught him the secrets of hunting and fishing. In return, using a ball of sago, he split them apart into two women, Asau and Oumo. In this way the two mothers became separate people (Landtman 1912b: 62). One day Sido went out hunting and met an old man who took Sido to his home. The old man had bananas and coconuts which Sido stole. He also stole the old man's magic but later took the old man to the house of the two women and they all lived together in one longhouse. In this way Sido was responsible for bringing together the knowledge of hunting, fishing and gardening. The old man made a drum which when beaten called out the name of Sido's future lover, Sagaru.

Sido was told to go to Iasa to a longhouse there. By magic Sido was transported across the island by a swinging tree that shot Sido into the air. At Iasa Sido met Sagaru his lover. Sido and Sagaru had sex and commenced their journeys around Kiwai Island but Sagaru ran away because Sido did not satisfy her. Sido followed Sagaru around the island and after he learnt to make a fine canoe that floated on the water he crossed to Mibu. Sido followed Sagaru to Mabudawan and there he climbed the rocky hill (Lawrence 1994: 403–05).

Figure 11. The imprint of Sido's foot at Paho Island near Mabudawan. Paho Island is only separated from Mabudawan by a small creek (VKK 248: 474. See also Schug 1995: 79)

From Mabudawan Sido went to Boigu. At Boigu a man named Meuri wanted Sagaru as his wife and fought with Sido for her. Meuri killed Sido and cut off his head. Sagaru then drank water from the head and then threw it away into the bush. The place where the head landed is now a well that is always filled with fresh water. Sagaru was killed after she ran away from Meuri and Sido's spirit returned to U'uwo where it lies near the village in a place that is always fresh and green. The place near U'uwo is considered to be an important site still and people are discouraged, politely, from visiting it. The large tree that shot Sido to Iasa is to be found near the present Sagapadi village. Under the tree are many large stone axe heads (Lawrence 1994: 403–05 and 1995: 39). Other versions of the legend state that Sido, called the first man to die, drank from his own skull and that he killed his two mothers and one became a turtle and one a dugong (Landtman 1917: 112–13 and 1927: 285–87). The story of Sido remains the most important legend told by the Kiwai as it legitimises Kiwai occupation of the places named in the legend.

The Legend of Kuiam

Contact between the people of the Western Islands of the Torres Strait and Cape York is told in the legends of Kuiam, a culture hero of mixed Islander and Aboriginal heritage. These legends were also collected by Haddon (1904, V: 67–83 and 1935, I: 380–85) as well as by Donald Thomson (1933), the Australian anthropologist who recorded detailed accounts of Cape York Aboriginal hero cults, totemism and initiation while undertaking ethnographic research with the people of Lloyd Bay on the east coast of north Queensland. Landtman's account of Kuiam states that Kuiam grew up as a small boy on the island of Mabuiag in the Western Torres Strait. He was cruel to his playmates and often teased them and hit them and he showed disrespect for elders by damaging the food and spoiling the camps. His mother was often angry with him. As he grew older, he continued to be cruel and his mother continued to be angry with him. One day he dressed as a warrior and waited for his mother. He killed her and cut off her head. He fought the Mabuiag people and killed many of them too. He cut off all the heads and decorated them and hung them on bush rope. With his mother's head he filled the eyes with beeswax and put shells in as eyes and placed clay in the nose and put a nose stick in it. Taking his young nephew with him, he sailed to Dauan and climbed one of the hills there.

Figure 12. The mark made by Kuiam's canoe when it landed on the shore of Dauan (VKK 248: 483)

Kuiam sailed with the boy to Boigu where he continued to kill people. They then crossed to the mainland and they started killing the bush people from the Buji area to Jibaru near Mawatta. After this they returned to Kagaro Point on Saibai. On the way the canoe was caught in strong seas and so Kuiam threw some of the heads overboard and they created the sandbanks and coral reefs between Saibai and Gimini reefs. On the return from Saibai to Mabuiag, Kuiam threw more heads overboard and they created the reefs between Mabuiag and the northern Torres Strait islands. The number of dead killed on Mabuiag matched the number of dead from the New Guinea side. After he had finished, Kuiam climbed the highest hill on Mabuiag and made his home there. Mabuiag remains the place of his spirit and the western Islanders claim ownership of these reefs and sandbanks that are important dugong and turtle hunting sites (Landtman 1917; Lawrence 1994: 293).

Mawatta

Mawatta proved to be a valuable research area for Gunnar Landtman. The most sustained exchange relationships between the Kiwai and the Torres Strait Islanders centred on this community on the strand at the mouth of the Binaturi River. It has previously been known as Kadawa and Katau. When H. M. Chester, the Police Magistrate from Somerset settlement on Cape York, and Captain William Banner, who had established the first bêche-de-mer station in the Torres Strait, landed at the mouth of the Binaturi River in 1870 they found a village of about 12 small houses and one longhouse parallel to the beach located near another coastal village called Toura Toura (Tureture) (Lawrence 1994: 269). The coastal Kiwai were descendents of Gamea, who founded Mawatta, and of Kuke, who founded Tureture. At that time the population of the two villages was about 900 people (Gill 1874).

Coastal Kiwai language is spoken by the inhabitants of the villages of Mabudawan, Mawatta and Tureture. Further towards Daru are the large coastal communities of Kadawa and Katatai. Together with Parama village, these communities speak Eastern Coastal Kiwai. However, all communities share the same origin story: the legend of Bidedu that was recorded by Landtman (1917: 85–88). The story tells that:

> Long ago at Mawatta, that is Tagara [old] Mawatta the area of beach and headland opposite Daru Island, people lived inside a creeper of a kind called *Buhere-apoapa*. When swimming in the sea at Dudu-patu [near the Oriomo River opposite Daru] they came across the intestines of dugong and turtle, which had been thrown away by the Daru people and had floated over to the opposite coast, and they ate them. A large hawk once flew away with a turtle bone and alighted on a *Kaparo* tree at Kuru [in the bush at the headwaters of the Binaturi River], close to a garden where a man named Bidedu was working. The hawk dropped the bone, and Bidedu, after picking it up and examining it, decided to go and find out where it came from. He found the people in the creeper and cut them out ... Both the Mawatta and Tureture people had been in the creeper. Their leader Bidja came out first, and Bidedu made friends with all of them. They used to eat poor kinds of fruits, roots and earth, and to smoke the leaves of a tree called *omobari*, but Bidedu gave them food of the right sort and showed them the use of tobacco. He taught them to build houses and the founded the village of Old Mawatta [opposite Daru].

In another version of this story, Bidedu from Kuru was in search of the origins of the turtle bone dropped from the sky when he heard the people in the vine tree. When he split the tree, Biza was the first man to come out, followed by his brothers one of whom was named Gamea. Bidedu made the first man out of the vine tree, Biza, go to sleep and caused him to dream of finding a way to the coast and other secret information. Biza moved to the coast and settled his people there. Biza named that place Mawatto, meaning to take someone and to cross to the other side of the river. While there they made rafts to cross the water. The people on Daru had canoes and hunted dugong and shared this knowledge with the people from the bush (Lawrence 1994: 408–11). The stories serve to illustrate the close connections between the people of the inland bush villages and the coastal Kiwai who established themselves on the coast after moving out of the Fly estuary. It was then that they learnt how to hunt dugong and turtle and to sail ocean-going canoes.

Having settled on the coast, the Kadawarubi began to grow in number. The headman, Gamea, who had gathered people from the Fly estuary, Parama and Daru then traveled westwards along the shore naming the coast, rivers and headlands and went as far as Saibai Island. From the Saibai Islanders Gamea and his men learnt many things to do with fishing, marine hunting, and making *narato* [dugong platforms]. He returned and later moved back along the coast in a canoe. Fighting broke out between the Kadawarubi (the descendants of Gamea) and the Tureturerubi (the descendants of his younger brother Kuke) and so the communities separated into the villages of Mawatta and Tureture (Lawrence 1994: 409–11).

Other stories and recorded history confirm these events. When the Kiwai began moving out from Kiwai Island some moved north across to the Manowetti coast and some west to the Dudi coast. One man, Sewota, sailed as far south as Koipomuba near the present village of Katatai. Another man, Bagari, was living there. Bagari gave Sewota fire but he told Sewota to go to live at Huboturi, near the entrance to Toro Passage. Bani, from Boigu Island, came from the west and he too went to live with Sewota. Later, Sewota gave his son to Bani to bring up and told them to go to Doridori. Gewi and Doridori are both on the Dudi bank just north of Toro Passage. At Doridori other people joined Bani and they established two longhouses called Kudin and Wasigena. These longhouses existed when the Rev. Samuel Macfarlane traveled up the Fly River with Luigi D'Albertis and Henry Chester in 1875 (Macfarlane and Rawlinson 1875–76). Macfarlane was not only exploring the country but looking for a suitable site for a mission in the lower Fly. However, following the abuse of one woman from Iasa, the warriors from Kiwai Island raided the two longhouses and drove the people south past Parama Island. From Doridori the people of the senior clans, the Gebarubi, went and established Parama village. The group of people in the junior clans, the Kadawarubi, went south back along the coast and established a village near Katatai. It was here that they came into contact with Bidedu from Kuru (Lawrence 1994: 412–16).

These stories illustrate how the Kiwai came to settle on the southwest coast of Papua, how they learnt the techniques of dugong and turtle hunting from the traditional inhabitants of Daru, the Hiamo-Hiamo, and the technique of building, and sailing ocean-going canoes from the Saibai Islanders. This mix of coastal and inland peoples separated into two different groups: the eastern communities of Parama, Kadawa and Katatai and the western section of Tureture, Mawatta and Mabudawan (Lawrence 1994: 302–03). There were most likely a series of migrations and back migrations as people searched for new land or occupied old village sites. While the historical record notes that small communities of Kiwai lived at Mawatta and Tureture before 1872, the migration of larger numbers of people from the Fly estuary certainly occurred after 1875.

In his report of a visit of inspection to the Western Division in 1895, the Administrator of British New Guinea, William Macgregor, noted that Tureture was a well established village of Kiwai-speaking people who wore European clothes and had many young men working in the Torres Strait pearling and bêche-de-mer fisheries. In Mawatta, Macgregor found the people had extensive contacts with European traders and fishers but the South Sea Islander mission teacher was reported to be demoralised. The teacher insisted that children attending school wear European clothing but the parents argued that if the mission wanted them to attend well dressed then the missionaries must find the clothing for the children. This very Melanesian debate remained unresolved (Annual Report of British New Guinea 1895/96: 40).

By settling on the coast at the mouth of the coastal rivers the Kiwai effectively controlled the customary exchange patterns that had been established between the Torres Strait Islanders and the inland bush dwelling Papuans. The Kiwai became, in effect, littoral dwelling entrepreneurs. The land they built on was owned by the inland Bine-speaking people of Masingara village. The Bine-speaking community of Kunini had moved close to Tureture but eventually they would move back inland to the banks of the Binaturi River when their houses were damaged by sea storms. Only recently has the good relationship between the Kiwai and Bine peoples broken down.

Kiwai villages today are still built close to the sea, or on narrow rivers and waterways. Houses are generally small, consisting of two to three rooms, and while they may look flimsy from outside they are strongly built. The nipa palm walls are made so that they open on the lee side and close on the windward side thus keeping the houses cool and weatherproof. In the northern part of the Fly estuary villages are physically different. People use plaited sago canes woven into broad screens for walls. This is a Gogodala custom that has been adopted by some Kiwai in the northern part of the estuary. These walls are more attractive but are not as water-proof as the closely folded nipa palm. Kiwai villages vary tremendously in their internal dynamics. Some are noisy and full of life, others quiet and sleepy. Landtman's period of research in the Fly region corresponded with that of the Resident Magistrate Wilfred Beaver who wrote that the Kiwai were 'most intelligent and forceful' (Beaver 1920: 154) and that they were the first to be recruited as members of the armed constabulary and in much demand as boat-hands both in Papua and in the Torres Strait. Beaver noted the vitality of the Kiwai village and wrote: 'a village is nothing but one continual state of chatter from dusk till dawn and the laughter is often as annoying as it is constant' (Beaver 1920: 155). Little has changed. By comparison with societies higher up the Fly, the Kiwai have a richer and more complex material culture — their canoes have elaborate rigging and they make and maintain a much wider range of baskets, nets and other fishing equipment — lending a 'busy' air to their villages. Consequently, their ability to travel within the estuary and by sea over considerable distances and their long tradition of contact with other cultures means that the Kiwai are unusually well-informed on many subjects, particularly the lack of development in the Western Province and have a good command of English (Lawrence 1994: 259–89). When Landtman arrived in Papua the Kiwai had been in touch with traders, missionaries and government officers for more than 30 years. They had learnt to adapt to changing social and economic circumstances. This is evident in their acceptance of new forms of hunting and fishing.

Figure 13. Coastal Kiwai dwelling for one or two families with storage and sitting area underneath (VKK 248: 37)

Hunting and fishing

Figure 14. Young men from Mawatta with hunting bows and arrows. Landtman's servant, Ganame, in the right is holding his Mauser hunting rifle (VKK 248: 150)

At Landtman's time, harpooning of dugong was undertaken in two ways. On nights with a full moon a hunter would climb onto the tall wooden platform erected over good patches of seagrass and where the men knew that dugong and turtle grazed (see illustrations in Landtman 1920 and 1933: 28 but originally from Haddon 1901: facing 123 and Haddon 1912; IV: plate xxiii). The hunter had a long wooden harpoon in his hand and in the head was the harpoon dart attached to a long rope made from eight-ply coconut fibre. Other men would wait in canoes nearby. When a dugong approached the platform the hunter would throw the harpoon at the animal. He had to throw it with all his might and dive onto the animal as well. If the head of the harpoon struck the animal and embedded itself in the flesh the animal would swim quickly away with the rope attached. Landtman records that 'at the present time [1910–12] the end of the harpoon line is generally tied to the platform, but formerly the harpooner had to catch hold of the line and allow himself to be towed away by the wounded animal' (Landtman 1927: 125–26). The hunter would be collected by the men on the canoes that would have to give chase. When they reached the dugong they would have to drown it by holding its tail in the air so that the breathing hole was submerged, or they would have to stun it by clubbing it to death. Landtman sailed with a hunting expedition where the men erected *narato* over the reef but this would have been one of the last times the platforms would have been used (Landtman 1913b: 167–68).

The use of the hunting platform declined because it was highly dangerous and could only be used on clear moonlit nights. The hunter could easily be caught in the long rope as it unwound, he could be drowned if the other men lost sight of him in the water at night and the blood from the wounded animal could attract sharks. One hunter, Maiva from Mawatta, drowned when he became entangled in the rope. Subsequently, when other hunters saw the ghost of Maiva he was surrounded by a pod of dugong and so they threw food into the ocean to ensure that fishing was good (Beaver 1920: 71).

The second method of hunting involved the use of the large double outrigger canoes. This form of hunting could be undertaken in all weathers and was more versatile as general reef fishing, turtle hunting and even communal travelling to other villages and the islands of the Torres Strait could be undertaken while lookouts, perched in the rigging of the masts and on the outriggers themselves, watched for the telltale signs of dugong in the sea.

Figure 15. Namai, Landtman's informant at Mawatta, demonstrating the use of a long fishing spear (VKK 248: 319)

It soon became the main method of marine hunting with a lugger being substituted for the canoe in the Torres Strait (Landtman 1913b: 31–35). The hunter would stand at the bow of the canoe with the *wapo* in his hand. When a turtle or dugong was sighted the canoe gave chase and the animal would easily tire after a long chase. The harpoon was hurled at the animals in the same way, it is still usual for the harpooner to dive into the ocean, and the hunter would quickly grab on to one of the outriggers as the canoe went past him in the water. The benefit of the canoe was that a number of men and women, and even children, could be together at one time so the men were safer than on the *narato* and the inside storage space of the large canoes would hold food, firewood, goods and sailing equipment (Lawrence 1994).

Figure 16. Man with dugong harpoon standing on the bow of a canoe while the lookout stands on the outrigger behind (VKK 248: 435)

Religious life in Mawatta

The London Missionary Society used Pacific Islander pastors from 1871 to 1915. Local evangelism was left to these pastors, many of whom subsequently intermarried into local communities and took over positions of local influence. Descendants of these pastors remain on both sides of the Australia/Papua New

Guinea border. As a result, Polynesian cultural influences have had a profound impact on the customary practice of the Torres Strait Islanders and the coastal Papuans.

The history of the Christian missions must be seen in terms of colonisation for mission paternalism mirrored the economic and political paternalism of the white administration (Beckett 1978). However, Islanders and coastal Papuans made considered judgments about the value of the missions for many communities welcomed the pastors as protection from the lawless behaviour of boat crews from the pearling and bêche-de-mer stations. With the establishment of the mission centre and trading post at Mawatta this village became the most important economic and cultural site on the southwestern coast. The community members acted as middlemen in trading all along the coast and long canoe-buying expeditions were undertaken during the calm weather before the northwest monsoons. When Landtman stayed at Mawatta, the village consisted of two streets of pile houses built off the ground generally containing two families, a flagstaff, a small village courthouse, the wooden LMS church and a trader's store (Beaver 1920: 61).

Figure 17. The LMS church at Mawatta (VKK 248: 538)

Figure 18. Samoan pastor, possibly Pastor Apineru, and his wife at Mawatta mission station (VKK 248: 544)

Ceremonial life in Mawatta

Ceremonial life continued despite the presence of the missions and administration but it occurred in seclusion. Landtman wrote to his family that he had to ask the men of Mawatta village to dress in ceremonial dance costume for him to photograph much to the disapproval of the local missionaries. It was acceptable for men and women to engage in approved introduced dances such as the formation dance, the *Taibobo*, and gradually a fusion of dances, ceremonies and costumes evolved. Men began to wear grass skirts over *lava-lavas* and in the formation dances the wearing of *dori* headdresses became common. Dances became competitive occasions with one section of a village or another village competing with another group for prizes.

Figure 19. Men from Mawatta dressed for ceremonial 'ship' dance wearing *dori* **headdresses made from woven cane and decorated with white reef heron feathers (VKK 248: 355)**

Figure 20. Man at Mawatta dressed for dance as warrior with cassowary feather headdress, chest ornament, arm bracer and *gabagaba* (fighting club) made with wooden head (VKK 248: 359)

Figure 21. Dance 'machine' in the shape of a crocodile. These objects were held in the hand of the dancer and moved with the music and singing. Dance machines form part of contemporary Torres Strait Islander cultural dance (VKK 248: 512)

Figure 22. Namai, playing a fine old style drum (*warupa*) decorated with a shark emblem (*baizam*) and cassowary feathers. This drum was known as 'Kowio' from the name of a mountain [Mt Yule] near Port Moresby where Namai had lived. Landtman stated that the drum was remodeled from a Buji *buruburu*. However, from the shape and style it is more likely that it was remodeled out of a large Morehead River drum (VKK 248: 324; Landtman 1927: facing 44 and 47)

The most important musical instrument of the Kiwai was the wooden hourglass-shaped drum. This remains the major accompaniment to dances and songs in the wide Torres Strait and Fly estuary region and is even used to accompany hymns in church. There are two types of drums: the older more finely carved and decorated *warupa* and the more modern often over-painted *buruburu*. Landtman's original comment (1927: 44) was:

> New drums are made at Mawatta like the Budji buruburu in shape, but provided with different decoration. It is also common practice at Mawatta to remodel imported Budji drums slightly by obliterating the original ornamentation and making the woodwork thinner by scraping them outside and inside (thereby improving the sound), then incising fresh ornamentation.

He was generally correct except that the drums originated further west of Boigu in the Morehead River region. This activity is still practiced and Papuan drums are still traded into the Torres Strait Islands were they are often again redecorated with bright paint.

Figure 23: Man at Mawatta burning the centre of a large drum (VKK 248: 323). One end, from the root end of the tree, is then covered with a tympanum made from lizard skin. The other end, from towards the branches of the tree, is left open. Thus the sound always comes from the 'top' of the drum. On the ground is a large *Melo* sp shell in use as a fire container.

Special ceremonies

Mawatta was an ideal place for Landtman to observe the still thriving ceremonial life of the coastal Kiwai. Spiritual beliefs and cult activities were recorded in some detail by Landtman no doubt at the specific request of Haddon. The goal of much of this data was to record the evolution of cultural forms, patterns of diffusion and migration across the ethnographic region (Knauft 1993: 31). While the Kiwai of the Fly estuary still practiced the *Mogeru* ritual, or what Landtman called the 'life giving ceremony' (Landtman 1927: 350–67), those on the coast celebrated the *Horiomu*, or more correctly, the *Taera* ceremony held before the onset of the southeast winds around April or May (Landtman 1927: 327–49, Knauft 1993: 195–201).

Figure 24. Men dressed as *Oromo-rubi oboro* in the *Horiomu* or *Taera* ceremony (VKK 248: 388)

The *Taera*, called by the missionaries 'The Great Pantomine Ceremony' was a celebration of the deaths that had occurred during the previous year and involved all the village men. Landtman considered it to be a ritual that aided in the access of marine hunting for turtle and dugong and as such had been borrowed from the Hiamo-Hiamo people of Daru and had spread along the southwest coast as far as Saibai and Boigu Islands in the Torres Strait and to Yam island and the western islands of the Torres Strait (Landtman 1927: 329–30). The *Horiomu* was in fact the name of the ceremonial ground near the beach that was screened off with bamboo and coconut leaf partitions for performers.

The ritual pantomime consisted of a long dance and performance cycle held at dusk over a number of days. Men dressed as a series of spirit figures and either wore simple masks of bast and leaves or complex ritual masks in the shape of fish and crocodiles made from turtle shell. These were worn over the head and required great physical effort by the dancer. Groups of men, dressed as dead warriors, the *Oromo-rubi oboro* [river-people-spirits], had an important place in the ritual (Landtman 1927: 338, 339, 342) It was believed that the dead spirits (*oboro*) can travel to Adiri, the land of the dead, but are able to return at certain times. Most likely Landtman had these men dress in ceremonial costumes for his photographs. Other collectors have also documented aspects of the *Horiomu*, though generally without any real understanding of the role, importance or the context of exchange of ceremonies and rituals across this vast region. In 1907 Charles Hedley and Alan McCulloch from the Australian Museum in Sydney photographed a Murray Island (Mer) man wearing *Horiomu* mask. They also purchased it for the museum (AM archives photograph no.vv2841 and Catalogue no. 176, AM E.17339; see Florek 2005: 39 and 60). McCulloch made a sketch of this mask that he called a 'çrocodile-kingfisher' mask. Hedley incorrectly noted that the ceremony was part of rituals promoting the fertility of the 'wangi palm tree' [wongai plum] (Florek: 2005: 60). However, this is probably the only complete extant *Horiomu* mask in any museum collection in Australia.

Figure 25. Mask in shape of human face photographed at Mawatta (VKK 248: 511)

Canoes and sailing

The first description of the impact of European tradestore goods into the customary exchange system that ran from Cape York to the Manowetti coast of the Fly estuary was written by Edward Beardmore, a small trader and buyer of pearl-shell and bêche-de-mer who had lived at Mawatta in 1890:

> Canoes are made at Kiwai and Paramoa [Parama] (Bampton Island) but not, I am assured, up the Maikusa [Mai Kussa] (Baxter River), where the people [Tugeri] are cannibals and deadly enemies to all the others this side of their country. Payments are made to suit the purchaser, sometimes in advance, but usually by three installments of shell ornaments (or in recent times of trade, such as tobacco, tomahawks, and calico). The unadorned canoes, with but a single flimsy outrigger, are transferred from one village to another until the destination is reached; each party receiving the canoe being responsible for the payment by the next. The builders, or rather diggers-out, usually deliver at Mowat [Mawatta], from thence the canoe travels to Saibai, then to Mabruag [Mabuiag] and from there to Badu, Moa [Mua], and ultimately say to Muralug [Muralag] or Nagir [Nagi]. In the case of evasion of payment a row ensues between the immediate parties and the delinquent is injured invisibly [by sorcery] in some way at the instigation of the sufferer. The wooden harpoon used in killing dugong and turtle is got and worked into shape about Mabruag [Mabuiag], Moa [Mua] and Badu and sent in the same manner as canoes to New Guinea, via Saibai (Beardmore 1890: 464–65).

The lines of exchange for canoes were also identified by James Chalmers during his work at Kiwai Island:

> They [the Kiwai] have canoes (pe) with one outrigger. These canoes are chiefly got from Dibiri, on the mainland, near the mouth of the [Bamu] estuary, and on its eastern side [the village of Maipani]. A few of the smaller ones are made by themselves. The large canoes obtained form Dibiri are traded to Parama, Tureture, Kadawa and Mawata [Mawatta]; and they trade them to Saibai, Dauan, Boigu, Mabuiag, Badu, Moa [Mua], Prince of Wales [Muralag], Waraber [Warraber], Damut [Dhamudh], Masig, Stephens Is [Ugar], Darnley [Erub], and Murray [Mer]. In all of these places, the single gives place to a double outrigger, with a platform in the centre, and a large amount of ornamentation fore and aft; these canoes are used for dugong fishing, and for going [on] long journeys (Chalmers 1903: 117).

Perhaps the most accurate and detailed report on the trading expeditions of the Kiwai was written by A. H. Jiear in 1904 (Annual Report on British New Guinea 1904/05: Appendix S: 69–71). Again, this was a public document that would have been readily available to Landtman on Daru.

Figure 26. Group of Mawatta villagers posed on a *motomoto*, a double outrigger canoe with a half-platform decking (VKK 248: 439)

Jiear noted that the 'most important form of native trading in this [Western] Division is that of buying and selling canoes'. He noted that the cash economy had made a significant impact into the barter economy with the Kiwai Islanders no longer interested in bows and arrows and shells and the bushmen having to buy their fish with cash rather than vegetables. However, the need for canoes was still strong. Katatai, Mawatta, Parama and Tureture villagers sent parties to Kiwai Island especially to Auti, Iasa and Sumai villages to buy canoes.

The price at that time still was measured in arm-shells (*mabuo*) but also European clothes, tools and tobacco were included as part of the payment. Jiear correctly noted that despite the impact of the European cash economy the demand for arm-shells and breast ornaments (*bidibidi*) had not decreased and that 'the wealth and importance of a family is gauged largely by the number of arm shells the members of it possess'. He reported that the ordinary sized arm-shell could be valued at £2: a large arm-shell at £4. At that time, a skilled Torres Strait

Islander on the pearling boats in the Torres Strait would have been fortunate to receive £2 per month but Papuans were only being paid £1 per month (Schug 1995: 152; Ganter 1994: 39).

Figure 27. Arrangement of *mabuo* **photographed at Mawatta (VKK 248: 514)**

From Kiwai Island, expeditions were made by canoe buying parties to the villages of Balamula, Domori at the mouth of the Fly and those along the Manowetti bank of the estuary. These expeditions could take between 14 and 24 days at all times of the year but the most usual time was during the northwest monsoon (the rainy season). At this time of the year the weather would be calm and the southeasterly trade winds would have dropped making travel safer. Following the rains the river would have been in flood and therefore the canoes would have been easier to manoeuvre down the narrow channels and creeks and into the estuary. Importantly most gardening and fishing would have been restricted at that time and men would have been able to devote time to long-distance sailing expeditions. From the villages along the Manowetti bank canoe buyers made the more dangerous trips into the lower Bamu River where villagers would have prepared canoe hulls for sale. Landtman, rather more concisely, wrote (1927: 213–14):

Since olden times an extensive trade has been carried on between different parts of the Kiwai region, as well as between these and the islands of Torres Straits. Different districts yield rather different kinds of produce, and, in addition, a certain distribution of labour exists as regards the articles manufactured by different tribes. The bushmen of the interior supply feathers of birds of paradise, cassowaries, parrots, etc, objects made of cassowary bones, bows, arrows, garden produce, *gamoda* [Piper methysticum: kava]; the Kiwai islanders [supply]: canoes, sago, garden produce, bows, arrows, mats, belts, women's grass petticoats, feathers; the Mawatta people [supply]: coconuts, certain shells, fish, dugong and turtle meat, etc; the Torres Strait islanders [supply]: stone axes, stone clubs, harpoon-shafts, all kinds of shell, dugong and turtle products, etc. The most important articles of barter are the canoes.

In fact, until recent times, the trade in canoes continued to be a significant part of the traditional economic system in the Fly estuary and southwest coast (Lawrence 1994).

Figure 28. The *motomoto*, Mauwa, being prepared for sail at the mouth of the Binaturi River (VKK 248: 431). At that time canoes were only fitted with half-platforms and small standing areas on the bow and stern. Later on the large ocean going canoes were fitted with full platforms and the inside of the canoe was used for storage and equipment

Figure 29. Photograph illustrating the method of steering using a movable steering board placed on the lee side of the canoe (VKK 248: 436)

Masingara

Inland only a short distance from Mawatta is the large, well-ordered and prosperous village of Masingara with its church and school that serves the neighbouring communities of Mawatta, Irupi and Kunini. The Bine-speaking people of this lower Binaturi region live along the river and inland in the villages of Bose, Giringarede, Masingara, Irupi, Drageli and Kunini. The people of Masingara have large gardens surrounded by high pig fences to protect the crops from wallabies, wild pigs and the Rusa deer that have migrated from West Papua where they were introduced by the former Dutch colonialists as sport for hunting. The Masingara people also built these fences for the Kiwai inhabitants of Mawatta.

The people refer to themselves as the Masa'ingle and the old village site of Masingle is located near the graveyard of the present village and about one to two kilometres from the present village church. Landtman (1917: 77–81) visited the old site and recorded the origin story of the people:

> The Masa'ingle were believed to be descended from the worms of a wallaby killed by the first woman on the earth, Ua-ogrere. She then taught these people how to make house and weapons and how to perform ceremonies. All garden foods, such as taro, yams and bananas, derive their origin from this woman, Ua-ogrere. When she died she returned to the sky. The people were all living together near Masingle but they fought among themselves and so separated into the various villages along the Binatruri River as far as Irupi, Tati, Jibara and Dirimo.

The Masa'ingle people were forced to move closer to the coast in former times to escape warfare inland. As they came near the coast they named the creeks and rivers around the Bullawe River and the larger Bineturi River [Kiwai for the Bine people's river]. From there they made contact with people in the central island of the Torres Strait islands of Yam and Tudu. Legend tells of people first being washed out to sea on the rafts used to cross the inland rivers: one day Omebwale, a young Bine man, went in search of his father who had been washed out to sea. He took with him a pig and as he went past the reefs and islands he threw out parts of the animal: the leg became a turtle, the skin a stingray and the head a dugong. The sea spirits gave him a hunting harpoon and when he reached Tudu the people there gave him a wife. Omebwale returned to the mainland with his wife from Torres Strait and they had many children. From the union came the close connections between the Bine and the central islanders of the Torres Strait. This connection was broken by the migration of the Kiwai who settled on the coast and interrupted the direct contacts between the islander and inland dwelling peoples (Lawrence 1994: 306–07). Connections with Yam

Island in the Torres Strait are now strongest between the Kiwai-speaking people of Mabudawan, Tuteture and Mawatta villages. Many Kiwai have intermarried with Yam Islanders and settled there (Fuary 2000).

Other legends continue the Masa'ingle journeys: one man, Soriame, journeyed east in search of a new place to live and met Bidedu at Kuru [also mentioned in the origin stories of the coastal Kiwai] and so he traveled southwest and finally at the mouth of Kura Creek, at Siblemete, he rested. He brought his people to the coast. It was here they first met with the Kiwai-speaking people but fighting broke out between the two groups and so the Masa'ingle again moved inland. While inland they made contact with Gamea who had settled his people at Mawatta. Eventually the dispersed groups of Masa'ingle came together and formed a new community at the site of the old Masingle village (Lawrence 1994: 307–08).

In 1891, when Sir William Macgregor (Annual Report on British New Guinea 1890/91. Appendix M: 46) visited the area he reported that the Masingle village was located about five kilometres from Mawatta and had a population of about 400 to 500 people and that their houses were a compromise between the longhouses of the Kiwai and small family houses. The men's houses were about 15 metres in length and decorated with trophies of hunting, mostly pig jaws.

Figure 30. Typical men's house of the Masa'ingle people with pig's jaw hunting trophies hanging from post (VKK 248: 33)

The small houses, often on the ground, were the homes of the women and children. About this time the government ordered the people to re-form near the site of the old graveyard and Hely in 1894 (Annual Report on British New Guinea 1893/94. Appendix E: 54–55) reported that the village of 400 people lived in 67 ordinary houses and four men's houses. The people, he reported, mixed and intermarried with the coastal Kiwai. When Landtman visited in 1910, the Masingara village was one large community that had relocated near the Binaturi River. [

Figure 31. Communal living house for women and children in Masingara village (VKK 248: 36)

The current Masingara village, with all houses of the coastal single-family type, was established closer to Mawatta with access to the mouth of the Binaturi River about 1950.

Dirimu Plantation

Figure 32. The Papuan Industries' manager's house at Dirimu. Landtman shared this house with the resident manager, G. H. Murray. Photo shows cookhouse at back and bathroom on verandah corner (VKK 248: 534)

The plantation of Dirimu [Dirimo] established by the Papuan Industries Ltd at the time of Landtman's visit was built on Bine land and its location near the intersection of the Bullawe and the Binaturi Rivers was an important story site. However, European visitors saw the region only for its commercial possibilities. Sir William Macgregor in his report of a visit of inspection to the southwestern coast in 1895 noted that the land around Dirimu village was fertile and a large number of coconut palms grew there. He stated that the land was ideal as a plantation and that: 'Along the Binaturi there is a belt of heavy forest timber, consisting of many different kinds of trees, and there are clumps of such wood at many places here and there amongst the undulating grassy ridges that give character to the district' (Annual Report on British New Guinea 1895/96: 40). Added to the image of fertile grassy inland ridges was the discovery that the Binaturi could be navigated as far as inland as Jibu village. When living at Dirimu plantation Landtman made frequent use of the Binaturi as a highway to the coast at Mawatta.

A story told to the Rev William Macfarlane (1928–29) and reprinted by Haddon (1935, I: 81–83) is similar to the story of Omebwale. At the site of the Dirimu plantation, in former times, many wild pigs roamed in the bush. One in particular was noted for its size and was feared for it ate people at the time. Amubalee, a man in that area, had a pregnant wife but one day when hunting his canoe was washed out to sea and it took him to Tudu [Warrior Island]. He was taken in by people there who wondered where he had come from for they did not know of Daudai. In the meantime, his wife had given birth to a son named Ui-balee. The boy grew and became a good hunter and eventually became so skilled that he killed the pig that threatened the people. The mother took the bristles of the pig and threw them around on the ground and the dead people were born again. The boy went in search of his father and he too travelled to Tudu. The father and boy were reunited and Ui-balee returned to the mainland to tell his mother. This original journey was the commencement of the bonds between the people of Tudu and the Bine.

Figure 33. Communal family house in Dirimu village (VKK 248: 39)

Figure 34. Boys with bows and arrows at Dirimu village (VKK: 248: 173)

Dudi

Koabu

Coastal Kiwai language is spoken by the communities of Sui and Daware near Parama Island, and at Severimabu, Koabu, Madame and Wederehiamo. Wederehiamo is the last Kiwai-speaking village on the Dudu, or western, bank of the Fly estuary. Koabu people originally came from Mugu near Teapopo on the Manowetti side of the estuary and the Wederehiamo people came from Sepe on Kiwai Island. When Sir William Macgregor came to the area in 1891 and 1892, the people of Koabu and Wederehiamo were still living as one community (Annual Report on British New Guinea 1888/89, 1889/90). But when Gunnar Landtman later visited Koabu he found a large village of people living in one long house and another located nearby at a community he called Ipidarimo [side or beside the men's house]. It is possible that Ipidarimo was the first longhouse of the Wederehiamo village. As warfare had been common between the people of the Dudi coast and the Kiwai Islanders, villagers all along the Dudi coast lived together for protection and only after good relations had been established were they able to build new villages along clan lines. As the earliest villages on the Dudi side were at Tirio, near Balamula, Madame and Meai near Severimabu it is reasonable to speculate that the establishment of the more recent communities at Koabu and Wederehiamo would have occurred sometime between 1891 and 1910.

Figure 35. Communal longhouse at Koabu (VKK 248: 47)

Currently, Koabu is the largest of the coastal villages and is located close to Severimabu. The village is built on flat, dry land about two to three metres above the river at low tide and consists of about 30–40 dwellings. Unlike Severimabu, the village runs at right angles to the river. Koabu is a well organised community with a school located at the back of the village beyond a large grassy paddock with a church and hall dividing the village into two areas. Most of the other communities, such as Severimabu, Madame and Wederehiamo, are smaller with fewer facilities.

Tirio, Balamula and Madiri

The village of Madiri is located on the site of the former Papuan Industries plantation and comprises people from the three neighbouring villages of Tirio, Balamula and Madiri. They mostly speak the local Bugumo language (Lawrence 1994). These villages were visited by Sir William Macgregor in 1898 who on his inspection of the Fly River noted that Madiri was the location of the largest longhouse yet seen in the Western District (Macgregor 1888–89). It measured 159 metres long and was 30 metres wide. Later, when this longhouse deteriorated, the people of Tirio built two smaller communal houses nearby (Beaver 1920: 133). The Kiwai would not go past this point for fear of sorcery but continued to obtain canoe hulls from the Bugumo-speaking people. Madiri people have traded inland with the communities of Iamega at the headwaters of the Oriomo River and with the people of Sepe on Kiwai Island who had extensive relations with the people of the Manowetti coast. Their external relations are wide and a number of communities now live in the Madiri region. From the inland people on the Oriomo Plateau they obtained drums, bows and arrows and exchanged in return sago, bananas and coconuts. Tirio and Balamula [also known as Odogositia] villages at the apex of the Fly estuary have always been in an advantageous position for customary exchange with their neighbours. Their position as a major site of canoe building was noted by Wilfred Beaver (1920: 139) who wrote: 'the Balamula [villagers] are among the best canoe-builders on the Fly. Pulling up the Baramura [Balamula] Creek I have seen scores of canoes of all sizes in the making. All are dugouts with the single outrigger, but without a platform'.Madiri plantation continued as a commercial copra and rubber venture until 1932. The Papuan Industries interest in Madiri was then sold to the Kwato mission but as the plantation was seen to be a suitable site for the development of a mission to the Gogodala it was gifted to the Unevangelised Fields Mission (UFM) the first 'faith' mission to operate in Papua. The introduction of the UFM in effect broke the sphere of influence agreement of the established churches (Wilde 2004; Dundon 2002). However, because the UFM was not an 'industrial mission' like the Kwato mission or Papuan Industries the operation of a plantation was seen to be irrelevant to their evangelical activities. Mission activity was disrupted in 1932 when the UFM missionaries at Madiri, Albert Drysdale, Len Twyman and Theo Berger, were forced to move to the relative safety of the northern Manowetti banks to escape potential threats from Suki raiders. Twyman later successfully established a UFM mission at the Suki lakes and converted many of the people there (Lawrence 1995: 63).

Mission activity among the Gogodala on the Manowetti coast was active before the Second World War. After the war Australian and New Zealander evangelical missionaries were successful in converting most of the remaining Gogodala living along the Aramia River further inland. The UFM changed its name to Asia Pacific Christian Mission in the 1960s and later the Evangelical Church of Papua New Guinea (ECPNG) was constituted but the ECPNG and the Asia Pacific Christian Mission are two parts to the one religious organisation (Crawford 1981: 40). After nearly 70 years in the field, the expatriate missionaries left the Balimo area in 2003 when the church to the Gogodala was fully localised (Wilde 2004: 34).

Manowetti

Gaima, Wariobodoro, Maipani

Landtman first visited Gaima, a Gogodala community on the Manowetti bank of the Fly estuary now known as Kaviapu, with Ben Butcher in 1910 (see Haddon 1916, Crawford 1981: 38, however Beaver 1914 confuses it with the second trip and states it was in 1911). Gaima was the first outlet to the Fly River for the Gogodala people and they maintained close trading relations with the Kiwai of Domori Island. The land is really owned by the Pagona Kiwai who inhabit Domori Island and who gave the Gogodala the village site on the river. The Kiwai of the Manowetti bank call the Fly River, Gimioturi, but the Gogodala name for the river is Kalama Wasewa. In fact, Landtman was the first person to photograph the Gogodala and his journey there was not long after the first government contact with the local people.

Gaima had been the location of a government police station established in 1903 and from there Butcher and Landtman walked to Balimo via Kubu. Contact with the Gogodala had only been made a few years before Landtman's visit. The Resident Magistrate at that time, C. G. Murray, visited Gaima in 1900 and headed a long inland expedition visiting Mida, Bida, Warigi, Dogona and Barimu [Balimo] that discovered the large freshwater lagoon areas around the Aramia River (Annual Report on British New Guinea 1900/01: 82). The next RM to travel to the Aramia was A. H. Jiear who made the journey inland from Gaima in 1902 covering the route taken by Murray. With the settlement and growth of Gaima it was decided to close the police post at Buji. The main reason was to stop the people from the middle Fly region raiding the coastal villages along the banks of the Fly estuary. The decision was not well received by the Boigu and Saibai Islanders who reported false sightings of 'Tugeri' raiders in the hope that the police post would be maintained at Buji.

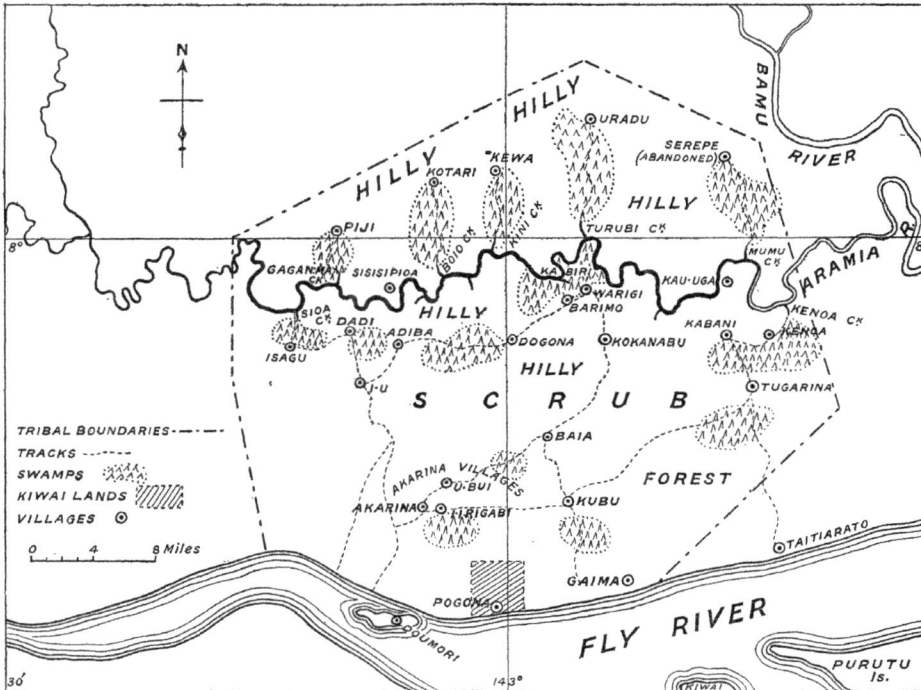

Map 4. Gaima and the Gogodala coast (Lyons 1926)

Crawford (1981: 38) also notes that Butcher and Landtman were in a party of men that reached the Bamu River in 1910. However, it appears that Landtman lost most of his Gogodala artefact collection in the canoe accident near the tidal mouth. Even so many objects were later donated to the Cambridge Museum. Presumably these were the artefacts retrieved from Gaima in 1911. Wilfred Beaver who was based on Daru at the time of Landtman's fieldwork there reported that: 'Messrs Butcher and Landtmann [sic] made a hurried journey from Gaima to Barimo [Balimo], there embarked in a canoe, and after two days and nights' paddling, reached the main Bamu river but unfortunately the trip was so hurried that no notes were taken and no traverse of the Aramia made' (Beaver 1914a: 410). Beaver repeated this account in his book (Beaver 1920: 199) but further explained that the 'party, however, had an exceedingly narrow escape in their canoe from the [tidal] bore which comes up the [Aramia] river from the Bamu' at full moon and high tide. The tidal bores in the Aramia, Bamu and Fly Rivers remain exceeding dangerous and unpredictable.

Figure 36. Gaima man in mourning net (VKK 248: 409)

Figure 37. Front of a Gogodala longhouse at Gaima (VKK 248: 121)

Considerable use of Landtman's photographs and collection was made by Haddon in his paper on the Gogodala, whom he incorrectly referred to as the Kabiri or the Girara (Haddon 1916). Haddon's terminology was corrected by the Lieutenant Governor no less (Haddon 1916; appendix). The word Kabiri [Kibili] is the actually the name of the large lagoon in front of Balimo and Dogona villages and Girara is the Gogodala word for 'language' (Lyons 1926). However the village of Gaima on the Fly was a logical place for Landtman and Butcher to begin an investigation of the inland wetlands and the well populated area along the Aramia River that gave access to the Bamu River.

The longhouses at Gaima, said to be between 60 feet (20 metres) and 130 feet (43 metres) in length and 50 feet to 60 feet (approximately 20 metres) in width, were built on the high ground of red clay between the river and the narrow band of rainforest behind. A. P. Lyons, who served for many years in the Western District, reported that longhouses of between 60 and 390 feet (20 to 130 metres) in length with a width of between 30 and 90 feet (10 to 30 metres) and a height of 30 feet (10 metres) were common in the region (Lyons 1926: 335). Longhouses of 100 metres in length were seen by J. H. P. Murray in 1916 at Balimo and Waligi villages (Crawford 1981) and Beaver (1914a), an accurate reporter, stated the longhouse of Dogona village was an astounding 500 feet (166 metres) in length,

117 feet (39 metres) in width and 70 feet high (23 metres). These longhouses were up to three storeys in height. Cooking was undertaken on the bottom, ground level, the men slept on the middle level near the fireplaces and the women and children slept in side stalls between the open centre and the sloping walls. Men could also sleep on the top level.

Figure 38. Side stall in Gogodala longhouse at Gaima (VKK 248: 125)

In his contribution to the Westermarck festschrift, Haddon (1912: 25) wrote: 'At Gaima and north of the Delta [estuary] between the Fly and the Bamu Rivers, the eaves of the roof [of longhouses] practically touches the ground, and the walled gable-ends are recessed to form a deep verandah, the angle of the outer gable being filled up with transverse bamboos'. Haddon's comments were largely taken from Landtman's notes.

The Aramia floodplain is wide and flat and in the annual rainy season it becomes a series of interconnected freshwater wetlands: one of the finest in the world. They can only be traversed by the long canoes without outriggers. In former times these were highly decorated, carved and painted. In the dry season the grasslands are burnt off and the isolated village communities can then be reached on foot. The Gogodala have a rich carving tradition and their distinctive style is readily recognised (see Crawford 1981; Beaver 1914a; Lyons 1926). During his patrols, Wilfred Beaver made a collection of artefacts which was later bought by Albert B. Lewis from the Field Museum of Natural History in Chicago who was later to criticize the quality of Landtman's photographs (Crawford 1981).

Figure 39. Children at Gogodala longhouse in Gaima. Most of the children exhibit signs of *kwashiorkor*, acute malnutrition caused by protein deficiency in infants no longer fed milk that leads to grossly distended stomachs (VKK 248: 251)

Maipani

The village of Maipani on Dibiri Island is the first contact point between the Island Kiwai and the Wabuda Kiwai and the Bamu Kiwai. While the people from Kiwai Island exchanged sago for canoe hulls with the people from Maipani they did not venture further along the Gulf coast from there. The area is considered 'spiritually' dangerous and even now the Bamu people are renowned for their magic and unusual customs such as offering their women to guests. A custom that so upset the missionary Ben Butcher. The first canoe, Burai, was said to be created by magic and young women with magic powers, the *Busere-busere*, made the canoe outriggers in the shape of the canoe. They taught the Bamu people how to paddle standing, first to make one long stroke, then to rest and to call out. The Bamu people still paddle like this. The route Burai took parallels the movement of canoe hulls from Dibiri Island and the migrations of people down the Fly estuary. From Bamu they traveled to Domori, the island near Sumogi Island, to Lewada, Tirio, Balamula, Wederehiamo, Severimabu, Daware, Sui and Parama. At that time the longhouses were still at Kudin and Wasigena just above Toro Passage. The story tells how the *Busere-busere*, after paddling down the coast finally reached Saibai. There they built a longhouse at Kagaro point that went as far as Otamabu Reef. The canoe, Burai, sank in the passage between Kagaro and Mabudawan. It is believed to be still there, its place marked by rocks (Lawrence 1994: 317).

Kiwai Island

Kiwai Island, the largest island in the Fly Estuary, is 60 kilometres long but only four kilometres wide and is generally more fertile at the southeastern end. The northwesterly end, near Sepe, is mostly sago swamp whereas in the south, between Sagapadi village and Samare, the inland is higher and covered by some good vegetation and tall trees. Sago from Kiwai Island is prized for its colour and taste. The population was recorded by Macgregor in 1889 at 5000 people and by Chalmers at 4000 people in 1903 (Macgregor 1888–89; Chalmers 1903). The legendary home of the Kiwai, Barasaro, was inland from Iasa village on the higher, more fertile land. It was estimated by Beaver, writing between 1910 and 1913, that the Kiwai moved out of Barasaro about 120 years earlier. This would estimate it to about 1800 and this would agree with the movement of the Kiwai along the southwest coast about 50 to 70 years later. The first move was made by one group to the northeast coast of Kiwai Island, near Doropo, and then to Wiorubi or Wapa-Ura. The next group to move went to Iasa on the southwest coast. From Iasa people moved north to Sumai or Paara, meaning death, for the leader remarked it was 'a good place to die in' (Beaver 1920: 156). The people in Iasa again separated and moved south to Saguane and Samare [Samari]. The most obvious reasons for the migrations was population growth, the resulting land pressure, growing food insecurity and social conflict.

However, legend illustrating the creation of Kiwai Island starts earlier. Stories say that once there were no islands in the estuary but the people from the Dudi and the Manowetti banks used to throw their rubbish into the wide river. The rubbish collected and eventually a sandbank formed. A dead nipa palm trunk became fixed on the sand and a hawk landed on the palm tree. It was carrying a fish in its claws and as it ate the fish bits of the flesh dropped onto the trunk and the sand. These pieces started to decay: women grew from this waste. From one worm came the first man: Meuri [the man who killed Sido was also called Meuri]. The hawk brought more food and other seeds grew. One day some men from the Manowetti bank came looking for the body of a boy taken by a crocodile and they met Meuri. They returned to their village and came back with more people. They built a village on the beach and the Kiwai people started from there. The sandbank still exists in the centre of a large swamp in the middle of Kiwai Island.

Landtman's informant at Mawatta, Namai, told him a second version. One day a log floated from Manowetti and became stranded in a tree near the site of the present Kubira village. In the tree was a ferocious, brightly coloured lizard. On Dibiri Island [near the Bamu River], a woman with a small son was going to her gardens and she asked her older sister, who was making a basket, to look after the small baby. The baby crawled into the basket and the sister, thinking it was a dog, hit it with a stick. She accidentally killed the child. When the mother returned home she grieved for the child so much that her husband decided they would move away from the other family. They sailed for a long time on the river and eventually came near the tree with the lizard in it. They became frightened by the animal but in a dream the lizard came to them and said it would help them. The couple buried their son near the tree and planted food and crotons. They subsequently had many children. These children were the beginnings of the Kiwai people. More Dibiri people came looking for the couple and they too saw the lizard and were afraid but the man and women explained that it was their protector. The lizard is still the protector of the Kubira people (Landtman 1917: 64–67).

The stories establish some common facts: some of the Kiwai people originally came from further along the Gulf of Papua coast from the area near Dibiri Island and settled at Kubira. Dibiri was also the source for canoe hulls and the origin of the first canoe, Burai. Other people first settled in the inland part of the island, near Barasaro, where they lived in the middle of the large marshlands protected from other peoples. From there, once they had established their position and the population had grown were they able to move out and settle on the coast and migrate further south.

When the first people moved out from Barasaro they dispersed and settled in various places along the banks of Kiwai Island at Sepe, Iasa, Kubira, Doropo, Sumai (Paara) and U'Uwo. From Sepe they again moved to Sumai (Lawrence 1994; Landtman 1917: 68). The elder brother clan remained there but the younger brother clan moved to Auti. The elder brother and younger brother clan separation usually describes the results of a breakdown in harmony between on two sections of a village: without resorting to violence the divisions agree to separate and build new villages and longhouses. From Auti people again moved to a new village at Sepe. Thus the people of Sepe, Auti and Sumai are all related. However other stories state that after they moved out of Barasaro, the people crossed to Mibu Island and went as far south as the present village of Sui but good land was scarce there and so they move back up towards the site of the present village of Severimabu. Sepe and Severimabu have one common origin and through this the Kiwai people of the Dudi coast and those of Kiwai Island are related.

Auti and Sumai (Paara)

In 1888 Sir William Macgregor on his tour of inspection recorded the presence of five large communal longhouses at Auti and stated that the Sumai area had a population of over 500 people (Macgregor 1888–89). By 1895 he could proudly state that Sumai was 'one of the most advanced communities in the colony, and one of the most powerful' (Annual Report on British New Guinea 1895/96: 44). In 1895 the Resident Magistrate Bingham Hely published a map of Kiwai Island which showed it divided into 'tribal areas' (Annual Report on British New Guinea 1895/96).

The map remains generally accurate despite nearly a century of migrations, village separations and amalgamations and the impact of missions and the government. The area called Auti is now the land of Sepe village, which originated from an amalgamation of the old Auti and Sumai villages. However, because of coastal erosion at Wamimuba [Wami Point] a new village has recently been formed as a break-away from Sepe and this has been re-established back at the old Auti site. The area called Doropodai is now the land of Doropo village formed from a combination of people from U'Uwo [Doropo] and Kubira villages. Wiorubi [sand beach people] is now the land of the Sagapadi village, a recent amalgamation of the Wapa'ura [Hely's Wapauura villages] and Sagasia villages that Hely recorded as the Doropotamurubi [branch of the Doropo people] and the Dameratamurubi [branch of the Damera people] communities. Wiorubi is an old name for the Wapa'ura communities and the area formerly had a population of 700 to 800 people (Macgregor 1888–89). The area marked Iasa remains the land of the present Iasa village. Prior to Landtman's visit, Macgregor had recorded the presence of six communal longhouses at this location that measured between 50 and 70 metres in length. Iasa then had a population of 500 people (Annual Report on British New Guinea 1889/90: 36–43; Macgregor 1888–89) and in 1895 Macgregor reported that the people of Iasa traded sago as far south as Saibai Island in the Torres Strait and to Tureture village and even to the eastern Torres Strait islands of Murray (Mer) and Darnley (Erub) (Annual Report on British New Guinea 1895/96: 45).

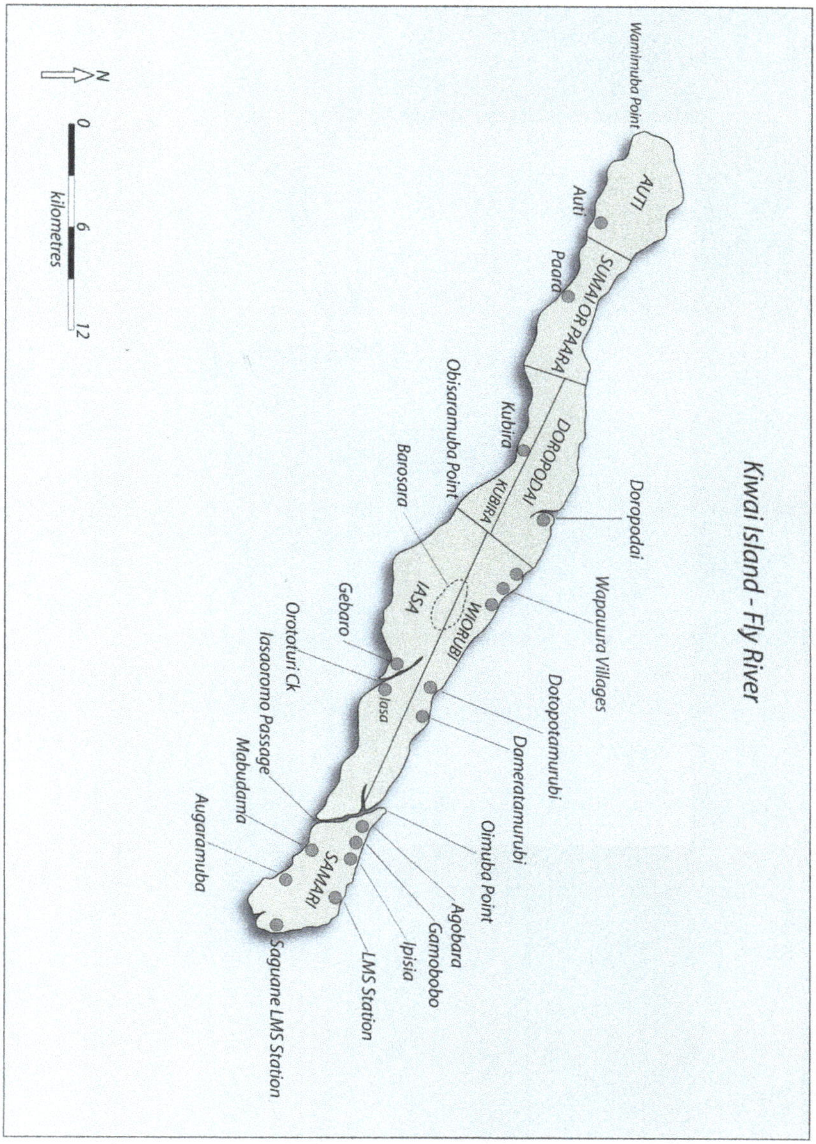

Map 5. Map of Kiwai Island prepared by Bingham Hely 1895 (Annual reports on British New Guinea 1895/96; Cartographic-GIS Services, College of Asia and the Pacific, ANU, 2009)

Figure 40. Group of longhouses at Auti (VKK 248: 81)

Figure 41. Interior of longhouse at Auti. Landtman was particularly pleased with the light effect that he achieved in the photographs of the dark and gloomy longhouses (VKK 248: 86)

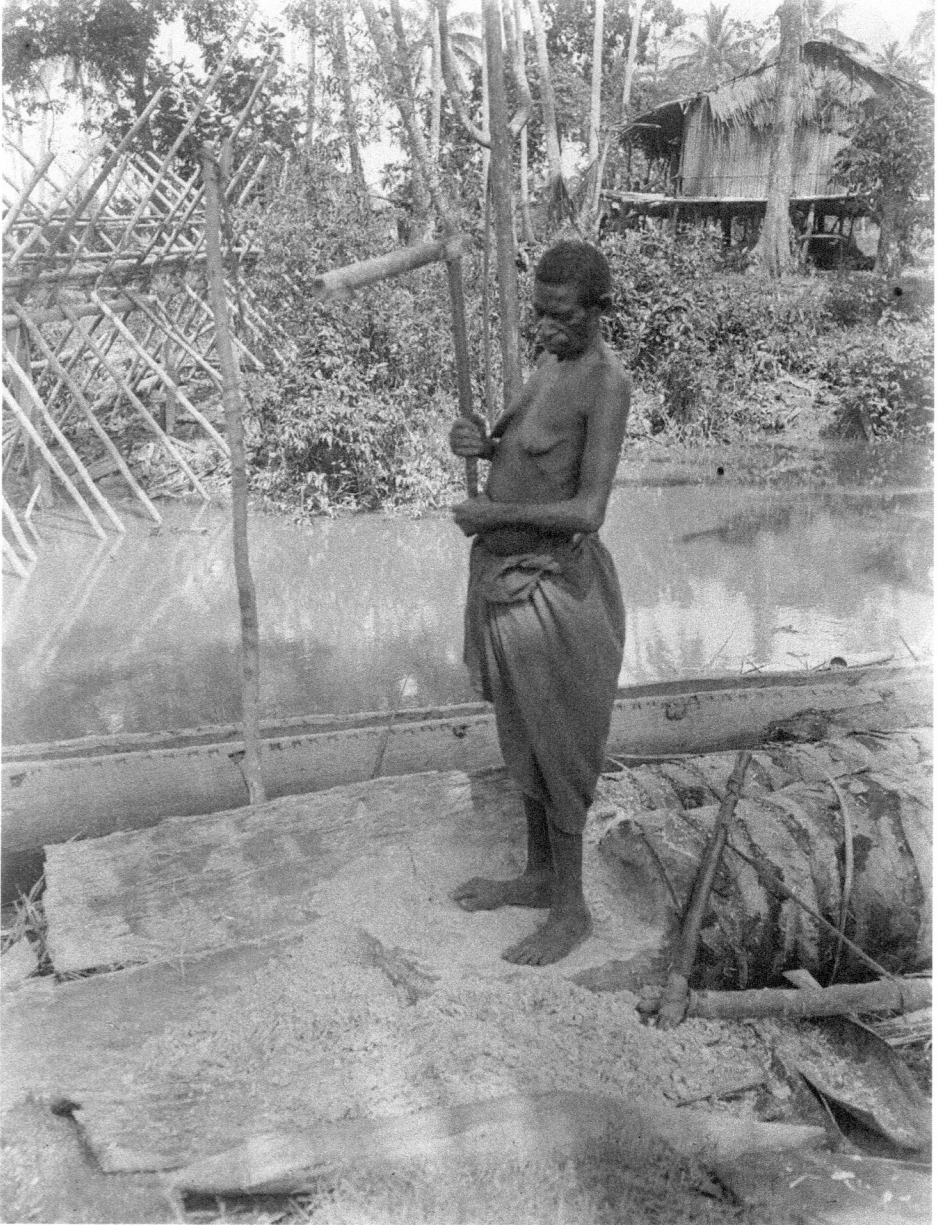

Figure 42. Woman from Sumai demonstrating the pounding of sago (VKK 248: 295). Sago is still made in exactly this method today

Figure 43. Sago strainer made from the outer bark of the sago palm
(VKK 248: 296)

Figure 44. Wooden bridge at Sumai crossing the canoe landing (VKK 248: 461). This bridge was especially noted as 'beautiful' by the Administrator, Sir William Macgregor in 1889 (Annual Report on British New Guinea 1889/90: 37)

Figure 45. Woman from Sumai preparing tobacco pipe (VKK 248: 310)[

Figure 46. Men dancing 'Taibobo' dance at Sumai (VKK 248: 369). The drummer is playing a hollow flour tin commonly called a 'Tinny'. These dances were learned from South Sea [Pacific] Islander crews of pearling and bêche-de-mer boats in the Torres Strait and from the Samoan missionary teachers. These dances are still performed today.

Figure 47. Boy paddling a single outrigger canoe (tataku) used in coastal creeks and rivers (VKK 248: 449). The bundles are old style tiro mats formerly used as sails but now used as sleeping rolls.

Figure 48. Longhouse at Iasa: considered the principal coastal village of the Kiwai Islanders (VKK 248: 59)

Figure 49. Front of longhouse at Iasa (VKK 248: 64)

Figure 50. Interior of longhouse at Iasa (VKK 248: 68). The box on the floor is a 'truck' or trade box of a returned indentured labourer

Figure 51. Framework of a new longhouse at Iasa (VKK 248: 77)

**Figure 52. Men performing a modern formation dance at Iasa
(VKK 248: 368)**

According to legend, after the people moved out of Barasaro they settled at Iasa
and from there some separated and went to Samare. Samare [Samari on Hely's
map] then divided into the Ipisia, Agobaro and Oromosapua villages all of which
were related. Samare was also related to Iasa. From Samare people moved to
Saguane and Ipisia. Saguane formerly had a population of about 250 but is now
considered an abandoned village. The mission station at Saguane was located on
a couple of acres near the village that contained two communal long houses and
a number of smaller huts (Annual Report on British New Guinea 1895/96: 45).
William Macgregor wrote bitterly that the sole missionary effort at Iasa village
was a case of the LMS 'holding the fort with a single sentry' (Annual Report on
British New Guinea 1889/90: 43; Wetherell 1996: 7). Early mission approaches
were unsuccessful and when Chalmers was appointed to revive the flagging
effort he based himself at Saguane in 1899 and 1900. Chalmers wrote that the
longest communal house on Kiwai Island measured 692 feet (230 metres) with
family stalls inside of 12 feet (4 metres) by 8 feet (3 metres). Communal feasting
and dancing took place in the wide central isle of the longhouse. Chalmers wrote
that the Kiwai were fine gardeners who built channels to drain the swamps and
planted gardens of taro, yams, sweet potatoes, bananas, sugarcane, breadfruit
and mangos (Chalmers 1903). Ipisia, which formerly had a large population

estimated at 1000 people and a small LMS post, is now a poor village of only about 15 houses built along the beach. However in the 1890s the Ipisia region contained the two closely related villages of Gamobolo and Agabara with over ten communal longhouses (Annual Report on British New Guinea 1889/90: 40). Landtman, in his travels from west to east, carefully documented the final stages in the construction of longhouses in the Fly estuary. With consolidation of colonial rule and missionary activity after the First World War, longhouses were considered unhygienic. Villagers were encouraged to build small coastal-style houses accommodating one or two families near latrines and to keep the village wells clean and tidy. The missions established churches, schools and medical aid posts near major villages with access to waterways.

Figure 53. Longhouse at Ipisia with decorated palm fronds and leaflets (VKK 248: 89)

Figure 54. Men in European clothing and waistcloths (*rami*) from Ipisia village on steps of longhouse (VKK 248: 216)

Figure 55. The longhouse at Oromosapua measured by Landtman at 154 metres (VKK 248: 107)

Figure 56. Man from Wapa'Ura in mourning costume (VKK 248: 404)

Chapter 4
Collecting and documenting the Kiwai

Gunnar Landtman was a dedicated and keen collector of artefacts. At first his collecting was carefully planned: 'Right from the beginning, too, I endeavoured to found two distinct main collections the principal one for the National Museum at Helsingfors [Helsinki], in case a complete duplicate set was not obtainable, and a similar one for the Cambridge University Museum of Archaeology and Ethnology [Anthropology]' (Landtman 1933: 10). However despite his plans Landtman could not control the accumulation of objects and when local people realised that he was paying good prices for artefacts he was inundated. Consequently, many objects are provenanced as 'mouth of the Fly', a generic term Landtman used to refer to his study region as he was unable to accurately document the origin of some pieces. This was not only a problem for Landtman. After the mid-1870s, when social, economic and political life in the Torres Strait was interrupted by the effects of pearling, missionary and administrative activities, the movement of Islanders and non-Islanders resulted in relocation of large numbers of artefacts and the Haddon collection also contains objects provenanced to places of purchase rather than place of manufacture (Kaus 2004: 95). Haddon at Cambridge had first choice of the artefacts collected by Landtman and this duplicate collection contains about 700 objects (Landtman 1927: ix Landtman 1910–12: letter dated 19 November 1912). In addition, Landtman gave artefacts to museums in Berlin and Stockholm and to his old school in Helsinki.

Both Haddon, as an avid collector also, and Baron Anatole von Hügel, the notable explorer of the Pacific, particularly Fiji, and first Curator of the Cambridge Museum of Archaeology and Ethnology [Anthropology], were generally pleased when the collection was unpacked. However, it appears the lack of decoration on the objects was one comment Landtman had to endure (Landtman 1910–12: letter dated 3 September 1912). On the return journey home Landtman stayed in Cambridge and in the time between sorting the artefacts for shipment to Helsinki, Landtman finalised a paper on the wandering of the dead in Kiwai folklore for submission to the festschrift celebrating Edvard Westermarck's birthday. In this, his first published paper on the Kiwai, Landtman described the legend of Sido as the story of the first man to open the road for humans to Adiri, the land of the dead. Landtman's rich folklore collection led him to understand that the beliefs of the Kiwai regarding their dead 'convey some idea of a people gifted with a singular power of imagination and displaying in various branches of folk-lore their astonishing faculty of interpreting, according to their own minds, the phenomena both of nature and their own lives. Their legends reveal to us the real Papuan Wonderland' (Landtman 1912b: 80). He understood the importance of the Sido story as one of a series of linked myths that serve to connect the peoples of the southern Papuan lowlands into concrete social relationships and patterns of communication. While we now know more about these interrelationships and are aware that people from different areas have ancestor hero legends that are not identical, that occasionally other people have different perspectives and often these stories may conflict, but there is a generally accepted common history of association between groups, and an exclusion of others (Busse 2005: 455), this early interpretation by Landtman was in marked contrast to contemporary writers who saw rituals and beliefs as evidence of primitive, irrational native minds.

Haddon's contribution to the Westermarck volume was a broad study in material culture describing housing styles from all known areas of New Guinea, both eastern and western, largely using secondary sources including Landtman's research notes. Landtman complained in his letters home that Haddon made frequent use of his material, photographs and quotes and that this was of some concern (Landtman 1910–12: Letter dated 3 September 1912). It appears that his relationship with Haddon was professional, formal and courteous but not intellectually stimulating.

Although Landtman was a protégé of Haddon and dutifully acknowledged his assistance in facilitating his research in Papua, he remained intellectually a student of the Frazer-Westermarck school. Westermarck's most influential work published in English at this time was *The Origin and Development of Moral Ideas* [*Moralens uppkomst och utveckling*] (1906–08) which was an attempt to rationalise the concept of moral philosophy. His conclusion was that morality is a social phenomenon and that moral judgments can be traced to altruistic and objective feelings of approval and disapproval, according to social rewards. Westermarck argued against the view that moral judgments were universal facts common to all people and he put forward the proposition that morality is a product of a long period of development, and ultimately based upon emotions and these vary in different individuals. This he based on anthropological, ethnological and historical data. Westermarck remained Landtman's intellectual guide. Westermarck also held a professorial position in sociology at the London School of Economics and Political Science between 1907 and 1931 at a time of the paradigmatic changes taking place in social anthropology that resulted in the ideological differences between the conservative evolutionists like James Frazer and the radical functionalists like Bronislaw Malinowski (Isotalo 1995). Landtman remained an ethno-sociologist despite his embryonic leanings towards anthropology (Wikman 1940).

The Landtman collection of Kiwai material culture

Landtman finally shipped his collection of 1326 objects home to Finland in 1913 and the Antell funds paid him 1700 Finnish marks (*Suomen markka*) for the artefacts and 300 marks for cataloguing the collection. The collection is now housed in the Museum of Cultures (*Kulttuurien museo*) in Helsinki, part of the National Museum of Finland (see Landtman 1933). It remains the most significant and comprehensive collection of Kiwai material culture available for research and complements the more famous Haddon collection of Torres Strait Islander material culture at Cambridge. The catalogue of the Kiwai ethnographic collection was not published until 1933 and this explains, in part, why Landtman used photographs of Torres Strait and Fly River material culture from the Haddon collection at the University of Cambridge Museum of Archaeology and Ethnology [Anthropology] in his main text published in 1927 (Landtman 1927 and 1933).

When Landtman made his collection of Kiwai material culture there was no philosophical separation between social and cultural anthropology and ethnology or the collection of artefacts for museum display. Fieldwork required the ethnologist to collect as much material culture, songs, stories, and documentation of a social and culture life of a people as was possible in a given time. At the time Landtman was collecting his Kiwai artefacts material culture was seen either as a measure of the developmental stages of cultures (social evolutionism) or as examples of the geographical spread and development of cultures (diffusionism). These theoretical aspects remained current until the 1920s and 1930s when anthropology moved in new directions (Kaus 2004: 100). Later, material culture came to be designated a kind of technological substrate that contrasted with the more abstract ideas of culture and the codes of social and spiritual life (Strathern 1990: 38). In a clear statement on tradition and transition in the Torres Strait, Florek (2005: 62) remarked that while material culture does not convey historical narratives, artefacts reflect change in the historical process. Significantly, artefacts, like photographs, cast light on the collector and on the collector's beliefs and expectations for 'the origin of artefacts and the mode of collecting strongly influence indigenous, historical and scientific values embedded in these collections'. Current museology is devoted to putting objects into their cultural context and producing functional and interpretative exhibitions where the artefacts are displayed as cultural objects and not as art (Strathern 1990: 39; Lahdentausta, Parpola, Vainonen and Varjola 2001). This is especially true of the Landtman collection and its links to the Haddon collections. Landtman's collection may be divided into four categories: subsistence, ornamentation and dress, ceremony and dance and warfare (Lawrence 1994).

Subsistence

This includes objects used as a means for supporting human life, in food getting, cultivation of the ground and for cooking and hunting. In the Torres Strait and Fly estuary dugong harpoons, bamboo water containers, mats, baskets, shell tools and utensils, stone-headed axes and adzes, coconut fibre fishing lines and brooms were all used during the pre- and post-contact periods. Following contact with European traders, more durable items like enamel bowls, knives, forks and spoons as well as rope and metal tools were gradually substituted for many of these artefacts. Also included in this category are watercraft such as canoes and canoe hulls. Other items such as bows, arrows, bamboo knives and spears may have been artefacts of warfare as well as subsistence.

Shell implements and shell utensils

The coastal Papuans employed shell hoes (*wedere moa*) for clearing gardens and digging in preparation for planting (Landtman 1933: 23; National Museum of Finland VK 4902: 563). Shell obtained from the Torres Strait Islanders were used for a variety of domestic utensils. Pottery was unknown in this region. The principal use for large bailer shells (*Melo* sp) was as a pot for boiling food or as a fire pot (VK 4902: 418) (see VKK 323). Old shells were often used as canoe bailers and other large shells such as *Fusus* sp. *Cassis* sp. and *Tridacna* sp. were used as water vessels (Haddon 1912, IV: 122 and Moore 1984: 64).

Illustration 1. Shell cooking pot (VK 4902: 418)

Stone tools

While smaller shell hoes were used to clear gardens and prepare areas for planting, heavier, hafted stone axes and adzes (*emoa*) were used for felling timber or for cutting and scraping wood. Landtman (1927: 33) was emphatic that the origin of all stone used by all coastal Papuan peoples was the Torres Strait, as the only naturally occurring stone along the southwest coast is the granitic outcrop of Mabudawan, and he wrote:

> According to what I was told at Mawata, the Torres Strait Islanders obtained the stones out of which axes (or adzes) and club-heads were made principally from the bottom of the sea, by diving. The diver had a long rope attached underneath one shoulder, by which his companions in the canoe helped him up to the surface when loaded with a heavy stone ... The shaping of the stone was effected by a hammer stone ... and the grinding by means of a somewhat softer stone (Landtman 1933: 45).

Landtman believed that Mabudawan was the principal centre where grinding stones were obtained by the Kiwai of Mawatta and these stones were exchanged with peoples further east and into the Fly estuary (Landtman 1933: 45). He would have based this on the evidence of being taken to see Wawa's grinding stone at Mabudawan. However, Haddon, on a later visit to Yam Island in 1914, was shown an isolated place in the bush called Konakan where large stone slabs with deep depressions, used as grinding stones for the manufacture of stone implements, were seen and photographed (Haddon 1935, I: Plate I, figures 1 and 2, and Plate II, figure 1). The stone slabs at Konakan may still be seen today and, according to the present day Yam Islanders, were places where the heads of stone axes (*gabagaba*) were ground.

The eastern Torres Strait Islanders brought armshells to Awridh Island and exchanged these for stone used in making club-heads and presumably stone axe and adze heads. Haddon (1935, I: 88) wrote that stone was obtained from the rocky Sir Charles Hardy and Forbes Islands off Cape Grenville on the coast of north Queensland. It would appear that the Torres Strait Islanders journeyed even further south than the Forbes Islands. The anthropologist, Donald Thomson wrote:

> The Koko Ya'o [Kuuku-Ya'u speaking people] of Lloyd Bay, which is the greatest stronghold on the [Cape York] Peninsula of hero cults of Papuan type [see Thomson 1933], stated that the people from Torres Strait came frequently in big canoes to Mitirindji (Quoin Island) off the mouth of the Pascoe River, to obtain supplies of stone for their axes (Thomson 1939: 82).

Thomson believed that this was further evidence of the contact and exchange between Torres Strait Islanders and the Aborigines of Cape York Peninsula. The large green turtle nesting sites of Eel Reef lie between Quoin Island and the mainland and it is likely that Torres Strait Islanders journeyed south on hunting and fishing expeditions long before European contact with Aboriginal groups along the eastern peninsula. The extent of this intermittent contact has been documented by Moore (1979).

The possibility that stone was transported down the Fly River was first mentioned by Haddon (1898: 221):

> In this district [Iasa on Kiwai Island] there are a number of very large stone implements (the largest I saw in Chalmers house [at Saguane] was 18 inches [46 cm] long). They are now placed round the graves but their significance is now entirely lost. The large implements are so cumbersome and heavy that it is difficult to see how many of them could ever have been used and I suspect that they were merely articles of barter — money in fact. As no stone occurs for many miles and none (of this kind) is known in the district — the implements have in all probability come down from the Fly River, and it is also probable that stone implements have been out of use for perhaps a century owing to the natives getting iron from passing ships and wrecks and then bartering it to their neighbours, thus in two or three generations the knowledge of stone implements could readily die out.

However, this was speculation as the possibility of stone being exchanged down the river is slight. Haddon changed his opinion largely on the basis of Landtman's research. The shape of all the larger axes or adze heads in museum collections is the same and quite distinctive. All are fine grained closely textured igneous rocks which appear to be holocrystalline. They are generally basalt or basaltic andesite, or andesite todacite but in general would appear to be volcanic or shallow intrusive rocks. It is more likely that stone was sourced within the Torres Strait or further south. As Landtman (1927: 34) remarked:

> As regards the shape of the stone axes, the Marindanim [the Tugeri] on the Dutch side of the boundary [now Indonesian Papua] have a tradition according to which, the first axe of this kind was obtained from one of the very large teeth of a certain being or man named Monubi [or Monuhi in Landtman 1933: 46], who had come from far away. The shape of an axe is in fact, very like that of a human front tooth.

Knowledge of their hafting and use was still strong when Landtman undertook his fieldwork in 1910–12. Among the Kiwai, an axe head was hafted with the cutting edge parallel to the handle between two blocks of timber, which were strongly bound on to an elbow or shoulder of timber. An adze head was hafted in a similar fashion, but with the cutting edge horizontal to the vertical wooden handle (VK 4902: 528). The size of the blade varies considerably with the largest stone blade in the Landtman collection almost 54 cm in length (VK 4902: 529) and the smallest only 8 cm in length (VK 4902: 559)(Haddon (1912, IV: 126 and Landtman (1933: 45-47).

Illustration 2. Stone adze (VK 4902: 528)

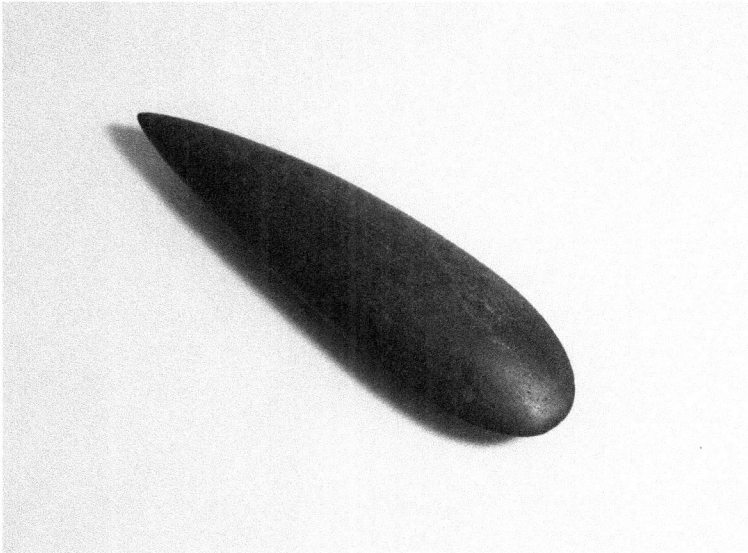

Illustration 3. Stone axe head (VK 4902: 529)

The true origin of stone axe and adze heads remains obscure although recent archaeological research in the Torres Strait (McNiven and Quinnell 2004) has broadened our understanding of the movement of stone across this region. Local quarry sites have now been investigated and the large stone heads from a number of collections have been examined. From this research it is becoming clear that stone was obtained principally from Dauan Island and from Moa [Mua] and Badu in the western Torres Strait and from the rocky volcanic eastern islands. Stone and stone axes were items of trade, exchange and looting and moved easily between ethnic groups (McNiven, von Gnielinski and Quinnell 2004: 271–89 and McNiven 1998).

Because of earlier contacts with Europeans and South Sea Islander maritime workers, the introduction of iron tools in the Torres Strait predated the introduction of iron into the coastal Papuan region. However, prior to European settlement the trade in stone tools was an integral part of customary exchange, and with the introduction of trade store tools, the replacement of iron for stone in the customary exchange system was a logical, rapid functional substitution.

Canoes

Formerly canoes (*pe*) were hollowed out, laboriously, using stone tools but the introduction of iron tools permitted easier and more sophisticated manufacture. The maritime technology of the Torres Strait Islanders and the Kiwai Papuans was of the highest order. Rutherford, a British naval officer passing through the region in the early 19th Century, wrote:

> the canoes are very long and narrow, swimmingly light, which renders the aid of outriggers necessary to prevent their upsetting. These outriggers consist of two long bamboo spars laid and fastened with grass ropes across the centre of the canoe, distant from each other about six feet [two metres], and on the outer ends of these two spars, on either side, another spar is tied parallel to the canoe itself, about seven feet [two and a half metres] from it, that is, beyond the gunwale or edge, and resting on the surface of the water, which, of course, must considerably impede the velocity of the vehicle, but which effectively prevents the risk of upsetting. The space between the cross spars on the canoe, and to the distance of about two feet [two thirds of a metre] beyond its gunwale or edge on each side is fitted or filled up with a bamboo hurdle, covered with a grass mat (Rutherford 1834: 195).

Decorated vertical boards were inserted in the bows and sterns of canoes of the Torres Strait Islanders (Haddon (1912, IV: 207 and 214, figure 209) and Landtman (1933: 77) reported that it was common practice for the people of the Fly estuary to place these oblong shield-like boards in the bows of canoes supported by stays and decorated with leaves or cassowary feathers. These carved and ochred *gope* were placed facing into the canoe for they served a practical purpose: they stopped water from splashing into the canoes (Landtman 1933: 21, figure 22). *Gope* were also hung outside longhouses as protection against illness.

In the Torres Strait this figurehead, there called a *dogai*, was fitted to canoes on Saibai on the journey from the place of origin in the Fly estuary to the eventual owner in the Torres Strait (Haddon 1912, IV: 207). Examples were collected by Haddon (Moore 1984: 50 and 59; plates 10 and 23; Haddon 1912, IV: 214, figure 209) from the Torres Strait islands of Saibai, possibly from Dauan, and from Mabuiag. The early descriptions of canoes described in detail the size of the canoes, the way in which they were well built and the sailing skills of the Islanders:

> Their canoes are very large, some being as much as 70 feet in length [20–25 metres], and capable of carrying from 25 to 30 people with ease, they are cut out of a single tree, broad and full in the bow, but narrower and rising out of the water abaft, with topgallant bulwarks of bark neatly sewed on and rising about a foot above the bow. Two outriggers extend about 6 feet [2 metres] on each side of the canoe amidships, to the ends of which is fastened a long canoe-shaped piece of light wood which prevents the narrow vessel from capsizing and also adds a good deal to buoyancy. The amidships part of these is decked over so as to form a kind of platform, on part of which some earth is usually laid by way of a fireplace. At the end of each side of the platform is built a sort of netting in which to keep provisions, fishing tackle &c ... They sometimes carry a large mat sail of an oblong shape which is stuck up in the bow of the canoe, there being two masts in one step but wide apart at the top, and the sail being trimmed by hauling of the masts aft, or vice versa (Sweatman 1842–47: 70–72; Allen and Corris 1977: 35).

Sweatman also described the use of large flat mat sails before they were replaced by cloth sails in lug rig copied from the pearling and bêche-de-mer fleets (see Haddon 1912, IV: 65 and 67; 1912, IV: Plate XXVI figures 1 and 2; Lawrence 1994: cover).

Before the introduction of fibreglass dinghies the main inshore and riverine watercraft in coastal Papua was the *tataku*, a small single outrigger canoe. It was long and narrow and used for fishing as well as for travelling to garden places along the rivers. Generally a *tataku* could take three or four people comfortably and could be either paddled or sailed, using a single cloth sail. The Kiwai from Katatai and Kadawa villages near Daru used a distinctive square cloth sail while the Fly estuary people, particularly the people from Kiwai Island, used an inverted triangular sail.

The second type of canoe using a dugout log was the *puputo*. This was principally used by the people living near Daru but also by some Oriomo River people and Binaturi River people who obtained their canoes from their Kiwai neighbours. The *puputo* had one mast, two sails, two outriggers, built up washstrakes and a large platform deck built over the raised planked sides. The main sail of the *puputo* was square. The *puputo* was used as an all-purpose fishing vessel and for carrying groups of people to and from the Torres Strait and Fly estuary villages. The *puputo* was similar to the larger *motomoto* but was lighter, could be used in coastal waters and be handled by a smaller crew. It was steered in the traditional fashion using a large, heavy, plank as both a rudder and centre board.

The *motomoto* (VKK 431) was the largest double outrigger canoe used in the Torres Strait and had two masts and three sails, a form adopted form the pearling luggers. While the *motomoto* was heavy and slow and required a large crew it was excellent for long trips, especially to the middle of the Torres Strait or the Warrior Reef. Turtles could be carried in the cargo area under the platform erected over the hull or on the outrigger booms although dugongs were usually carried on top of the platform due to their bulk and weight. *Motomoto* were almost exclusively used by the Kiwai from Mabudawan, Mawatta and Tureture villages who had to travel long distances over difficult waters to reach Daru or the Torres Strait islands. It was ideal in bad weather and although the ride was wet and cold the canoe was stable. They were ideally suited for carrying large cargoes of artefacts, people, foodstuffs and raw materials. Canoes were made from a variety of timbers: tall straight trees suitable for canoe hulls were generally only found in the well-timbered country along the northern Manowetti coast. Softer timbers, such as *Bombax* sp and *Erythrina* sp, were more common along the southwestern Daru coast and this material could be used for outriggers and planking needed to raise the decking high above the rough ocean of the Torres Strait.

Landtman took numerous photographs of canoes, both large and small, and they illustrate the gradual change in form of the *motomoto* that was previously sailed without a full platform. The canoe was the most important item of material culture for both the Torres Strait Islanders and the coastal and riverine dwelling people of the southwest coast of Papua prior to the introduction of European maritime technology. Occupation of island, inter-ethnic contact and the maintenance of some form of equilibrium in the subsistence pattern across Torres Strait would not have been possible without a sufficiently sophisticated maritime technology.

Both Haddon (1908, VI: 186) and Landtman (1927: 214–15) recorded descriptions of formal or ceremonial practices associated with the exchange of valued items. Although Landtman stated that 'in the canoe traffic, as in any other form of barter, there is no clearly marked difference between actual commerce and the exchange of friendly presents' (Landtman 1927: 215) he recorded precisely the formality of such an 'exchange of friendly presents' in the westerly movement of canoes from the Fly estuary and into the Torres Strait and the easterly movement of a variety of artefacts in 'payment' or exchange. The formality of exchange partnerships stimulated and activated the flow of other material culture. Along the lines of exchange also moved food, plants, animals and marriage partners.

Mats and baskets

Mats and baskets, as well as other plaited articles, such as belts and bands, continue to be made by Islanders and Papuans. The variety of forms and manufacture was noted by Quiggin (1912: 63) who remarked: 'Basketry and plaitwork are the most important of the native arts of the Torres Strait Islanders, though here also, as is found to be the case with so many other artefacts now in use, importations from New Guinea are met'.

Plaited mats, from both coconut and pandanus leaf, are still items of daily use in Islander and Papuan homes. This applies even in mainland Australian cities where Islanders have settled and in towns and cities in Papua New Guinea. The spreading of mats has social as well as practical meaning. Guests are welcomed in Islander and Papuan homes by placing clean, often new, mats on floors or on outside seating platforms. It signifies welcome and hospitality and as Landtman (1933: 64) stated, in former times, a man conducted into a men's house would have been filled with foreboding if no mats had been spread for him for it signified that blood could be shed without fear of soiling the flooring.

Mats are cool and soft to sleep on particularly in hot and rainy times and are still preferred to European-style beds and mattresses that cannot be aired or dried easily in the tropics. A common form of sitting mat used outside can be made by plaiting trimmed coconut leaves. A form of pandanus mat was made from slips of pandanus leaf sewn together, not plaited (Quiggin 1912: 67–68). This mat could be folded lengthwise and rolled up for storage (see Landtman 1933: 21, figure 22). In Kiwai it is referred to as a *tiro* and Landtman (1927: 41) states that this form of mat came originally from Kiwai Island (VK 4902: 736). Such mats are no longer made or used in the Torres Strait but are still used in coastal Papua where they are principally used as 'sleeping bags' because they are warm and waterproof if used outside or on the deck of a canoe. Landtman (1927: 41) illustrated that they could also be used as rain hoods (*hoboro*).

Illustration 4. Tiro mat (VK 4902: 736)

The now commonly used pandanus leaf mat (*hawa*) was introduced to Kiwai Island from Mawatta (VK 4902: 732 and 733). It is therefore possible that the *tiro* was introduced into the Torres Strait from the Fly estuary along with canoe hulls and other exchange items. Conversely, the *hawa* commonly made in the eastern and central islands may have been introduced to the coastal Papuan region from the Torres Strait for it is generally considered to be more recent in origin than the *tiro* mat.

Illustration 5. Hawa mat (VK 4902: 732 and 733)

Coconut leaf baskets (*sito*) were, and still are, made and used in both the Torres Strait islands and in Papua (VK 4902: 394). They are used principally for carrying garden foods and personal belongings. One form of basket, made from the green coconut leaf, is used as a disposable rubbish basket. However, the plastic supermarket carry-bag is replacing this form of basket and, along with the disposal of cans, bottles and containers, is adding to environmental problems around village areas.

Illustration 6. Coconut leaf basket (VK 4902: 394)

Another type of fine grass or tuberous root basket (*gatere*) is readily available on Daru. These soft and beautifully decorated baskets were noted and collected by Landtman (1927: 41) and were, and still are, used largely by men for personal articles and by some older men as 'magic' bags (VK 4902: 402) (Moore 1984: 42; Plate l). These bags are brought through the Agob and Bine areas from the Suki Lakes in the middle Fly and for this reason are generally referred to as 'Suki bags'. A similar bag called by Quiggin in Haddon (1912, IV: 84, and Plate XVII figure 2) a 'check basket of Flagellaria' was obtained on Mer. Suki bags were important exchange items and continue to be popular accessories.

Illustration 7. Suki basket (VK 4902: 402)

Dugong harpoons

The principal tool used by both Islanders and coastal Papuans in hunting dugong was the harpoon (*wapo*) that consisted of a harpoon dart (*kuior*), a small barbed head inserted into a terminal hole in the butt end (*kumu*) of the main harpoon shaft *(paike)* (Haddon 1912, IV: 166, as well as Plate XXIII, figure 1–4, and Landtman 1933: 27 and 28). The ends of the harpoons were often decorated with cassowary feathers and the butt end finely carved or incised.

The harpoon, especially the butt end, was often made from *wongai* wood and the best wood came from the Torres Strait islands particularly Muralag and Mabuiag (Haddon (1912, IV: 169 and Plate XXIII, Figure 4). A fine harpoon from Muralag is illustrated in Haddon (1912, IV: 169) and a number of harpoon darts are in the Haddon collection (Moore 1984: 43 and Haddon 1912, IV: Plate XXIII, Figure 2). Landtman collected a similar harpoon from Mawatta. This was cut into three main parts for transportation to Finland: only the dart, the butt end and the base of the shaft are in the Landtman collection (VK 4902: 588, VK 4902: 586, and VK 4902: 587)(see Landtman 1933: 27). As items of exchange the dugong harpoon was highly regarded:

The Miriam [eastern Islanders] valued them [harpoons] more as ornaments or works of art, and like the imported spears they indicated the wealth of the owner; they were exchanged or given as presents at marriages. The wooden shafts of fishing spears, likewise, constituted important items of exchange (Haddon 1912, IV: 169).

Ropes

Ropes made from lawyer cane (*Calamus* sp.) or possibly coconut root fibres as well as eight-ply dugong ropes (*amo*) made from the tough climbing *Apocynaceae* plant were taken from Papua into the Torres Strait (VK 4902: 527) (Moore 1984: 43 and Plate 2). This buoyant rope was an essential part of the dugong harpoon equipment but at present hunters use strong nylon ropes readily available in tradestores on Daru. Other fine quality ropes were also made by the Kiwai from bush materials (VK 4902: 525).

Illustration 8. Dugong rope (VK 4902: 527)

Brooms

Brooms (*mihere* or *koumiri*) made from coconut leaf midribs have always been important items in Islander and Papua households. Brooms continue to be significant items of material culture although they are rarely collected by museums. It is still common for both Islander and Papuan women to use coconut leaf brooms both indoors and outdoors in preference to European style brooms.

Bamboo water containers

Bamboo water containers (*obo-marabo*) (Landtman 1933: 61) were used on canoes and by people travelling to gardens and fishing places (VK 4902: 412). They could be easily cut from the large bamboo stands growing along the coastal waterways. A small hole was cut in one end node and the container filled with fresh water. It could be stoppered with clay or grass A cord of bamboo was then tied to each end of the bamboo stick that could be carried over the shoulder. A similar, decorated, object in the Haddon collection was obtained on Mer (Moore 1984: 64, Plate 28).

European tradestore goods and tools

The introduction of European tradestore goods and tools, such as metal axes, knives, metal spikes, ropes, sails and textiles, resulted in the substitution of many material culture items used and made by both Islanders and Papuans prior to European contact. The trader, John Cowling who had operated a pearling station and store on Mabuiag in 1898 commented on the long distances over which tradestore goods passed from hand to hand across the Torres Strait when he wrote:

> ... when I first went to the Bamu in [18]98 I was surprised to see the prints the natives were wearing that I had sold in Mabuiag. I know they were mine as I bought them from patterns sent from Manchester and imported direct, no other store had them, but this is only one instance of the distance trade-goods travel and change hands ... (Haddon 1898: 225).

This was the same John Cowling who was Landtman's host at Mibu Plantation in the Fly estuary.

Ornamentation and dress

Fibre skirts, plaited belts and bands were used as clothing. However, a great variety of objects were used as personal adornment for the head, arms, body, legs and feet. This included various types of marine shell ornaments, dogs' teeth and boars' tusks, plaited and feather headdresses, plaited frontlets, armguards and leglets. The range of bird plumes used was considerable: feathers from cassowaries, birds of paradise, Torres Strait pigeons, herons, and parrots were worn and exchanged. In addition coloured ochres, threaded seeds and bone ornaments were used for personal adornment, as markings of status or as decoration. Following contact with European traders, and the introduction of Christianity, cotton calico or *rami* [turkey red cloth] became important items of dress.

Pubic Shells

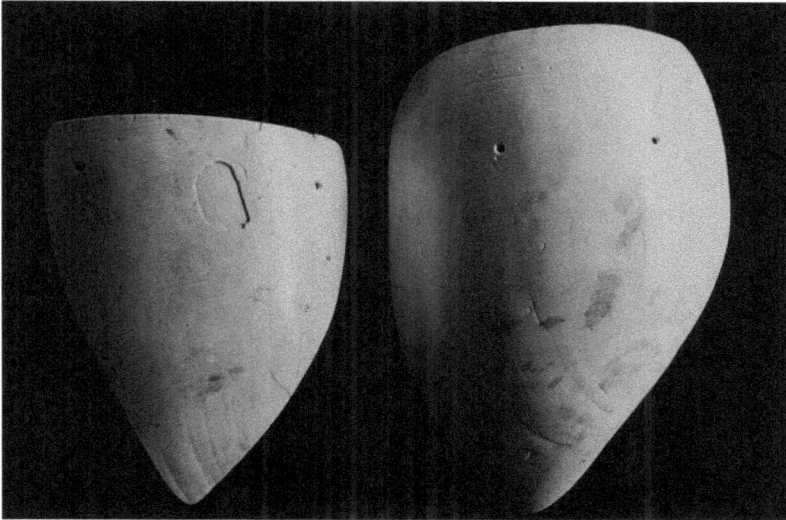

Illustration 9. Shell pubic covers (VK 4902: 231 and 232)

Both Landtman (1933: 33) and Haddon (1935, I: 297) noted that a common item of men's dress in Papua and in the Torres Strait was the pubic shell (*wedere*) usually made from the bailer shell (*Melo sp*) often incised with designs. This was not worn at all times and the people living in the inland region did not wear pubic shells at all. In most cases the pubic shell covered the genitals although a Landtman (1933: 34, Figure 40) photograph taken at Buji shows the pubic shell worn as a cover only over the penis. Other men wore the shell over a cotton calico wrap. For warfare or for ceremonial occasions and dances, temporary coconut leaf skirts and belts were worn with a variety of other, often elaborate, ornamentation, such as arm, leg, nose and ear decorations, masks, headdresses, necklaces and breast ornaments.

Landtman was able to collect pubic shells (VK 4902: 232) and Haddon collected a shell pubic cover in 1898 on Mer similar to those from Kiwai Island and the Fly River (Moore 1984: 97 and Plate 76). Other examples in the Landtman collection are not decorated with incised designs and show the usual variety in size (VK 4902: 231). A similar pubic shell in the Australian Museum collection (E 17284) in Sydney was collected at Mer in 1907 by Charles Hedley and Allan McCulloch, zoologists at the Australian Museum, and has been decorated with buttons and calico attachments. It was most likely traded from Papua to be worn in dances. The introduction of European clothing, and mission control, led to the demise of both the shell pubic cover worn by men and the fibre skirt worn by women, on all occasions except when dance dress was acceptable, in which case the shell was worn on men's hips. It became common for the fibre skirts to be worn by women over cotton dresses and for men to wear the pubic shells over cotton *lava-lavas* at dances.

Fibre skirts

From puberty Kiwai women wore a fibre skirt (*wapa* or *eere*) as a covering. These fibre 'petticoats' consisted of two fringes, one longer than the other, joined by a plaited band (VK 4902: 275 and 276). The longer fringe worn at the back was brought forward between the legs and tucked into the waist band forming a thick fibre apron in front. In the Torres Strait sometimes more than one fibre skirt was worn to make this 'petticoat' continuous around the body (Haddon 1912, IV: 60). In the 'top' western islands of Boigu, Dauan and Saibai the band of fibre was not continuous and the right thigh was shown.

Illustration 10. Fibre skirt (VK 4902: 275)

Women's skirts were made from a variety of fibres, such as the swamp grass (*Philydrum* sp.), *Ficus* sp., *Hibiscus* sp., or even banana (*Musa* sp.) and sago basts. The use of the leaves of the 'waterwort or flag' plant, possibly the *Philydrum* sp., was common for fibre skirts in both the Torres Strait islands and even among the Aboriginal people of nearby Cape York (Haddon 1912, IV: 61). The fibres were either left in their natural dried colour or marked with vegetable dyes, the more common being red dye from crushed mangrove roots. The connection between Papuan and Islander women's coverings was documented by Landtman (1933: 34):

> The same type of petticoat is seen in Waboda, Sageru [Wabuda Island, Segera village near Dibiri Island] and Mawata and is said by my Mawata informants to have been worn in ancient times by the women in the Torres Strait islands.

Hair and nose ornaments

The hair of both men and women was adorned with combs (*ipegi*) and ochres or clays. Women generally clipped their hair and wore it short. Both Islanders and Papuans wore a wide variety of ornaments, notably those made from shells and teeth. In early times the septum of the nose was pierced and smooth curved pieces of clam shell (*Tridacna* sp.), cone shell (*Conus* sp.), *Cassis* sp., or even bailer shell (*Melo* sp.) pointed at both ends, were inserted. Thick stubs of clam or *Cassis* sp. shell were worn as common daily ornaments but long nose sticks (*ini*) were worn on ceremonial occasions (Haddon 1912, IV: 39; Moore 1984: 69 and 45, and Plates 5 and 33; VK 4902: 168 [nose stick], VK 4902: 160 [nose plug]).

Necklaces and breast ornaments

Many types of necklaces worn close to the throat and chest pendants or breast ornaments attached to a cord and hung to the middle of the chest were worn by men and women. Necklaces were usually fashioned from shell, teeth or seeds and necklaces made from dogs' teeth attached to fibre cords (*genaio* or *gesa*) were highly valued for only the four canine teeth could be taken from one dog. Strings of teeth were worn by women and girls on ceremonial occasions and formed a 'considerable part of the price of a canoe or of the gifts given in exchange for a bride' (Landtman 1933: 41; Haddon 1912, IV: 41). Necklaces of dogs' teeth were commonly worn by people along the whole southwest coast as far as present day West Papua (VK 4902: 203). Other necklaces were made from reef shells and one form, made from 'olive' shells (*Oliva* sp.), was of considerable value. It too could be used as part of exchange for canoes (Haddon 1912, IV: 41 and 44).

Illustration 11. Dogs' teeth necklace (VK 4902: 203)

Crescent-shaped breast ornaments of pearl-shell (*nese*) constituted important exchange items right across the Torres Strait and Fly estuary region. Usually, most of the shell was left undecorated and only the outer edge incised or lightly decorated. A small hole, for attachment of a cord or fibre, was bored through the base but the shape of the pearl-shell itself was generally retained (VK 4902: 183).

The circular polished bases of the cone shell (*Conus* sp.) termed *bidibidi* (Kiwai) [*dibidibi* (Meriam) or *dibidib* (Kala Lagaw Ya) in the Torres Strait] were one of the most valuable breast ornaments worn by Islanders and coastal Papuans and of singular value in the exchange of shells for canoe hulls. The whole of the flattened base of the shell was removed and ground down to make a thin white disk with the upper surface generally convex. Occasionally the edge was nicked and a hole was bored into the side. Fibre or cloth was attached as a cord. Haddon (1912, IV: 44) wrote:

> The *dibidibi*, even more than most ornaments, except the *waiwi* or *wauri* [*mabuo* (Kiwai) armshells] … served also as a kind of currency. They varied much in size and finish and had a corresponding value, thus no table of equable exchange can be drawn up. I [Haddon] gathered that

ten or twelve *dibidibi* of fair size would be equal in value to a large shell armlet ... to a canoe, to a dugong harpoon, or to a wife. Three or four *dibidibi* would constitute an annual instalment for a canoe ...

Cone shell breast ornaments were collected by Haddon and his associates on Mer (Moore 1984: 70 and Plate 36) and other examples of cone shell breast ornaments can be found in the Landtman collection (VK 4902: 189). One example, consisting of six cone shell bases strung together on a plaited base forms part of the Landtman collection (VK 4902: 194). However, strings of *bidibidi* were not as common as the single *bidibidi* breast pendant.

Illustration 12. Breast ornament (VK 4902: 189)

Other breast ornaments of shell, European tradestore cloth and even boars' tusks were worn as ornaments. Boars' tusk breast ornaments were obtained from the coastal Papuans who hunted in the open savanna lands between the inland riverine swamps and these tusks were worn on Mer at initiation ceremonies by the men who controlled the Malo-Bomai cult ceremonies (see Haddon 1912, IV: 50–51, and in Moore 1984: 78 and Plate 47). Boars' tusks were worn as armlets. Imitation boars' tusk pendants could be made from the shell of the giant clam (*Tridacna* sp.) or, in the Torres Strait, from the shell of the large *Trochus* sp. (Haddon 1912. IV: 51).

Belts

Varieties of shell and seed ornaments were attached to belts (*bata* or *bage*): the more usual being of cowrie shells (*Cypraea* sp.) or *Coix* sp. seeds. Many of the shells which hung from belts served as rattles especially in dance for the collective coordinated sound of the rattles could be very impressive. In coastal Papua various seeds and shells, most commonly small cowries, were attached to belts and armlets as decoration (Landtman 1933: 44).

Armlets and leglets made from fibres

Plaited armlets and leglets (*susare*, *tusare* or *tutabe*) made from plaited rattan or coconut leaves were also worn for dances and warfare. At dances crotons or other coloured leaves were inserted in the arm and leg bands which, like belts, could be plain or decorated. Plaited armlets were often ornamented with shells, seeds or calico (VK 4902: 327). The Haddon collection contains numerous examples of armlets plaited from cane, coconut midrib or fibre from the swamp grass that were worn right across the region (Moore 1984: 46, 47, 58, 72 and Plates 5, 6, 21 and 37).

Illustration. 13 Plaited arm decorations (VK 4902: 319, 331, 317, 336, 337, 335) and leglets (359, 360)

Forearm bracers (*adigo*), usually worn as protection against the recoil of bow strings, and made from sago palm spathe or plaited rattan, were worn by men both in warfare and in ceremony (VK 4902: 311 and 314). Commonly a decorated plume of cassowary feathers (*kioma*) was inserted into the forearm bracer. Into the armguard could be inserted a loop or a series of loops of cane decorated with cloth or cassowary and pigeon feathers (Haddon 1912, IV: 57–58). This cane loop was representative of one or more spare bowstrings worn by coastal Papuans on the lower arm, but had become a 'functionless dance ornament' in the Torres Strait islands (Haddon (1912, IV: 58; D'Albertis (1881, II: 173). Landtman (1933: 43) noted that the *koima* was commonly worn by all those Papuan peoples who habitually carried bows and arrows for hunting and fighting and agreed with Haddon's interpretation that the *koima* represented a spare bowstring modified to become a dance ornament.

Armlets made from shell

Pigs' tusks (*boromo kokai*) could be used as armlets on the upper arm. Haddon collected examples of these armlets from Mer that were decorated with *Coix* sp. seed and seed tassels and bound with calico (Haddon 1912, IV: 55 and figure 75). A fine example is illustrated and documented in Moore (1984: 77 and Plate 46). A similar object in the Landtman collection (VK 4902: 380) consists of two boars' tusks bound with fibre. Hanging from a cord attached through a hole in one tusk is a variety of decorative items including a European button, a crustacean claw and a *goa* seed (*Pangium edule*).

Undoubtedly, the most prized armlets, and the most important artefacts in the pre-European exchange of shells for canoe hulls, were armshells made from cone shells (*Conus* sp.) called *wawri* by the western Islanders and *wauri* by the eastern Islanders of the Torres Strait and *mabuo* by the Kiwai. Both Haddon (1912, IV: 56) and Landtman (1933: 43) noted the prized value of these arm ornaments that were largely obtained by the central Islanders from the reefs around Tudu or the Warrior Reefs. While the base of the shell could be made into a valued breast ornament, the remaining cone could be cut off. If the shell were large then a circlet of shell, with faint black spots, could be removed and used as an upper arm ornaments (see VKK 513 and 514).

Even more prized were the top portions of the cone after the removal of the bases. Part of the cone could be removed and the remaining conical shell with a strong circlet base could be worn as an upper arm decoration. Few examples of these valued armlets have been collected by museums. The Landtman collection has no examples of *mabuo* armlets although they were obviously seen and photographed by Landtman in the field (see Landtman 1933: 44, Figure 52 and VKK 513 and 514)[see Figure 27]. It is perhaps indicative of the high value placed on such objects that Landtman was not able to obtain examples for those photographed are fine specimens. Haddon collected examples of the base-ring shell armlet in 1889 from Mer and he was able to procure an unmodified *Conus* sp. shell from Mer in 1898 (Moore 1984: 73 and 74 and plates 37 and 41). However, one full set of cone shaped *mabuo* and one circlet of shell was collected in 1986 during research in the Fly estuary (Lawrence 1994: 358 and 437–38).

Headdresses made of cassowary feathers: the *daguri*

Illustration 14. Daguri headdress (VK 4902: 13)

The most commonly worn men's headdress made of black cassowary feathers was the *daguri* and this was most commonly worn by men of the southwest coast of Papua and the Fly estuary during warfare. Young boys first put on the headdress at initiation (Haddon 1912, IV: 36; Landtman 1933: 37). It is now worn for special dances and ceremonies. The basic form of the headdress was common throughout the region. Small bunches of plain, undecorated cassowary feathers were bound together tightly and inserted into a plaited headband usually stiffened with rattan. The shape of the headband varied only slightly but the usual ceremonial or dance band was a lozenge-shape with curved sides. Two thin cords attached at the sharpened edges tied it to the head. The cassowary feathers were tightly plaited into the woven fibres at the back, and the front was often decorated with over-plaiting and coloured with ochre. These headdresses are still made in the inland villages, notably near Wipim. Haddon and Landtman both collected a number of examples of *daguri* headdresses (Moore 1984: 48, 76, 77, and 102 and Plates 7, 45 and 78; VK 4902: 13/14/20 and 26). Variety was added to these headdresses by the addition of bird of paradise plumes, pigeon or cockatoo feathers, or pieces of European tradestore cloth. In some cases the whole bird of paradise was used, its beak being used as a pin (VK 4902: 94/95 and 99, 101 and 103). These plumes are now extremely rare.

Illustration 15. Bird of paradise plumes (VK 4902: 99)

Headdresses made of reef heron feathers: the *dori*

The finest headdress worn by the Torres Strait Islanders and coastal Kiwai-speaking peoples was the *dori* (Kiwai). Its importance as a cultural item is still such that it is a most visible symbol of Islander culture, particularly for the eastern Islanders and the *dari* (eastern islands) is the most prominent symbol on the officially recognised Torres Strait Islander flag.

The headdress consists of a woven rattan frame in either an 'n' or an 'm' shape. Cords at the feet of the frame were tied around the forehead so that the rattan frame stood high above the head. The feathers of the white reef heron (*Demigretta sacra*) or the Torresian pigeon (*Ducula bicolor*) were inserted into the frame to form a fan shape. Often one long frigate bird feather, preferably black, was inserted in the top so as to extend vertically. At the base of the feather a red bean (*Mucuna* sp,) was placed. The white feather tips were clipped into various stylised shapes for effect and two long feathers projected from the base almost at the level of the wearer's cheeks. Both Haddon and Landtman collected examples of *dori* headdresses and the cane frames for the feathers (VK 4902: 121; Moore 1984: 76 and plate 44).

Illustration 16. Dori headdress (VK 4902: 121)

The *dori* were often quite large and elaborate. When worn in night dances with the dance ground illuminated with small fires or torches, the actions imitating the movements of the reef heron could be most spectacular and effective. Like the *dari* used in 'Island dance' the headdresses serve to frame the face and special dance effects are achieved by turning the head suddenly so that the image of the reef heron appears and disappears.

The most complete details of the construction of the headdress was given by Haddon (1912, IV: 37-39) who stated that all such headdresses were imported from New Guinea. However, as only the coastal Kiwai perform dances with *dori*, and generally they refer to this style of dance as Islander-style dancing, it would appear that the style of dance and the use of the headdress were borrowed from the Torres Strait and was incorporated into coastal Kiwai dance culture. The Torres Strait Islanders have elaborated the *dari* dances into an art form.

Frontlets

Other items of ornamentation and dress included a large variety of stiff frontlets (*makeso*) made from rattan or fibre plaited on to a bamboo frame that were worn across the forehead and tied at the back of the head. Frontlets were made in a variety of designs: triangular, semi-ovoid or even a lozenge shape (VK 4902: 108 and 109) (see also Haddon 1912, IV: 39 and Moore 1984: 76 Plates 43 and 44). Landtman (1933: 38) wrote that these frontlets could be used both with and without cassowary feather decorations. A variety of headdresses were made from plaited fibres, rattan and feathers and even cuscus fur (*Phalanger* sp.) was worn as a decorative fillet. Haddon (1912, IV: 35) collected one cuscus fur head decoration at Tudu in 1888 which he stated had come 'from New Guinea' and Landtman (1933: 39) collected from Kiwai Island a similar head decoration, with shells and rattles made from *goa* seeds attached (VK 4902: 113).

Recreation, ceremony and dance

The objects used on ceremonial occasions, such as masks and drums, are included in this category along with other sound-producing instruments and ornaments specifically made for dance performance such as dance-wands seed pod rattles and shell trumpets. Raw material for masks, such as turtle shell, was an important trade item and bamboo tobacco pipes were highly regarded.

Drums

Torres Strait Islanders obtained all their waisted drums from coastal Papua (Haddon 1912, IV: 278) and the common Torres Strait drum used on all present day dancing and music occasions is still obtained from Papua. Originally there were two different types of waisted drums. The first, the older form, the *warupa* consisted of a hollowed out single piece of wood, with a definite, waisted central portion and a bowl-like tympanum end. Landtman (1933: 68) stated that the *warupa* originated in Saibai:

> According to tradition, the first drum in Mawata was a warupa, and it came from Saibai, which is said to be the original home of all drums in that part of the country, the inhabitants of that island not having learnt the art of making drums from any other people.

These older waisted drums are still referred to as 'Saibai drums' even though they are no longer manufactured there. A fine *warupa* illustrated in Edge-Partington (1969, I: Plate 332 No. l) now located in the British Museum was made for Rev. Samuel Macfarlane on Saibai. These drums were distinctive for their open 'shark' or 'crocodile' mouth ends and were described by Jukes (1847, I: 176) and Haddon (1912, IV: 280). However, few remain, even in museum collections. Fine old drums, like canoes, often had individual names and, like famous canoes, were often mentioned in stories.

Haddon noted that the average length of the *warupa* was about one metre with a diameter at the tympanum end of about 20 cm. The tympanum could be covered with file snake (*Acrochordus spp.*), land lizard (*Varanus spp.*) or wallaby skin, although lizard skin was the most common. While wallaby skin gave a deeper sound it could not be tightened for long. Beeswax added to the tympanum was heated over a fire in front of the drummer and the small pieces acted both to tighten the lizard skin and to give the skin and the hand a sticky surface which made drumming more effective. The outer surface of the old drums was heavily ornamented and often cassowary feathers and shells decorated the open end.

The sacred Malo drum of the Miriam people, Wasikor, is still kept on Mer under the protection of the Noah family of Kewaid village. It belongs to the Zagareb clan and was used in the last re-enactment of the Malo/Bomai dances performed by Murray Island people in 1977 for the St James Church building fund. Originally part of a pair of drums, the companion, Nemau, was burnt by the crew of the bêche-de-mer boat the 'Woodlark' about 1860 (see Haddon 1908, VI: 43, 190 and 296; Fisher 1856/57). It is the most famous ceremonial drum in the region.

Other open-mouthed drums, simpler in form were obtained from Kiwai Island (VK 4902: 622; Haddon (1912, IV: 280). This type of drum is known as *buruburu* (western islands), *boroboro* (eastern islands) or generally *gama* among the Kiwai but the onomatopoeic nature of the word *buruburu* makes it the more popular term. These are more cylindrical in shape, with a waist generally central across the drum. The open circular end is not cut into a 'shark' mouth. A *buruburu* was collected by Haddon on Yam Island (Haddon 1912, IV: 279) and Landtman collected typical 'contemporary' drums from Kiwai Island (VK 4902: 625, 626 and 628). Photographs from Mawatta (VKK 323) show that Kiwai men had the knowledge of manufacture of *buruburu* or at least how to improve the sound of the drum but now obtain them from inland.

Illustration 17. Old style drum (VK 4902: 622)

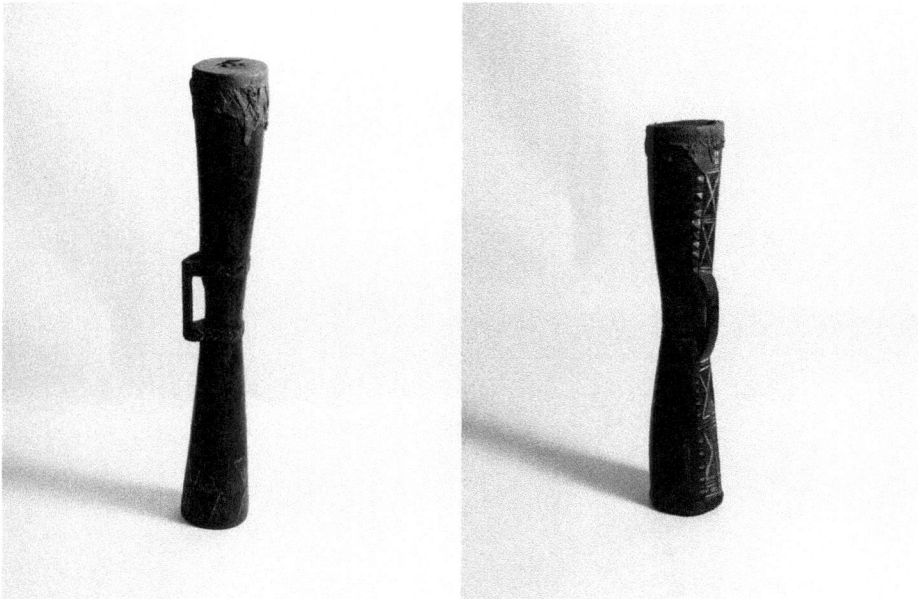

Illustration 18. New style drum (VK 4902: 626 and 628)

Drums of this type, now used throughout the Torres Strait, originate from the villages located in the well-wooded inland region at the headwaters of the Pahoturi, Binaturi and Oriomo rivers. Waisted drums from the inland region all have handles carved from the same piece of timber as the body of the drum. They are generally about one metre in length with an even symmetrical shape, decorated at the base with carved diamond and triangular patterns. These carvings are usually repeated around the handle boss. The drums are left unpainted although the outer surface is usually blackened with charcoal before carving. At the present time these drums are used by most Torres Strait Islander dance groups both on the Australian mainland and in the islands although they are often recarved and overpainted with bright acrylic paint which adds to their visual impact during competitive dance performances.

Drums have been, and still are, important items of material culture in the Torres Strait and Fly estuary region. Perhaps the reason for this is that no readily transportable, functional substitute has been found that could reproduce the quality of sound and visual impact of the wooden hand drum.

Shell trumpets

Shell trumpets, *tuture*, were made by boring a lateral mouth hole in the whorl of a *Fusus* sp., *Syrinx* sp., or *Triton* (*Charonia tritonis*) shell (VK 4902: 637). They were used by men in canoes for signaling success in hunting and warfare but they were also used to decorate burial places (Landtman 1933: 73) or placed on the central poles of the old style round houses of the eastern Torres Strait Islanders (Haddon 1912, IV: 283).

Illustration 19. Shell trumpet (VK 4902: 637)

Rattles

Hand held rattles (*kokare*) made from the shells of seeds of the *goa* (*Pangium edule*) tree were used in both action and 'sit down' dances by the Torres Strait Islanders. They are still used by both Islanders and Papuans. Landtman (1933: 72) collected examples of *goa* and shell rattles from the mouth of the Fly River (VK 4902: 655) and Haddon collected an example on Mer (Moore 1984: 83 and Haddon 1912, IV: 272). Rattles have an important place in coordinated dance movements that add sound and drama to performances.

Masks

Haddon noted (1912, IV: 296–97) that two varieties of mask existed: those made either from a single block of wood (*mooa*) (see VKK 511) or those constructed from pieces of turtle shell (*karara*) stitched together. Turtle shell, especially from the less common Hawksbill turtles, was traded across the Torres Strait. In the Queensland Museum, one beautiful turtle shell mask on a wooden base, with a fillet of cassowary feathers and other adornments, was acquired on the southwest coast of Papua late last century (Queensland Museum E 4777) and a similar mask in the collection (QE 4668 also numbered E 5929) was obtained on Erub. In the same way one well-made wooden mask with pearl-shell buttons for eyes in the Landtman collection (VK 4902: 135) collected at Mawatta, is similar to objects in the Queensland Museum obtained from on Mer (E 5930) and Saibai (E 5488). A heavily decorated piece of turtle shell, most likely part of a turtle shell mask, was obtained at Mawatta by Landtman (VK 4902: 1318). In 1888, Haddon (1888: 5 and 6) obtained turtle shell masks, drums, armlets and breast ornaments, as well as tobacco pipes, bows and arrows on Nagi in the Torres Strait but noted that all these objects originated on the Papuan mainland.

In addition, Haddon collected a number of fine turtle shell masks from the central, western and eastern islands (Moore 1984: 48, Plate 7; 59, Plate 22; 75, Plate 41 and 42). Landtman (1933: 75 and 76) collected wooden masks at Mawatta, on Kiwai Island, and at Kubu between Gaima and the Aramia River. Of masks and masking in general Haddon (1912, IV: 296) remarked:

> Highly characteristic of Torres Straits are the numerous masks and effigies which have been obtained on the islands. This art extends to Daudai [Papua], and it is probable that some specimens labelled "Torres Strait" in museums have come from the mainland, it is easy to determine whether a given unlabelled specimen came from the district generally, but not whether it belongs to the [Torres Strait] islands or to Daudai.

While material, such as cassowary feathers and *goa* shells, were probably obtained from Papua, it is likely that important ceremonial masks used on the mainland were made from turtle shell and ochres obtained from Torres Strait Islanders.

Illustration 20. Wooden mask with pearl-shell button for eyes (VK 4902: 135)

Bamboo tobacco pipes

Tobacco was the only narcotic used by the Torres Strait Islanders (Haddon 1912, IV: 141) and although it was used in coastal Papuan and the Fly estuary, the Kiwai also used *gamoda* (*Piper methysticum: kava*) made from tapping into the soft stalks at the crown of a coconut palm. *Gamoda* can be drunk at an early stage with no ill effects, but over time becomes highly fermented if left in its container on the palm. It is potent and may cause blindness if drunk in quantities. 'Native' or bush tobacco was probably introduced into the Torres Strait from the mainland north of the Fly and was generally known as *sukuba* (Haddon 1912, IV: 143). The introduction of European tradestore tobacco in the form of 'black stick' tobacco had an immediate social and economic impact. When Landtman conducted his field research stick tobacco had become a virtual currency and had quickly entered the customary exchange system:

Nowadays trade-tobacco, manufactured in Australia under Government control, is almost exclusively used among the natives. It is much in demand among them and constitutes one of the principal articles of barter with them. (Landtman 1933: 65–66)

Landtman paid his informants and servants in stick tobacco. Although he thought he made good bargains with his informants, they no doubt made even better deals with their own people or with the people in the interior who had limited access to the European wage system. *Sukuba* is still used as the general name for tobacco or cigarettes among the coastal Kiwai.

The tobacco pipes (*waduru*) used throughout the region consisted of a length of stout bamboo containing two or more nodes. In the node at one end a hole was bored, and near the other end on the side, a hole was cut in the surface. A thin wooden tube, with a slightly curved-in base, was filled with tobacco which was lit and inserted into the hole on the side. Smoke was either sucked into the bamboo pipe or blown into the pipe through the small tobacco bowl and the pipe passed to another who inhaled the smoke. The exterior of the pipe, but not the small bowl, was most often heavily decorated with pecked or incised designs representing animals, or geometric and stylised patterns.

Considerable variety exists in decoration on tobacco pipes held in museum collections. Tobacco pipes in the Queensland Museum (E 13/257 and QE 4288) were collected on to Mer and a similar pipe in the National Museum of Finland (VK 4902: 658/662 and 665) was collected from the Fly estuary. This type of pipe was to be found throughout the whole Kiwai district and neighbouring districts, and both Haddon (1912, IV: 141) and Landtman (1933: 66) referred to them as 'Papuan pipes.'

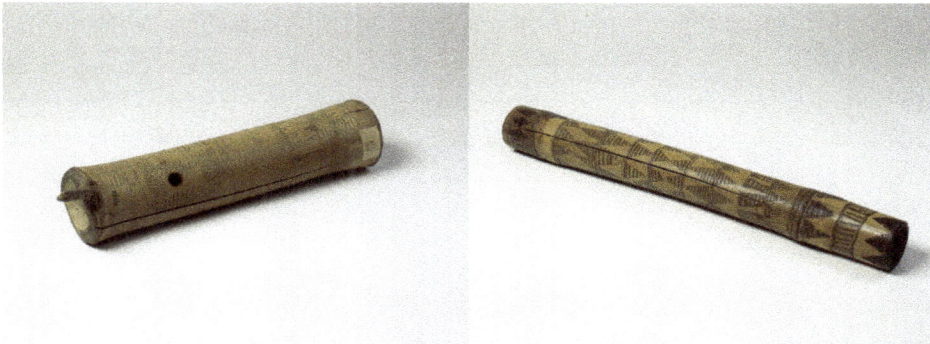

Illustration 21. Bamboo tobacco pipes (VK 4902: 658 and 662)

A sketch made in 1845 shows men from Masig Island in the central Torres Strait near a village on Nagi with a bamboo tobacco pipe as well as bows and arrows

(McNiven and Quinnell 2004: cover illustration) and another particularly fine pipe now in the Queensland Museum collection (formerly James Cook University collection 80.4.1.) was obtained by Captain V. Lovett-Cameron, in or before 1876, from the western islands of the Torres Strait. Documentation associated with the pipe states that it belonged to a member of the Baidam [Baizam: shark] clan that was represented on Mabuiag, Moa [Mua], Muralag, Nagi, Tudu, Yam and Saibai as well as among the Kiwai of Mawatta and Tureture (Haddon 1904, V: 151–57). Among the Miriam-speaking eastern Islanders the *baizam boai* [shark men] were among the most important members of the Malo/Bomai cult (Haddon 1908, VI: 285–86). However many tobacco pipes are decorated with shark designs and this may have led to a belief that they only belonged to members of the Baidam clans.

The fact that Papuan tobacco pipes were also common among the Australian Aboriginal people of Cape York was noted by Moore (1979: 27–28, 98–99, 222, 281–82), Haddon (1947: 79) and Thomson (1939: 82). Tobacco pipes were observed in use among the Aboriginals on Cape York by Moseley (1892: 356) who stated that they were obtained by the Gudang people of Cape York from the Murray Islanders through 'barter'. Landtman collected tobacco pipes and photographed men and women smoking and preparing pipes (VKK 310).

Warfare

Artefacts of warfare used included bows, arrows, bamboo knives, cassowary bone daggers, human skulls and heads, cane loops for holding human heads, spears and stone-headed clubs. Some objects may belong to more than one category: bows and arrows were used both as weapons of war and as hunting implements for killing fish and wild animals and cassowary bone daggers were also used as coconut huskers.

Inter- and intra-ethnic warfare was endemic prior to the consolidation of European administration and mission control. Warfare consisted of sporadic surprise raids on isolated groups or villages and the history of these raids is still told in story, song and dance. The memory of specific raids, particularly those of the 'Tugeri' from the Dutch territory to the west, is still keen among the coastal Papuans near Buji and the Pahoturi River as well as among the nearby Saibai and Boigu Islanders. These raids were usually made by groups of armed men in canoes accompanied by their women carrying digging sticks or cassowary bone knives (Landtman 1933: 31). The object of these quick sporadic attacks was to kill as many people as possible and obtain a number of human heads before retreating in their fast war canoes.

Cassowary bone daggers

The Landtman collection contains examples of fine cassowary bone daggers (*wagi* or *soke*) (VK 4902: 493 and 494). These have been decorated with crabs-eye seeds (*Abrus precatorius*) although cassowary bone daggers were used by both men and women to disable prisoners taken during raids. More generally they were used as coconut huskers (Landtman 1933: 57). One example in the Haddon collection (Moore 1984: 64 and Plate 20) is recorded as 'imported from New Guinea' and having been used as a coconut husker on Mer.

Illustration 22. Cassowary bone dagger (VK 4902: 494)

Bows and arrows

Split bamboo bows (*gagare*), often up to two metres in length, were in common use as weapons prior to pacification (Haddon 1912, IV: 174). Bows are today used only as dance accessories in the Torres Strait but are still used for hunting wallaby, cassowary and wild pigs in coastal Papua. The principal manufacturers of high quality bows were, and still are, the Agob, Gizra and Bine people of Papua although some bows are now obtained from the Morehead River area to the west. The best bamboo in its green pliable state comes from the swampy wetlands behind the Papuan coast. The bowstring is made from a thin (approx. 125mm wide) strip of green bamboo, knotted into two loops at either end and pulled over the points of the bow stave. Contrary to Haddon's (1912, IV: 174) poor opinion these bows are very accurate and powerful. At close range they can drive a steel tipped arrow completely through a small wallaby.

A number of bamboo bows in the Landtman collected are provenanced to Kiwai Island (VK 4902: 759). These bows are of a form common throughout the coastal Papuan region west of the Fly estuary. The bows and arrows observed by Cook in 1770 at Possession Island near Cape York (Haddon 1935, I: 4, and Flinders 1814, I: xv) were most likely in the hands of western Islanders rather than Cape York Aboriginals.

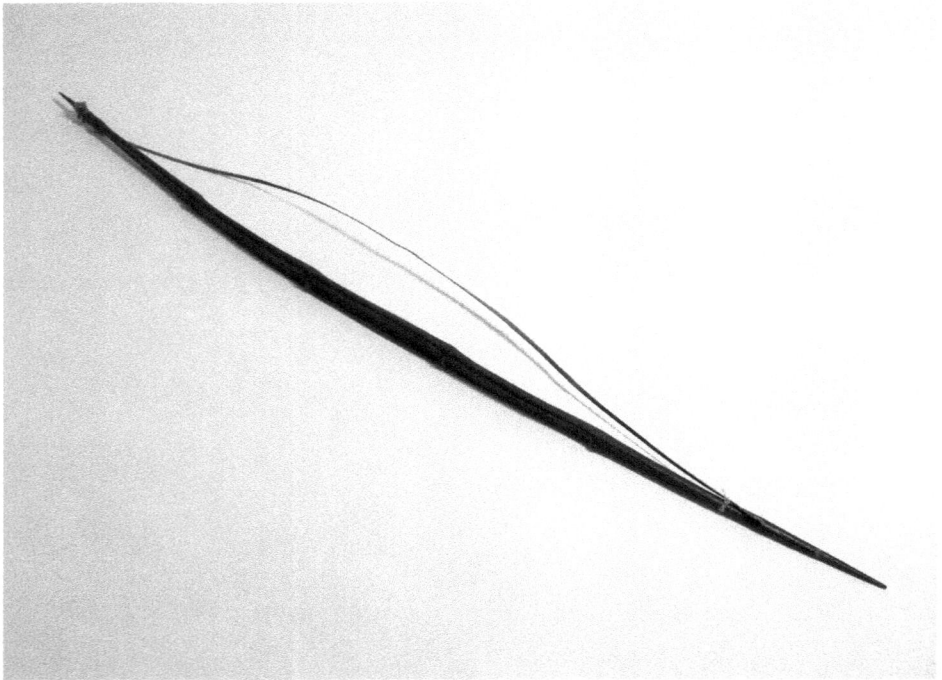

Illustration 23. Bamboo bow (VK 4902: 759)

All arrows (*tene*) used by Torres Strait Islanders came from Papua (Haddon 1912, IV: 175). There were two reasons for this. Firstly, the thin reed used for making arrow shafts grows in the riverine swamps and marshes of coastal Papua, not on the islands of Torres Strait and, secondly, arrow-heads were made from cassowary or wallaby leg bones, animals that can only be hunted in the bush lands of coastal Papua. Arrows of this region were all constructed from a reed shaft and a separate arrow-head. The variety of arrow was very wide for the type of arrow-head was directly related to its function. Among the inland and riverine dwelling people, this functional classification of arrows still applies and this classification was documented by Haddon (1912, IV: 175–90) and Landtman (1933: 50–55).

The most attractive and highly prized arrows came through Buji and were made by the Agob-speaking people who lived between the Mai Kussa and the Pahoturi River. The Agob continue to make these fine arrows and they are still used by neighbouring groups who refer to them as 'Buji arrows'. These arrows are decorated with an infinite variety of designs using the three colours: red, black and white. The red dye is made from mangrove root, black from charcoal mixed with juice and white from lime made by baking and crushing shells.

'Man-arrows'

The most distinctive arrow of the region has been called the 'man-arrow' (*otame*) (Haddon 1912, IV: 184–86 and Landtman 1933: 50). The man-arrow, like other arrows, is constructed from two different materials, forming the shaft and the head, but the lower portion of the arrow-head is finely carved to represent the culture hero Muiam who was heavily tattooed. Man-arrows belong to specific clan groups. Contrary to the statement in Moore (1984: 103) they were never used in warfare or hunting. However, they retain the ceremonial role of a weapon for they were used in ritual wounding and killings particularly in cases of adultery. Their full practice and use is still guarded. Man-arrows are specifically objects of ritual and ceremony for the Gizra and the neighbouring Bine peoples. They originate among the clan groups of Waidoro and Kulalae (Togo) area and as Dirimu and Masingara villages have kinship ties with the Gizra, clan arrows were distributed through these groups.

Haddon (1912, IV: 184–86) described the general characteristics of man-arrows in considerable detail but made no comment on their origins, meanings or uses. One example in the Haddon collection (Moore 1984: 103 and plate 79), attributed to the Torres Strait in general, was collected in 1888 and Haddon in an early paper (Haddon 1894: 51) remarked that man-arrows were known in both the western and the eastern islands of the Torres Strait as *parulaig* (Kala Lagaw Ya) or *opop* (Meriam) meaning that 'it had a face'. The Landtman collection contains numerous examples of man-arrows (VK 4902: 929) that are often included in bundles of other arrows.

Stone-headed clubs

The most common weapon of the Kiwai in former times was the stone-headed club (*gabagaba*). Stone heads were usually flat or biconvex stones with a hole in the centre through which a stout rattan stick was inserted. Clubs were often carried in the hand, or over the shoulder by means of a cord loop. Stone-headed clubs were used as a weapon by Torres Strait Islanders and their use was noted by Jukes (1847, II: 19). The most common form used (Haddon 1912, IV: 191–92) was biconvex and disc-shaped with a central hole. This common form was collected by Haddon from Muralag (Moore 1984: 52 and Plate 13) and Yam in 1888 (Moore 1984: 57 and Plate 20), and from Mer in 1898 (Moore 1984: 96 and Plate 75).

The second form collected by Haddon was the star-shaped stone-headed club (Moore 1984: 52 and Plate 13; 96 and Plate 75) may have been used in ceremonies, particularly the Malo/Bomai cult in the eastern islands, or in dances (Haddon 1912, IV: 192). The Landtman collection contains a number of plain bi-convex stone-headed clubs (VK 4902: 569) and one star-shaped stone-headed club (VK 4902: 573)

Haddon (1912, IV: 191) recorded information collected by his associate Wilkin in Mabuiag that stated that stone-headed clubs came from Dauan, Saibai and Mer. Haddon (1912, IV: 191) doubted this information but noted that a disc or star stone-headed club cost one dugong harpoon or one armshell. Recent archaeological evidence supports a Torres Strait origin for stone used in *gabagaba* (McNiven and Quinnell 2004).

Unusual examples of clubs were collected from the mouth of the Fly River by Landtman (1933: 55) (VK 4902: 574 and 575). These clubs incorporated metal heads in place of stone heads. One example (575), possibly a brass plate from a ship, had a metal head, attached by three iron nails, with three large screw and bolt holes and a small piece of angled metal attached by two screws to the plate.

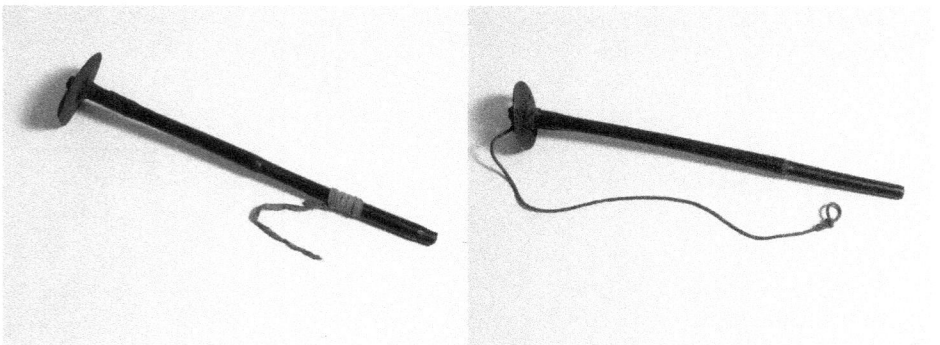

Illustration 24. Gabagaba clubs (VK 4902: 574 and 575)

Bamboo headcarriers

A distinctive artefact of warfare found in museum collections and definitely Kiwai in origin is the bamboo headcarrier (*gara oro*) that consists of a loop of rattan with the ends tightly lashed to a cross-piece sometimes made from the dart of an old dugong harpoon (Haddon 1912, IV: 199–200). Supplementary bindings made of coconut fibre held the rattan and cross-bracing together. This simple but distinctive object was used during former times to carry severed heads. The loop of rattan was passed either through the mouth of the severed head and the cut neck, or through the floor of the mouth, so that the cross-piece rested against the lower jaw (Landtman 1933: 57 and Haddon 1912, IV: 200).

Headcarriers were valued by families and clans as reminders of past glories of ancestors and were even included in ceremonies and dances. Three fine examples in the Landtman collection were collected from Kiwai Island (VK 4902: 581–83) all of which incorporate old dugong harpoon darts as cross-pieces.

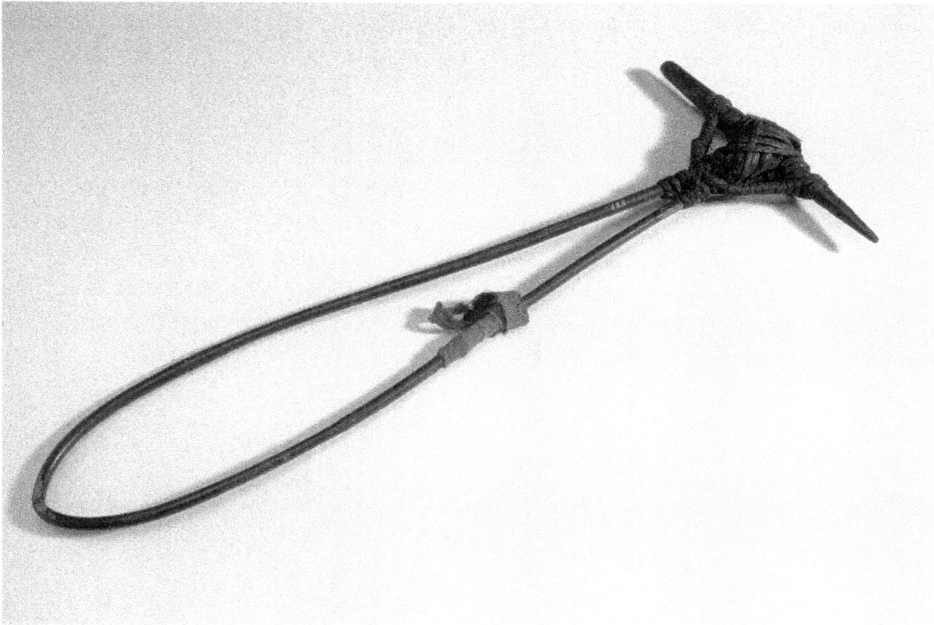

Illustration 25. Bamboo headcarrier (VK 4902: 582)

Bamboo knives

A second distinctive artifact of warfare from coastal Papua, and associated with the bamboo headcarrier, was the bamboo 'headhunting' knife (*uere*). Haddon collected one example at Mabuiag in 1898 (Moore 1984: 52 and Plate 13), a 'model' of a beheading knife and headcarrier at Mer in 1889 (Moore 1984: 84 and Plate 55) and another bamboo knife at Tudu in 1888 (Haddon 1912, IV: 199).

The bamboo knife consisted of a split piece of stout bamboo about 30–50 cm. in length. Into one concave end a piece of wood or pith was placed and this was bound patterned into a handle with fine cord or string. The edge of the knife was sharpened by cutting a notch near the handle and removing a sliver of bamboo (Haddon 1912, IV: 200). This left the blade with a sharp clean-cutting edge but had to be done regularly as the bamboo blade become blunt and dull quickly. Bamboo knives could be used for cutting other flesh, for example, dugong or fish, though Haddon (1912, IV: 199) reported that the number of notches in the handle indicated the number of heads cut. According to Landtman (1933: 55–56), the Kiwai of Iasa village previously employed shells as knives but learnt the art of making bamboo knives from the people of Kubira village who are said to have originated in Wabuda and Dibiri Islands near the intersection of the Fly and Bamu estuaries. Landtman (1933: 56) described with some colour the various methods used in severing heads.

The Landtman collection contains some fine examples of old bamboo knives, one of which (VK 4902: 580) has a finely plaited cord handle. This example, as with others in the collection (VK 4902: 576 and 578), was collected on Kiwai Island. Beheading knives, like headcarriers, were valued objects and were possibly objects of exchange between close kin for they were closely associated with respected ancestors among both Islanders and Papuans. Many of the items worn as dress in warfare, such as cassowary feather headdresses, boar's tusk ornaments, fibre skirts and pubic shells have been discussed previously. Ceremonial dress and decoration were carefully made and were of high value, for a man's renown and style was tested by his skill as a warrior and a warrior wore only his finest ceremonial dress and accoutrements into battle.

Illustration 26. Bamboo knife (VK 4902: 580)

The Landtman collection is an important one and complements the more famous Torres Strait collections held at the Cambridge Museum of Archaeology and Anthropology. Together with smaller collections in Australia, they comprise the most significant examples of Torres Strait and Kiwai material culture available for research today.

Conclusion:
A witness to change

In his two years in Papua, Gunnar Landtman managed to record a large collection of valuable legends and stories, many of which are still told today. He travelled widely throughout the Torres Strait, southwest coast of Papua and the Fly estuary and even managed a short trip to the Gulf District. He made a comprehensive collection of Kiwai material culture now housed in the Museum of Cultures in Helsinki and a second, duplicate set for the Cambridge Museum. He also collected some of the earliest examples of Gogodala material culture available for research. He was remarkably productive. Landtman returned with his draft manuscript largely written and although the English language version was not published until 1927, Landtman published his large volume of Kiwai legends and stories in 1917 only four years after he returned home. In 1913, following Haddon's example he published, *Nya Guinea färden* [New Guinea expedition], a detailed travelogue of his work and life among the Kiwai (Landtman 1913b). Over the next 20 years he wrote a substantial corpus of work on the Kiwai in English, Swedish and Finnish.

Landtman's career after Papua

Landtman returned to the University of Helsinki where he served as Docent in sociology from 1910 to 1927. This would have been an interesting time in Finnish academic circles: in 1917 Salkari Pälsi produced the first silent movie of the everyday life of the Tjukts hunters and fishers who lived on the Tjukotka [Cukockij] Peninsula in northeast Russia (Crawford 1993: 12). Before the disruptive effect of the post-Independence civil war, and for a brief period, ethnology flourished in Finland.

Landtman was granted a post as a Personal Extra Professor of Sociology that he retained from 1927 to his death in 1940. This position, within Finnish academic institutions, was one rotated within the faculty. It was granted to a person who was recommended a professorial chair but who does not hold the head of department status. Landtman was also a keen nationalist. He had been a member of *Nylands Nation*, a Swedish students' association for southern Finland, and sat briefly in the national Diet as representative for the Swedish party in 1922–23. Landtman remained an active member of social movements between the two world wars and supported humanist programs and opposed capital punishment. His work extended beyond the confines of his Papuan ethnology for he also collected folklore and ethnography of the Swedish-speaking Finns (the *finlandssvenskar*) for the *Svenska litteraturesällskapat i Finland*, the Swedish Literature Society.

Although Landtman made a name outside the study of Finnish-Swedish folk tradition, he was especially interested in the people, landscape and villages of the province of Nyland (Uusimaa), one of the southern provinces of Finland. In the beginning of the 20th Century he contributed to the Brage Society's collection of folklore and was generally interested in the folklore of the Swedish-speaking Finns. As a supporting member of the *Svenska litteratursällskapet* he became one of the editors for its publication *Finlands svenska folkdiktning* (Finnish–Swedish folklore). The section entitled *Folktro och trolldom* (Folk belief and magic), planned by him, was published in two volumes in 1919 and 1925. He found ethnography of the rural people interesting and collected pictures and artefacts during his summer holidays for a small local museum. Even though ethno-sociology was his main intellectual focus it had a strong philosophical foundation that took the form of philosophical criticism and ethic utilitarianism. The questions of rights and justice had a particular dominance. These thoughts are expressed at their clearest in his work *Det rättas värde* (Wikman 1940. Translated from the Swedish by Pirjo Varjola).

Value and significance of the Kiwai collections

Landtman's pioneering research with the Kiwai has provided the foundation for much recent ethnographical and geographical research along the Daru coast. Roy Wagner (1978 and 1995), Billai Laba (1995) and Mark Busse (2005) have undertaken research on hero cults, Tom Eley (1988) focused on the marine geography of the Kiwai dugong and turtle hunters, Don Schug (1995) also followed this complex web of maritime resource exploitation and Kiwai participation in the early pearling and bêche-de-mer industries.

In a different vein Lawrence Hammar (1999) investigated the often dangerous and socially stigmatising world of the local Daru sex industry and Bruce Knauft (1993 and 1999) explored homosexuality among southwest coastal cultures. There is little evidence to support the idea that homosexuality is more prevalent in Kiwai culture than any other in the region. However, Daru remains a dangerous place for the uninitiated. Knauft's (1993) often quoted study argued against conceptualising south coast New Guinea cultures as bounded units existing in the timeless ethnographic present has been subjected to some considerable critical attention by Busse (2005: 448). Busse's complaint was that Knauft then proceeded to do just that: define regional cultures in terms of physical geography, linguistic classifications and practical realities of ethnography (Busse 2005: 449).

My own research with the Kiwai (Lawrence 1994) and the subsequent social mapping studies conducted as part of submissions to the legal claim for compensation from the Ok Tedi mine (Lawrence 1995 and see also 2004) were largely informed by the material Gunnar Landtman left to us. Other significant research in the region has also been supported by Landtman's research. McNiven and Quinnell (2004) have produced a comprehensive study of the archaeology and material culture of the Torres Strait that includes particular reference to trade links with the top Western islands (Vanderwal 2004: 257–70), the origin of large stone axes from Kiwai Island (McNiven, von Gnielinski and Quinnell 2004: 271–90) and the origin of stone headed clubs from the Torassi/Bensbach River area in the Trans-Fly (Hitchcock 2004: 305–15). Garrick Hitchcock has also undertaken important research into the political ecology of the Wartha people living along the Torassi/Bensbach River borderlands of Papua (Hitchcock 2004)

The value of Landtman's work transcends the bounds of interdisciplinary and philosophical discourses. It is true that Landtman and his mentors, Haddon and Westermarck, remained entrenched within evolutionary theory and the comparative method of research when others, like Malinowski and Radcliffe-Brown moved on to functionalism (Suolinna 2000: 317–18). Malinowski (1929: 109–12) damned Landtman's book with faint praise. He most certainly considered the 'descriptive' text lacked a dynamic and critical analysis. Certainly Landtman's book lacks the style of Malinowski's work but it is based on sound scientific principles where objective description is combined with deductive reasoning: a hallmark of early ethnology that grew out of the natural sciences (see Kuper 1988). The delay between the conclusion of Landtman's fieldwork in 1912 and the publication of his monograph in English in 1927 most certainly acted to Landtman's disadvantage. Now, however, the value of Landtman's books and papers is just that very descriptive content that Malinowski criticised.

Landtman's journey to Papua was in many ways extraordinary. Culturally and socially the Papuans were far removed from his comfortable life in Finland. Life in coastal villages would have been hot, uncomfortable and stressful: even his accommodation at the various mission stations and plantations in the regions would have been trying. Travel in the Fly estuary remains exhausting and at times physically dangerous. At times, life in the villages would have been confronting. Life in Kiwai villages can be hard, there is little gender equality. With the impact of alcohol and drugs the threat of violence is always apparent. Landtman's letters to family and friends rarely document daily problems and they are deliberately cheerful and optimistic.

However, his writings show an empathy with the Kiwai and, perhaps despite himself, he warmed to the people and they warmed to him. The Kiwai would have found this strange foreigner complex and demanding although his regular habits and rituals would have been found amusing. Landtman sub-titled his

1927 monograph on the Kiwai with the cryptic phrase: 'A Nature-born instance of Rousseau's ideal community'. A clue to the origin of this phase lies in an earlier publication that presented a detailed study of social inequality and the rise of social class through investigation of social relations, ranking, status and wealth among many societies drawn from a theoretical examination of sources available at the turn of the 20th Century. Here Landtman (1909: 1) wrote 'Anthropology shows us that the savage is not even that child of an Elysian liberty which writers of Rousseau's school conceived him to be. Absolutely free in the sense of being independent of masters, he is bound hand and foot by custom'. In this paper Landtman paid homage to Westermarck's teachings but also wrote 'Yet we should be judging the lower races wrongly if we should deny them every approach to the Utopian social state of philosophy. ... Apart from all Utopian affinities in general we cannot help noticing that among the most primitive peoples there is found an equality of rank which is generally considered to be the attribute of a perfect social state' (Landtman 1909: 2).

Landtman's search for the perfect social state commenced long before he even reached Papua. Certainly, the idea that the Kiwai societies are constituted of free and equal individuals who banded together to form a civil society through a social contract and, by submission to the authority of the general will of the people remain untouched and uncontaminated, seems to be more a statement of late-19th Century romanticism than one grounded in empirical facts. Early sociologists, and Landtman can be included, set out to show that 'native' or 'primitive' cultures, with a supposed lack of sophisticated technology and less integrated economies like those of Europe, were prime examples of the ideal human societies. However, even Rousseau's notion that people are good because they are self-sufficient and by being self-contained are not subject to the vices of a wider political society is not applicable to the Kiwai.

Coastal and island Kiwai have a long and complex history of customary exchange and cultural interaction with their neighbours over a vast area of sea in a socially and politically volatile world. They are an outgoing and worldly people. Landtman's principal monograph on the Kiwai (1927b) certainly presents the people in an untouched and unchanging cultural environment. This was a common methodology used at that time. Now, the idea of 'salvage' anthropology is unacceptable. The Kiwai, like other people in Papua New Guinea, live in a society where the internal social and cultural values are being shaped, often violently upset, by outside influences. It is important to show that even when Landtman was undertaking fieldwork among the Kiwai they were actively interacting with missions, traders and government officers. As Hitchcock (2004: 24) explains it is important to review Landtman's work in the light of a new paradigm, critical anthropology:

Critical anthropology is a broad and increasingly important movement in the discipline, directing our attention to the wider socioeconomic formations in which small, local-level community groups operate. These wider sets of social and economic relations include interactions with the capitalist world system, in the past a largely neglected study area as a result of the tendency to present social formations and cultures as ahistorical, static and disconnected entities.

In his principal monograph, his ethnographic catalogue and his wonderful collection of myths and stories Landtman carefully removed himself from the picture. This is unfortunate for he was a keen witness to social and cultural change among the Kiwai. Fortunately the real Gunnar Landtman is always present in his travel memoirs and it is here that some clue to his use of the term Fairyland (1913b: 155 and 1932b) or Paradise (1913b: 166). It is apparent that there were times, when comfortable and established among local people who understood his reason for being there, or when out hunting with the men, that Landtman did find the experience of life in Papua almost close to ideal. These times were brief.

Perhaps Landtman's contribution to Melanesian ethnology is that he shows us in words, photographs, folklore, songs and artefacts that Papuan communities are not elaborate, abstract ideological constructions but societies of ordinary people deriving a hard living from a particular area of land and sea in their own way and, in doing so, are attempting to live together, as best as they can, according to local laws and customs. The Kiwai would be the first to admit that they are not an ideal society and that they do not live in an ideal world.

But, like Landtman, I find something strong and often noble in the Kiwai soul. Seventy years later I too worked in these villages and grew to love and respect the 'dear and difficult' Kiwai.

David Lawrence

Bibliography of writings on the Kiwai by Gunnar Landtman

The National Museum of Finland holds four separate collections relating to Landtman's work in the Fly River region. They are referenced as:

NMF VK 4902: 1–1326. The 1326 artefacts collected between 1910 and 1912.

NMF VK 4919: 1–3; 6–14; 17–39; 40–41 and 45–46. The 38 phonograph recordings made in 1910 and 1911 in Ipisia and Mawatta.

NMF VKK 248: 1–572. The 572 photographs taken by Landtman in the field.

NMF VKKA Landtman. The three volumes of original correspondence either in English or Swedish.

Gunnar Landtman was a prolific writer and from 1912 to 1934 wrote more than 20 book and papers in English, Finnish and Swedish on Kiwai culture. They are:

Landtman, Gunnar (1912a). '[Review] *The Mafulu Mountain People of British New Guinea* by Robert W. Williamson [and] *Papua or British New Guinea* by J. H. P. Murray', *Folklore*, 23 (4): 522–24.

Williamson undertook research in the Central District of Papua in 1910. This was Landtman's first paper in English and presumably written from the field.

——(1912b) 'Wanderings of the dead in the folklore of the Kiwai-speaking Papuans', In: Castrén, Ola (ed.). *Festskrift tillegnad Edvard Westermarck*. Helsingfors, J. Simelii Arvingars Boktryckeriaktiebolag: 59–80.

——(1913a). *En Papuansk saga*. Helsingfors, Frenckellska Tryckeri-Aktiebolaget [A Papuan legend].

——(1913b). *Nya Guinea färden*. Helsingfors, Sönderström and Co [New Guinea expedition].

——(1913c). 'The poetry of the Kiwai Papuans', *Folklore*, XXIV(3): 284–314.

——(1913d). 'Två Papuanska sagor', *Särtryck ur Svenska Folkskolans Vänners Kalander* 1913: 1–9.

——(1914a), 'Cat's cradles of the Kiwai Papuans, British New Guinea' *Anthropos*, 9: 221–32.

——(1914b). *Kiwai Papuanernas sätt att färads-how the Kiwai Papuans travel.* Helsingfors, Centraltryckeri och Bokbinderi Aktiebolaget.

——(1914c). 'Papualaisten parissa oleskelustani Uuden Guinean alkuasukkaiden keskuudessa', *Kansanvalistusseuran Toimituksia*, 2: 1–7.

——(1914d) 'Uudenguinean alkuasukkaiden keskuudessa [Among the natives of New Guinea]', np.——(1916a). *Techningar utförda av infördingar i Nya Guinea.* Helsingfors, Frenckellska Tyrckeri-Aktiebolaget.

——(1916b). 'The magic of the Kiwai Papuans in warfare', Journal of the Royal Anthropological Institute of Great Britain and Ireland, XLVI: 322–33.—— (1917a). *The Folk-Tales of the Kiwai Papuans.* Helsinki, Finnish Society of Literature.

In his review of *The Folk-Tales of the Kiwai Papuans*, Haddon (1920: 44) wrote that: The collection should be compared with the tales narrated in Volumes V and VI of the 'Reports of the Cambridge Expedition to Torres Straits' as both areas constitute one ethnographic province'

——(1917b). *Ur sagans barndom berättelser av vildfolket i Nya Guinea.* Helsingfors, Holger Schildts Förlag.

——(1918a). 'Min första färd uppför Fly-floden i Nya Guinea', *Terra, Geografiska Fören i Finland Tidskrift*, 30: 13–18 [My first journey up the Fly River in New Guinea].

——(1918b). 'The Pidgin English of British New Guinea', *Neuphilologische Mitteilungen*, 19: 62–74 [An edited and more complete version of this paper was later published in Landtman 1927b: 453–61].

——(1919a). 'Om folksagans underbaradaning', *Ofverstryck ur Finsk tidskrift*, LXXXVI: 130–51.

——(1919b). 'Orsakerna till Kiwai-papuanernas vandringar', *Särtryck ur 'Terra'*, *Geografiska fören i Finland Tidscrift*: 27–51.

——(1920a). 'Papuan magic in the building of houses', *Acta Academiae Åborensis-Humaniora*, 1: 1–28.

——(1920b). 'Religious beliefs and practices of the Kiwai-speaking Papuans', In: Beaver, W. *Unexplored New Guinea*. 2nd.ed. London, Seeley Service: 300–16.

Landtman contributed this chapter to Beaver's largely anecdotal but noteworthy account of his service as a Resident Magistrate in the Western Division of Papua that was published following Beaver's death on the Western Front during the

First World War. In the paper Landtman defines magic as 'the employment of supernatural mechanical power without appeal to any supernatural being' (Beaver 1920: 300). Landtman contributed a number of photographs to Beaver's book: notably those of a Tirio woman in full mourning, the *Horiomu* spirits at Mawatta and one of the interior of a Kiwai long house.

——(1920c). 'Stenåldersvedskap i användning bland papuanerna i Nya Guinea', *Terra: Geografiska Fören i Finland Tidskrift*, 32: 1–12.

——(1925). *Naturfolkens diktning och dess betydelse*. Helsingfors, Söderström and Co. (Finska Vetenskaps-Societeten Minnesteckningar och Föredrag, III (5).

——(1926). 'The origin of images as objects of cult' [*Sonderabdruck aus*] *Archiv für Religionwissenschaft*, XXIV (1/2): 196–208.

——(1927a). 'Barens lekar bland Kiwai-papuanerna i Nya Guinea', *Särtryck ur Svenska Fröbelförbundets Tidskrift*, 3: 1–4.

——(1927b). *The Kiwai Papuans of British New Guinea*. London, Macmillan.

Seligman, who had accompanied Haddon to the Torres Strait in 1898, wrote in his review of *The Kiwai Papuans of British New Guinea* that it was the 'first monograph to appear on any of the true Papuan of that territory [Papua]' (C. G. S[eligman] 1928: 496–97) and that Landtman is to be congratulated for surviving two years at the Fly River for despite the abundance of fish, dugong and turtle it is necessary to live on tinned foods.

Malinowski was less congratulatory in his review of the book (Malinowski 1929: 109–10) for although he stated that: 'Professor Landtman has written one of the very best descriptive books if anthropology on one of the most interesting peoples of the world' and considering he liked the sociological analysis of kinship, totemism, the ways of governance and administering justice, the book lacked the 'dynamic aspect'. Malinowski particularly disliked the use of Pidgin-English and remarked that: 'Pidgin-English is a caricature of human speech'. In this Landtman would have disagreed for he felt correctly that '[Pidgin-English] is on the contrary an actual language founded on principles which, simple though they be, yet give to it a certain extent a distinctive character of its own' (Landtman 1918b: 64).

Perhaps the most comprehensive review of his book was written by the Cambridge anthropologist, Camilla Wedgwood, herself a protégé of Haddon who was to gain considerable experience on Manam Island off the coast of northern New Guinea (Wedgwood 1933–34, Lutkehaus 1986). Wedgwood complimented Landtman generally and made the most appropriate examination when she said: 'Dr Landtman has confined himself to pure description [especially in the section on ceremonies and rituals]. He refrains from theorizing either as to the meaning of those things which he recounts or as to those things which he recounts to other New Guinea tribes. ... Heralded by such a general survey this full ethnographic account of a people in this all too-little studies area is of estimable value.'

Stocking (1992: 31) was also disparaging of Landtman's book: 'The closest approximation to Malinowski's *Argonauts* [1953 c. 1922] is Landtman's flat-footedly descriptive (and rather cumbrously titled) *Kiwai Papuans of British New Guinea: A Nature-Born Instance of Rousseau's Ideal Community'*. Landtman was accused of working with individuals and paid informants as well as using Pidgin English rather than Kiwai. Regardless of these criticisms Stocking had to agree that Landtman had entered the field a full five years before Malinowski who by the 1920s had assumed the status of the master of the ethnographic field-work tradition. Undoubtedly the delay in publishing the English version of Landtman's book lessened its impact in the world of British anthropology.

——(1931a). *Ett Sagoland och dess infödingar*. Helsingfors, Sönderström and Co.

——(1931b). 'Folklig metreologi, väderlekskunskap och tidräkning bland Kiwai-papuanerna', *Särtryck ur 'Terra', Geografiska Sällskapets i Finland Tidskrift*, 2: 82–90.

——(1932a). 'Rättsförhållandena bland Kiwai-papuanerna', *Särtryck ur Tidskrift utgiven av Juridiska Föreningen i Finland*, 374: 176–97.

——(1932b). *Satumaa ja sen asukkaat: kiwai-papualaiset Uuden-Guinean jättilässaarella*. Porvoo and Helsinki, Werner Sönderström Osakeyhtio.

——(1933). *Ethnological Collection from the Kiwai District of British New Guinea*. Helsingfors, Commission of the Antell Collection.

——(1934). 'The origins of sacrifice as illustrated by a primitive people' In: Evans-Pritchard, E. E., Firth, R., Malinowski, B., and Schapera, I. (eds), *Essays presented to C.G. Seligman*. London, Kegan Paul, Trench, Trubner: 103–12.

——(1953). 'Initiation ceremonies of the Kiwai Papuans', In: Mead, Margaret and Calas, Nicolas (eds), *Primitive Heritage: an anthropological anthology*. London, Victor Golancz: 179–86.

Margaret Mead and Nicolas Calas published a wide ranging anthology of excerpts from anthropological texts but also included some unusual examples of other authors works, such as Herodotus writing on the Egyptians and their relationship with domestic animals and D. H. Lawrence's description of Australian scenery near Sydney. Landtman's piece was taken from his main text

(1927b) and covered aspects of the *horiomu* and *moguru* ceremonies and sexual instruction of young boys and girls in Kiwai society. It was reproduced with permission of St Martin's Press as Landtman had died in 1940.

References

Abel, Charles (nd) Photograph collection. (UPNG NG collection ALX-1).

Allen, J. and Corris, P. (eds) (1977). *The Journal of John Sweatman*. St Lucia, University of Queensland Press.

Annual Reports on British New Guinea (1886/87–1905/06). Votes and Proceedings of Queensland, Parliament. Brisbane, Government Printer.

Annual Reports on Papua (1906/07–1919/20). Votes and Proceedings of Queensland, Parliament. Brisbane, Government Printer.

Anttonen, V. (2007). Comparative religion at the University of Turku and the University of Helsinki: a brief survey. Unpublished paper (http://www.hum. utu.fi/oppiaineet/uskontotiede).

Austen, L. (1925). 'D'Albertis exploration of the Upper Fly River', *Royal Australian Historical Society, Journal and Proceedings*, 11: 251–62.

Austin, T. (1972). 'F.W. Walker and Papuan Industries Ltd', *Journal of the Papua New Guinea Society*, 6: 38–62.

Barham, Anthony J., Rowland, Michael J. and Hitchcock, Garrick. (2004) 'Torres Strait *bepotaim*: an overview of archaeological and ethnoarchaeological investigations and research', In: McNiven, Ian J. and Quinnell, Michael (eds). 'Torres Strait Archaeology and Material Culture', *Memoirs of the Queensland Museum. Cultural Heritage Series*, 3 (1): 1–72.

Barthes, Roland (1993). *Camera lucida: reflections on photography*. London, Vintage. (Translation of *Chambre claire* c.1980).

Baxter-Riley, E. (1925). *Among Papuan Headhunters*. Philadelphia, Lippencott.

Bayton, J. (1969). 'Missionaries and Islanders', *Queensland Heritage*, 1: 16–19.

Beardmore, E. (1890). 'The natives of Mowat, Daudai, New Guinea', *Journal of the Royal Anthropological Institute of Great Britain and Ireland*, 19: 459–66.

Beaver, W. N. (1914a). 'A Description of the Girara District, Western Papua', *The Geographical Journal*, 43 (4): 407–13.

Beaver, W. N. (1914b). 'Some Notes on the Nomenclature of Western Papua', *Man*, 14: 135–36.

Beaver, W. N. (1920). *Unexplored New Guinea*. 2nd.ed. London, Seeley Service (see also: www.archive.org/details/unexplorednewgui00beavnoft).

Beckett, J. R. (1972). 'The Torres Strait Islanders', In: Walker, D. (ed.). *Bridge and Barrier*, Canberra, ANU Press, 307–26.

Beckett, J. R. (1977). 'The Torres Strait Islanders and the pearling industry: a case of internal colonialism', *Aboriginal History*, 1: 77–104.

Beckett, J. R. (1978). 'Mission, church and sect: three types of religious commitment in the Torres Strait Islands', In: Boutilier, J. A., Hughes, D. T., and Tiffany, S. W. (eds). *Mission, Church and Sect in Oceania*, Ann Arbor, University of Michigan Press, 209–29.

Beckett, J. R. (1987). *Torres Strait Islanders: custom and colonialism*. Cambridge, Cambridge University Press.

Breinl, A. (1913). *Port Moresby to Daru: an account of a journal on foot and by canoe*. Townsville, Australian Institute of Tropical Medicine.

Burnett, F. (1911). *Through Polynesia and Papua: wanderings with a camera in Southern Seas*. London, F. Griffith.

Busse, M. (2005). 'Wandering hero stories in the southern lowlands of New Guinea: culture areas, comparison, and history', *Cultural Anthropology*, 20 (4): 443–73.

Busse, M., Turner S. and Araho, N. (1993). *The People of Lake Kutubu and Kikori: changing meanings of daily life*. Port Moresby, Papua New Guinea National Museum and Art Gallery.

Butcher, B. T. (1963). *We lived with headhunters*. London, Hodder and Stroughton.

Chalmers, James (1887). *Pioneering in New Guinea*. London, Religious Tract Society (see also: www.archive.org/details/pioneeringinnewg00chaliala).

Chalmers, James (1903). 'Notes on the natives of Kiwai Island, Fly River, British New Guinea', *Journal of the Royal Anthropological Institute of Great Britain and Ireland,* 33: 117–24.

Chester, H. M. (1870). Account of a visit to Warrior Island in September and October 1870 with a description of the pearl fishery on the Warrior Reef, together with: account of a visit to New Guinea in September 1870. Unpublished manuscript QSA COL/A151 Letter 3425 of 1870 [Brisbane, Queensland State Archives].

Crawford, A. L. (1981). *Aida: life and ceremony of the Gogodala*. Bathurst, Robert Brown.

Crawford, P. I. (ed.) (1993). *The Nordic eye: proceedings from NAFA 1*. Højbjerg, Denmark, Intervention Press.

D'Albertis, L. M. (1881). *New Guinea: What I did and what I saw*. 2nd ed. London, Sampson Low, Marston, Searle and Rivington.

Davies, A. (1986). The location and identification of Australian photographs, particularly of the Nineteenth Century, in British institutions. Canberra, up.

Dempwolff, O. (1929). '[Review]Landtman, G.: *The Kiwai Papuans of British New Guinea*', *Orientalistische Literaturzeitung*, 32: 217.

Dundon, Alison (2002). 'Dancing around development: crisis in Christian country in Western Province', *Oceania*, 72 (3): 215–30.

Edge-Partington, J. (1969). *An album of weapons, tools, ornaments, articles of dress of the natives of the Pacific Islands*, London, Holland Press [facsimile edition].

Eley, T. J. (1988). Hunters of the Reef: the marine geography of the Kiwai, Papua New Guinea. Unpublished PhD thesis, University of California, Berkeley.

Everill, H. C. (1885/86). 'Explorations of New Guinea, Captain Everill's report', *Transactions and Proceedings of the Royal Geographical Society Australasia, NSW Branch*, 3/4: 170–87.

H.O.F. (1902). '[Review] *Head Hunters, Black, White, and Brown* by Alfred C. Haddon', *The Geographical Journal*, 20 (4): 444–46.

H.O.F. (1920). '[Review] *Unexplored New Guinea: A Record of the Travels, Adventures, and Experiences of a Resident Magistrate Amongst the Head-Hunting Savages and Cannibals of the Unexplored Interior of New Guinea* by Wilfred N. Beaver', *The Geographical Journal*, 55 (3): 226–27.

Fife, W. (2001). 'Creating the moral body: missionaries and the technology of power in early Papua New Guinea', *Ethnology*, 40 (3): 251–69.

Fitzpatrick, Judith (1991). 'Maza: a legend about culture and the sea', In: Lawrence, D. and Cansfield-Smith, T. (eds). *Sustainable development for traditional inhabitants of the Torres Strait region: proceedings of the Torres Strait Baseline Study Conference*. Townsville, Great Barrier Reef Marine Park Authority: 335–46.

Flinders, M. (1814). *A voyage to Terra Australis…in the years 1801, 1802 and 1803 in His Majesty's Ship the Investigator*. London, G. and W. Nicol (see also: www.archive.org/details/avoyagetoterraau12929gut(volume1) www.archive.org/details/avoyagetoterraau13121gut(volume2)

Florek, S. (2005). *The Torres Strait Islands Collection at the Australian Museum*. Sydney, Australian Museum.

Fisher, J. W. (1856/57). Logbook of the Barque Woodlark 1856–57, Unpublished manuscript 196, Pacific Manuscripts Bureau, Canberra, ANU.

Fuary, Maureen (2000). 'Torres Strait and *Dawdhay*: Dimensions of self and otherness on Yam Island', *Oceania;* 70 (3): 219–30.

Ganter, Regina (1994). *The Pearl-Shellers of Torres Strait: resource use, development and decline, 1860s–1960s*. Melbourne, Melbourne University Press.

Garran, A. (ed). (1868–88). *Picturesque Atlas of Australasia*. Sydney, Picturesque Atlas Publishing Co. (3 volumes).

Gash, Noel and Whittaker, June (1975). *A Pictorial History of New Guinea*. Milton, Jacaranda Press.

Gill, W. W. (1874). 'Torres Straits and New Guinea and notes in New Guinea', *Leisure Hour,* 1: 217–20; 2: 245–48; 3: 775–79; 4: 822–23.

Grainger, E. (1978). *Hargrave and Son*, Brisbane, University of Queensland Press.

Haddon, A. C. (1888). Journal [of a trip to Torres Strait]. Unpublished manuscript, Cambridge University.

Haddon, A. C. (1890a). 'Ethnography of the western tribes of the Torres Straits', *Journal of the Royal Anthropological Institute of Great Britain and Ireland*, 19: 297–442.

Haddon, A. C. (1890b). 'Legends from Torres Straits [I]', *Folklore*, 1 (1): 47–81.

Haddon, A. C. (1890c). 'Legends from Torres Straits. II', *Folklore*, 1 (2): 172–96.

Haddon, A. C. (1894). *The decorative art of British New Guinea: a study in Papuan ethnography*. Dublin, Academy House.

Haddon, A. C. (1898). Journal [of a trip to Torres Strait]. Unpublished manuscript, Cambridge University.

[Haddon, A. C.] (1899). 'The Cambridge Anthropological Expedition to Torres Straits and Sarawak', *The Geographical Journal*, 14 (3): 302–06.

Haddon, A. C. (1900a). 'A classification of the stone clubs of British New Guinea', *Journal of the Anthropological Institute of Great Britain and Ireland*, 30: 221–50.

Haddon, A. C. (1900b). 'Studies in the Anthropogeography of British New Guinea', *The Geographical Journal*, 16 (3): 265–91.

Haddon, A. C. (1900c). 'Studies in the Anthropogeography of British New Guinea (Continued)', *The Geographical Journal*, 16(4): 414–40.

Haddon, A. C. (1901). *Headhunters: black, white and brown*. London, Methuen (see also: www.archive.org/details/headhuntersblack00haddnoft).

Haddon, A. C. (1916). 'The Kabiri or Girara District, Fly River, Papua', *The Journal of the Royal Anthropological Institute of Great Britain and Ireland*, 46: 334–52.

Haddon, A. C. (1920). '[Review] *The Folk-Tales of the Kiwai Papuans*. by Gunnar Landtman' *Man*, 20: 43–45.

Haddon, A. C. (1947). 'Smoking and tobacco pipes in New Guinea', *PhilosophicalTransactions of the Royal Society of London*, series B 232: 1–278.

Haddon, A. C. (ed.)(1901/03–1935). *Reports of the Cambridge Anthropological Expedition to Torres Straits*. Cambridge, Cambridge University Press (Referenced as Haddon 1901/03, II; Haddon 1904, V; Haddon 1907, III; Haddon 1908, VI; Haddon 1912, IV; and Haddon 1935, I; Vol III also referenced as Ray 1907) (see also: www.archive.org/details/ for online versions of the Reports).

Haddon, A. C. and Hornell, J. (1936–1938) *Canoes of Oceania*. Honolulu, Bernice P. Bishop Museum.

Hammar, Lawrence (1999). 'Caught between structure and agency: the gender of violence and prostitution in Papua New Guinea', *Transforming Anthropology*, 8 (1 and 2): 77–96.

Harder, B.(1885). Views of British New Guinea [photographs]. (Mitchell Library PicAcc1191). Herle, Anita and Rouse, Sandra (eds) (1998). *Cambridge and the Torres Strait: centenary essays on the 1898 anthropological expedition*. Cambridge, Cambridge University Press.

Hitchcock, G. (2004). 'Torres Strait origin of some stone-headed clubs from the Torassi or Bensbach River area, southwest Papua New Guinea'. In: McNiven, I. J. and Quinnell, M. C. (eds). 'Torres Strait Archaeology and Material Culture', *Memoirs of the Queensland Museum. Cultural Heritage Series*, 3 (1): 305–15.

Hitchcock, G. (2004). *Wildlife is our gold: political ecology of the Torassi River borderland, southwest Papua New Guinea.* Unpublished PhD, University of Queensland (www.papuaweb.org/dlib/s123-png/hitchcock/phd.pdf).

Hocking, Paul (1992). 'The Yellow Bough: Rivers's use of photography in *The Todas*', In: Edwards, Elizabeth (ed.). *Anthropology and Photography: 1860–1920.* New Haven, Yale University Press in association with the Royal Anthropological Institute, 179–86.

Hughes-d'Aeth, Tony (2001). *Paper Nation: the story of the Picturesque Atlas of Australasia: 1868–1888.* Melbourne, Melbourne University Press.

Hurley, Frank (1924). *Pearls and Savages: adventures in the air, on land and sea in New Guinea.* New York, Putnam's Sons.

im Thurn, E.F. (1893). 'Anthropological use of the camera'. *The Journal of the Royal Anthropological Institute of Great Britain and Ireland*, 22: 184–203.

Isotalo, Riina (1995). 'Edward Westermarck and Hilma Granqvist in the field of Orientalist discourse in Finland', paper presented to the third Nordic conference on Middle Eastern Studies: 'Ethnic encounter and culture change', Joensuu, Finland, 19–22 June 1995.

Jiear, A. H. (1904/05). 'Addendum to annual report of resident magistrate, Western Division', *Annual Report on British New Guinea*, Votes and Proceedings of Queensland, Parliament. Brisbane, Government Printer, Appendix S: 69–71.

Jukes, J. B. (1847). *Narrative of the surveying voyage of HMS Fly during the years 1842–1846.* London, T. & W. Boone.

Kaus, David (2004). 'Material culture collections and research from Torres Strait' In: McNiven, I. J. and Quinnell, M. C. (eds). 'Torres Strait Archaeology and Material Culture', *Memoirs of the Queensland Museum. Cultural Heritage Series*, 3 (1): 93–104.

Kirsch, Stuart (2006). *Reverse anthropology: indigenous analysis of social and environmental relations in New Guinea.* Stanford, Stanford University Press.

Knauft, B. (1993). *South Coast New Guinea Cultures.* Cambridge, Cambridge University Press.

Knauft, B. (1999). *From primitive to postcolonial in Melanesia and anthropology.* Ann Arbor, The University of Michigan.

Kuklick, Henrika (1996). 'Islands in the Pacific: Darwinian biogeography and British anthropology', *American Ethnologist*, 23 (3): 611–38.

Kuper, Adam (1988). *The invention of primitive society: transformations of an illusion*. London, Routledge.

Laba, B. (1995). 'Oral traditions about early trade by Indonesians in southwest Papua New Guinea'. In: Swadling, Pamela (ed.). *Plumes from Paradise: trade cycles in outer Southeast Asia and their impact on New Guinea and nearby islands until 1920*. Coorparoo, Q., Robert Brown, 299–308.

Landtman, Gunnar see bibliography of writings on the Kiwai.

Landtman, Gunnar (1905). *The Origin of Priesthood*. Ekenaes, Ekenaes Printing (see also: www.archive.org/details/originpriesthoo00langoog).

Landtman, Gunnar (1909). *The primary causes of social inequality*. Helsingfors, Finska vetenskaps-societeten. (Öfversigt af Finska vetenskaps-societetens förhandlingar Afd B: Humanistiska vetenskaper: 2) (see also: www.openlibrary.org/details/primarycausesofs00landrich).

Lahdentausta, Heli & Parpola, Marjatta, Vainonen, Pilvi and Varjola, Pirjo (eds). (2001). *Satumaa ja sen asukkaat — Gunnar Landtman Papua-Uudessa-Guineassa 1910–1912, Paradise and the People Who Lived There — Gunnar Landtman in Papua New Guinea 1910–1912*. (Kulttuurien museon näyttelyjulkaisu 1, Exhibition publication of the Museum of Cultures 1). Helsinki: Museovirasto.

Larsen, Peter [2006]. 'Individual and type: early ethnographic photography' (http://nordik.uib.no/nordik2006/papers/PeterLarsen.pdf).

Lawrence, David (1991). 'The subsistence economy of the Kiwai-speaking people of the southwest coast of Papua New Guinea', In: Lawrence, D. and Cansfield-Smith, T. (eds). *Sustainable development for traditional inhabitants of the Torres Strait region: proceedings of the Torres Strait Baseline Study Conference*. Townsville, Great Barrier Reef Marine Park Authority: 367–78.

Lawrence, David (1994). 'Customary exchange across Torres Strait', *Memoirs of the Queensland Museum*, 34 (1):241–446.

Lawrence, David (1995). *Lower Fly area study: 'You can't buy another life from a store'*. Canberra, Resource Management in Asia Pacific Program, The Australian National University (Ok-Fly Social Monitoring Project; 9) (http://rspas.anu.edu.au/rmap/projects/Ok-Fly_social_monitoring/Ofsamp09-Lawrence 1995-Lower-Fly.pdf).

Lawrence, David (2004). 'Shared space: Papuan perspectives of the Torres Strait' In, Davis, Richard (ed.). *Woven Histories, Dancing Lives: Torres Strait identity, culture and history*. Canberra, Aboriginal Studies Press: 190–206.

Lawrence, D. and Cansfield-Smith, T. (eds)(1991). *Sustainable development for traditional inhabitants of the Torres Strait region: proceedings of the Torres Strait Baseline Study Conference*. Townsville, Great Barrier Reef Marine Park Authority. (http://www.gbrmpa.gov.au/corp_site/info_services/publications/workshop_series/Ws016/index.html).

Lawrie, M. (1990). 'Zahel, Ethel May Eliza (1877–1951)', *Australian Dictionary of Biography*, Volume 12: 604–05.

Lett, Lewis (1944) *The Papuan achievement*. 2nd ed. Melbourne, Melbourne University Press.

Lewis, Albert B. (1934). '[Review] Ethnographical Collection from the Kiwai District of British New Guinea, by Gunnar Landtman', *The American Anthropologist*, ns 36: 606.

Lindt, J. W. (1887). *Picturesque New Guinea*. London, Longmans, Green and Co. (Photographs held at Mitchell Library Q988 4/L).

London Missionary Society. nd. Photograph collection. (University of London, School of Oriental and Asian Studies. World Mission Archives Boxes 1-10).

Lutkehaus, N. (1986). '"She was 'Very' Cambridge": Camilla Wedgwood and the history of women in British social anthropology', *American Ethnologist*, 13 (4): 776-798.

Lutton, N. (1979). 'Abel, Charles William (1862-1930)', *Australian Dictionary of Biography*, Volume 7: 5-6.

Lyons, A. P. (1921). 'Animistic and Other Spiritualistic Beliefs of the Bina Tribe, Western Papua', *The Journal of the Royal Anthropological Institute of Great Britain and Ireland*, 51: 428-37.

Lyons, A. P. (1926). 'Notes on the Gogodara Tribe of Western Papua', *The Journal of the Royal Anthropological Institute of Great Britain and Ireland*, 56: 329–59.

MacFarlane [Macfarlane], S. and Rawlinson, H. C. (1875–76). 'Ascent of the Fly River, New Guinea', *Proceedings of the Royal Geographical Society of London*, 20 (4): 253–66.

Macfarlane, W. (1928/29). Correspondence with Haddon dated 1928/29. (Unpublished manuscript PMB MF 959. Canberra, Pacific Manuscripts Bureau).

Macgregor, [Sir] W. (1888/89). Dispatch respecting visit of inspection to island of Kiwai at mouth of Fly River, together with vocabulary of the Kiwai language, British New Guinea, *Annual Report on British New Guinea*, Votes and Proceedings of Queensland, Parliament. Brisbane, Government Printer, Appendix E: 36–43; 124–31.

Macgregor, [Sir] W. (1899). Map of the western part of British New Guinea from the latest astronomical observations surveys and explorations by His Excellency Sir William Macgregor and Officers of the British New Guinea Government; D. J., Brown & W. MacKay, draftsmen (Scale [1:253,440] 4 statute miles to an inch). Brisbane, Surveyor-General's Office, 1899. (http://nla.gov.au/nla.map-rm2733). [Note: together with maps of the Papuan Gulf and eastern part of British New Guinea [Papua].

Macintyre, Martha and MacKenzie, Maureen (1992). 'Focal length as a analogue of colonial distance', In: Edwards, Elizabeth (ed.). *Anthropology and Photography: 1860–1920*. New Haven, Yale University Press in association with the Royal Anthropological Institute, 158–64.

McNiven, I. J. (1998). 'Enmity and Amity: reconsidering stone-headed club (gabagaba) procurement and trade in Torres Strait', *Oceania*, 69 (2): 94–115.

McNiven, IJ. and Quinnell, MC. (eds) (2004). 'Torres Strait Archaeology and Material Culture', *Memoirs of the Queensland Museum. Cultural Heritage Series*, 3 (1): 1–386.

McNiven I. J, von Gnielinski, F. and Quinnell, M. C. (2004). 'Torres Strait and the origin of large stone axes from Kiwai Island', In: McNiven, I. J. and Quinnell, Michael (eds). 'Torres Strait Archaeology and Material Culture', *Memoirs of the Queensland Museum. Cultural Heritage Series*, 3 (1): 271–89.

McPhee, Ewen (2004). 'Archaeology of the pearl shelling industry in Torres Strait', In: McNiven, I. J. and Quinnell, Michael (eds). 'Torres Strait Archaeology and Material Culture', *Memoirs of the Queensland Museum. Cultural Heritage Series*, 3 (1): 363–77.

Malinowski, B. (1929). '[Review] *The Kiwai Papuans of British New Guinea. A Nature-Born Instance of Rousseau's Ideal Community* by Gunnar Landtman', Folklore, 40 (1): 109–12.

Malinowski, B. (1935). *Coral Gardens and their Magic*. 2 vols. London, Allen and Unwin.

Malinowski, B. (1953 [c. 1922]). *Argonauts of the western Pacific*. London, Routledge and Kegan Paul.

Mead, Margaret and Calas, Nicolas (eds) (1953). *Primitive Heritage: an anthropological anthology*. London, Victor Gollancz.

Moore, D. R. (1979). *Islanders and Aborigines at Cape York*. Canberra, Australian Institute of Aboriginal Studies.

Moore, D. R. (1984). *The Torres Strait Collections of A.C. Haddon*. London, British Museum.

Moseley, H. N. (1892). *Notes by a naturalist: an account of observations made during the voyage of HMS Challenger …1872–1876*. New York, Putnam.

Mullins, Steve (1995). *Torres Strait: a history of colonial occupation and culture contact 1864–1897*. Rockhampton, Central Queensland University Press.

Mullins, Steve (1996). 'Haddon, Alfred Cort (1855–1940)', *AustralianDictionary of Biography*, 14: 349–50.

Mullins, S[teve]. (1997). 'Internal colonialism, communalism, institutionalized racism, progressive reform, clash of administrative cultures, or all of the above', *The Electronic Journal of Australian and New Zealand History*(http://www.jcu.edu.au/aff/history/articles/mulllins.html).

Murray, A. W. and Macfarlane [MacFarlane], S. (1872). *Journal of a missionary voyage to New Guinea*. London, Snow.

Neuenfeldt, Karl and Costigan, Lyn (2004). 'Negotiating and enacting musical innovation and continuity: how some Torres Strait Islander songwriters incorporate traditional dance chants within contemporary songs', *Asia Pacific Journal of Anthropology*, 5 (2): 113–28.

O'Hanlon, M. (1999). '"Mostly Harmless?" Missionaries, Administrators and Material Culture on the Coast of British New Guinea', *The Journal of the Royal Anthropological Institute*, 5 (3): 377–97.

Pacific Manuscripts Bueau (2006). Sample catalogue of South Seas Photograph Collections 30 June, 26 July 2006 (www.rspas.anu.edu.au/pambu/Onlinematerial).

Parkinson, Richard (1999). *Thirty years in the South Seas*. Edited by B. Ackerman. Honolulu, University of Hawai'i Press (Translation of *Dreißig Jahre in der Südsee* 1907).

Pawley, A. and others (eds) (2005). *Papuan Pasts: cultural, linguistic and biological histories of Papuan-speaking peoples*. Canberra, Pacific Linguistics, The Australian National University.

Pinney, Christopher (1992). 'The parallel histories of anthropology and photography', In: Edwards, Elizabeth (ed.). *Anthropology and Photography: 1860–1920*. New Haven, Yale University Press in association with the Royal Anthropological Institute: 74–95.

Poignant, Roslyn (1992). 'Surveying the field of view: the making of the RAI Photographic Collection', In: Edwards, Elizabeth (ed.). *Anthropology and Photography: 1860–1920*. New Haven, Yale University Press in association with the Royal Anthropological Institute: 42–73.

Quanchi, Max (2007). *Photographing Papua: representation, colonial encounters and imaging in the public domain*. Newcastle, UK, Cambridge Scholars Publishing.

Quiggin, A. H. (1912). 'Textiles', In: (Haddon, A. C. (ed.) (1912). *Reports of the Cambridge Anthropological Expedition to Torres Straits, Volume IV* Cambridge, Cambridge University Press: 63–88.

Quiggin, A. H. And Fegan, E. S. (1940). 'Alfred Cort Haddon, 1855–1940', *Man*, 40: 97–100.

Ray, S. H. (1895). 'The Languages of British New Guinea', *The Journal of the Anthropological Institute of Great Britain and Ireland*, 24: 15–39.

Ray, S. H. (1923). 'The Languages of the Western Division of Papua', *The Journal of the Royal Anthropological Institute of Great Britain and Ireland*, 53: 332–60.

Riley, E. B. see also Baxter-Riley, E.

Riley, E. B. and Ray, S. H. (1924). 'Kiwai Seasons', *Man*, 24: 73–75.

Riley, E. B. and Ray, S. H (1930/31). 'Sixteen vocabularies form the Fly River', *Anthropos*, 25: 173–94, 831–50; 26: 171–92.

Rivers, W. H. R. (1906). *The Todas*. London, Macmillian.

Rivers, W. H. R. (1914). *The History of Melanesian Society*. 2 vols. Cambridge, Cambridge University Press (see also: www.archive.org/details/Historyofmelanes02riveruoft (volume 2 only).

Roth, Jane and Hooper, Steven (1990). *The Fiji journals of Baron Anatole von Hüge: 1875–1877*. Suva, Fiji Association in association with the Cambridge Museum of Archaeology and Anthropology.

Ruby, Jay (1996). 'Visual anthropology' In: David Levinson and Melvin Ember (eds). *Encyclopedia of Cultural Anthropology*. New York, Henry Holt and Co. Volume 4: 1345–351.

Rutherford, D. (1834). 'Some account of the natives of Murray's Island in the Torres Strait', *United Service Journal*, 2: 194–202.

Schieffelin, E. L. and Crittenden, R. (1991). *Like people you see in a dream: first contact in six Papuan societies*. Stanford, CA, Stanford University Press.

Schnukal, A. (2004). 'The post-contact created environment in the Torres Strait Central Islands', In: McNiven, I. J. and Quinnell, Michael (eds). 'Torres Strait Archaeology and Material Culture', *Memoirs of the Queensland Museum. Cultural Heritage Series*, 3 (1): 317–46.

Schug, D. M. (1995). The marine realm and a sense of place among the Papua New Guinean communities of the Torres Strait. Unpublished PhD thesis, University of Hawai'i, Honolulu.

Schug, D. M. (1996). 'The trade of our ancestors', *Journal of Pacific History*, 31 (1): 58–69.

Schug, D. M. (1997). 'The politics of Papuan labour in the Torres Strait marine industry', *Journal of the Royal Australian Historical Society*, 83 (1): 59–70.

Seligman, C. G. (1910). *The Melanesians of British New Guinea*. Cambridge, Cambridge University Press.

C. G. S[eligman]. (1928). '[Review] *The Kiwai Papuans of British New Guinea* by Gunnar Landtman', *The Geographical Journal*, 71 (5): 496–97.

Seligmann, C. G. and B. Z. (1911). *The Veddas*. Cambridge, Cambridge University Press.

Singe, John (1989 rev. ed.). *The Torres Strait*. St Lucia, University of Queensland Press.

Specht, Jim and Fields, John (1984). *Frank Hurley in Papua: photographs of the 1920–1923 expeditions*. Bathurst, Robert Brown in association with the Australian Museum Trust.

Spencer, Herbert (1873–81). *Descriptive Sociology, or groups of sociological facts*, parts 1–8 classified and arranged by Herbert Spencer. Compiled and abstracted by David Duncan, Richard Scheppig and James Collier. London, [William and Norgate].

Stocking, G. W. (1992). *The Ethnographer's Magic and Other Essays in the History of Anthropology*. Madison, University of Wisconsin Press.

Stone, O. C. (1880). *A few months in New Guinea*. London, Sampson Low.

Strachan, J. (1888). *Explorations and adventures in New Guinea*. London, Sampson Low (see also: www.archive.org/details/explorationsand01stragoog).

Strathern Marilyn (1990). 'Artefacts of history: events and the interpretation of images', In: Jukka Siikala (ed.). *Culture and History in the Pacific*. Helsinki, Suomen Anthropologinen Seura.

Staniforth Smith, M. (1912). 'Exploration in Papua', *The Geographical Journal*, 39 (4): 313–31.

Suolinna, Kirsti. (2000). 'Hilma Granqvist: a scholar of the Westermarck School in decline', *Acta Sociologica*, 43: 317–23.

Sweatman, J. (1842–47). Surveying voyage of Her Majesty's Schooner Bramble 1842–1847. Unpublished manuscript A1725, Mitchell Library, Sydney [Published in part in Allen and Corris 1977].

Tayler, Donald (1992). '"Very lovable human beings": the photography of Everard im Thurn', In: Edwards, Elizabeth (ed). *Anthropology and Photography: 1860–1920*. New Haven, Yale University Press in association with the Royal Anthropological Institute, 187–92.

Thomas, Nicholas (1992). 'Colonial conversions: difference, hierarchy and history in early Twentieth-Century evangelical propaganda', *Comparative Studies in Society and History*, 34 (2): 366–89.

Thomson, D. F. (1933). 'The Hero Cult, Initiation and Totemism on Cape York', *The Journal of the Royal Anthropological Institute of Great Britain and Ireland*, 63: 453–37.

Thomson, D. F. (1934). 'The dugong hunters of Cape York', *The Journal of the Royal Anthropological Institute of Great Britain and Ireland*, 64: 237–62.

Thomson, D. F (1939). 'Notes on the smoking-pipes of north Queensland and the Northern Territory of Australia', *Man*, 39: 81–91.

Thomson, J. P. (1892). *British New Guinea*. London, George Philip and Sons.

Urry, J. (1972). '"Notes and Queries on Anthropology" and the development of field methods in British anthropology, 1870–1920', *Proceedings of the Royal Anthropological Institute of Great Britain and Ireland*, no.1972: 45–57.

Urry, J. (1984). 'Englishmen, Celts and Iberians', In: Stocking, G. W. (ed.). *Functionalism Historicized*. Madison, University of Wisconsin Press: 83–105.

Vanderwal, R. (2004). 'Early historical sources for the top western islands in the western Torres Strait exchange network'. In: McNiven, I. J. and Quinnell, M. C. (eds). 'Torres Strait Archaeology and Material Culture', *Memoirs of the Queensland Museum. Cultural Heritage Series*, 3 (1): 257–70.

Vuorela, Toivo (1977). *Ethnology in Finland before 1920*. Helsinki, Societas Scientiarum Fennica (The History of Learning and Science in Finland 1828–1918).

Wagner, R. (1995). 'Mysteries of origin: early traders and heroes in the Trans Fly'. In: Swadling, Pamela (ed.). *Plumes fromParadise: trade cycles in outer Southeast Asia and their impact on New Guinea and nearby islands until 1920*. Coorparoo, Q., Robert Brown, 285–98.

Wedgwood, Camilla H. (1929). '[Review] *The Kiwai Papuans of British New Guinea* by Gunnar Landtman', *Man*, 29: 40–41.

Wedgwood, Camilla H. (1933–34). [Unpublished] fieldnotes: Manam Island (January 1933-February 1934). Archives of the University of Sydney, Sydney.

Westermarck, Edward [Edvard] (1900). 'Remarks on the Predicates of Moral Judgments', *Mind*, New Series, 9 (34): 184–204.

Westermarck, Edward [Edvard] (1906–08). *The Origin and Development of the Moral Ideas*. London, Macmillan (see also: www.archive.org/details/originanddevelop029351mbp (volume 1) and originanddevelop014110mbp (volume 2).

Wetherell, D. (1993). 'From Samuel McFarlane to Stephen Davies', *PacificStudies*, 16 (1): 1–32.

Wetherell, D. (1996). *Charles Abel and the Kwato Mission of Papua New Guinea 1891–1975*. Melbourne, Melbourne University Press.

Wetherell, D. (2004). 'The Bishop of Carpentaria and the Torres Strait Pearlers' Strike of 1936', *Journal of Pacific History*, 39 (2): 185–202.

Wheeler, G. C. (1926). *Mono-Alu folklore: Bougainville Strait, western Solomon Islands*. London, Routledge.

Wikman, K. Rob. (1940). 'Gunnar Landtman: Några minnesord' [Some words in his memory], *Budkavlen*, 19.

Wilde, Charles (2004). 'Acts of Faith', *Oceania*, 75 (1): 32–49.

Williams, F. E. (1928). *Orokaiva Magic*. Oxford, Clarendon Press.

Williams, F. E. (1930). *Orokaiva Society*. Oxford, Clarendon Press.

Williams, F. E. (1936). *Papuans of the Trans-Fly*. Oxford, Clarendon Press.

Williams, F. E. (1976). *The Vailala Madness, and other essays*, edited by Erik Schwimmer. London, Hurst.

Williamson, R. W. (1912). *The Mafulu: mountain people of British New Guinea*. London, Macmillian (see also: www.archive.org/details/mafulumountainpe00willuoft).

Wilson, P. D. (1978). Chester's report on a voyage to the Fly River, Papua, in December 1875', *Queensland Heritage*, 3 (9): 18–24.

Wirz, P. (1933). 'Headhunting expeditions of the Tugeri', *Tijdscrift voor Indische Taal-, Land- en Volkenkunde*, 73: 105–22.

Wurm, S. A. (1973). 'The Kiwaian language family', In: Franklin, K. (ed.). *The linguistic situation in the Gulf District and adjacent areas, Papua New Guinea*. Canberra, The Australian National University.

Yonge, C. M. (1930). *A year on the Great Barrier Reef*. London, Putnam.

Young, M. W. (1998). *Malinowski's Kiriwina: fieldwork photography, 1915–1918*. Chicago, University of Chicago Press.

Young, M. W. and Clark, J. (2001). *An anthropologist in Papua: the photography of F.E. Williams, 1922–39*. Adelaide, Crawford House. Publishing.

Index

Abel, Charles (missionary) 19, 64

Åbo Academy, Turku, Finland 9

Aboriginal Protection Act of 1897
(Queensland) 21

adigo (forearm bracer) 153

Adiri, land of the dead 47, 94, 131

Agabara village 128

Agob people 4, 71-74, 143, 165, 167

Aird Hills 17, 57

Aird River 43

amo (dugong rope) 145

Amubalee (culture hero) 104

Antell, Dr Herman Fritiof 29

Antell Commission, Helsinki, Finland 29,
40, 64, 133

Apau (Daniel) (servant) 31, 40

Apineru (pastor) 42, 88

Aramia wetlands ix, 32, 33

archaeology and material culture of the
Torres Strait 175

Argan (boat) 25, 27

Armstrong, W. E. (Government
Anthropologist) 11

Army and Navy Stores, London x, 10, 28

Asau (culture hero) 76

Asia Pacific Christian Mission 108

Australian Immigration Restriction Act of
1901 13

Australian Museum, Sydney 94, 148

Auti village 53, 96, 115, 116, 118, 119

Badu Island 16, 19, 20-25, 37, 38, 40-42,
61, 63, 71, 72, 95, 138

Badu Native School 37, 61

Bagari (culture hero) 81

Baidam (pastor and teacher) 35

baizam boai (shark men) (cult) 164

Balamula village 61, 97, 106, 107, 114

Balimo (Barimu) village 34, 108, 109, 111

Bamu River 32, 49, 58, 97, 109, 111, 112,
115

Bani (culture hero) 81

Banner, Capt. William 14, 80

Baramura Creek (see also Balamula Creek)
107

Barasaro (Kiwai Island) (village site) 114,
115, 127

Barthes, Roland 68

Basipuk [Basir Puerk] 74

bata or bage (woven belts) 152

Baxter-Riley, Rev. Edward (missionary)
12, 13, 17, 20, 24, 28

Beardmore, Edward (trader) 95

Beaver, Wilfred (Resident Magistrate) 43,
60, 74, 83, 107, 108, 109, 111, 113,
114, 180, 181

bêche-de-mer fishing 12, 14, 21, 61, 80,
82, 87, 95, 124, 139, 158, 174

Berger, Theo (missionary) 108

Bida village 108

Bidedu (culture hero) 80, 81, 101

bidibidi (breast ornaments) 96, 150, 151

Binaturi [Bineturi] River 4, 12, 29, 41, 45,
46, 47, 49, 80, 98, 100, 102, 103, 140,
160

Bine people x, 4, 41, 47, 82, 100, 103,
104, 143, 165, 167,

boats

    Argan 25, 27

    Goodwill 21, 22, 2, 29, 30, 31, 53

    Louisa 40

    Merrie England 58

    Olive Branch 20

    Pearl 31, 32, 34, 36

    Tamate 54, 56, 57

Boigu Island 1, 2, 51, 71, 72, 73, 78, 79,
81, 92, 93, 95, 109, 148, 164

boroboro (drum) 158

boromo kokai (pigs' tusks ornament) 153

Bose village 100

Brage Society, Finland 174

British evolutionary anthropology and sociology 5, 7, 8, 19, 175

Broome, Western Australia 14

Buji village 51, 52, 69, 71, 72, 73, 79, 91, 109, 147, 164, 167

Bullawe River 100, 103

Burai (name of a magic canoe) 113, 114, 115

Buru Reef 72

buruburu (drum) xi, 91, 92, 158, 159

Busere-busere (young women with magic powers) 113, 114

Butcher, Rev. Ben (missionary) 12, 17, 20, 24, 28, 31-36, 52, 54, 56-58, 64, 108, 109, 111, 113

Cairns, North Queensland 37

Cambridge Anthropological Expedition to Torres Straits, 1898 4, 7, 64

Cambridge Anthropological Expedition to Torres Straits, 1898, material culture collection see Haddon collection

Cambridge Anthropological Expedition to Torres Straits, 1898, reports 8

Cambridge Museum of Archaeology and Anthropology (see also Cambridge Museum of Archaeology and Ethnology) x, 171

Cambridge Museum of Archaeology and Ethnology (see also Cambridge Museum of Archaeology and Anthropology) x, 6, 109 133, 173

Cambridge University ix

Cameron, J. B. (Resident Magistrate) 73

canoe trade, description of 87, 95-98, 107, 113-115, 139-141

Cape York–Oriomo Ridge (see also Oriomo Plateau) 1

ceremonies
Horiomu 93, 94, 181, 183
Mogeru 93
Taera 93

Chalmers, Rev. James (missionary) 13, 24, 38, 54, 57, 95, 114, 127

Chester, H. M. (Police Magistrate) 80, 81

Christmas on Badu, description of 38, 40-41

coastal Kiwai people 3, 13, 28, 47, 80, 81, 83, 93, 101, 102, 156, 157, 163

comparative religion 8, 9

Congregation of the Sacred Heart, Yule Island (mission) 12

Council for World Mission Archives 164

Cowling, J. (trader and planter) 24, 30, 48, 49, 51, 146

critical anthropology 176, 177

Cults
baizam boai (shark men) 164
Malo/Bomai cult 151, 158, 164, 168

Culture heroes
Amubalee 104
Asau 76
Bagari 81
Bani 81
Bidedu 80, 81, 101,
Gamea 80, 81, 101
Geadap (Gidap) 74, 76
Hido 76
Iko 76
Jabi 75, 76
Kuiam 73, 75, 76, 78, 79
Kuke 80, 81
Meuri 78, 114
Muiam 74, 76, 167
Omebwale 100, 104
Oumo 76
Sagaru 77, 78
Sewota 81
Sido 73, 75-78, 114, 131, 132
Soriame 101
Souw 76
Ua-ogrere 100
Ubrikubri 71, 72
Ui-balee 104
Wawa 73, 75, 76, 135

202

Dabu (cultural site) 74

daguri (headdress made from cassowary feathers) 154, 155

D'Albertis, Luigi 12, 81

Damera Point 28

Dameratamurubi (branch of the Damera people) 116

dari (headdress) (see also dori (headdress)) 30, 156, 157

darimo (communal men's house) xi, 106

Darnley Island (see also Erub) 95, 116

Daru island and town vii, xii, xiii, 1, 2, 4, 12, 13, 17, 22, 24, 28, 32, 40, 42, 43, 46, 52, 58, 60 73, 80, 81, 82, 93, 96, 109, 139, 143, 145, 174

Daru, crime and poverty 174

Daru sex industry 174

Dauan Island 1, 51, 73, 78, 79, 95, 138, 139, 148, 168

Daudai 1, 70, 104, 161

Daware village 106, 141

Descriptive Sociology (book title) 7

Det rättas värde (book title) 174

Dhamudh Island 95

dibidib [dibidibi] (breast ornament) 150, 151

Dibiri Island 2, 76, 95, 113, 114, 115, 149, 170

diffusionism 93, 113

Dirimu (Darimo) village and plantation 23, 29, 42, 44-47, 49, 52, 60, 61, 103-105, 167

dogai (oblong shield-like boards used in canoes) (see also gope) 139

Dogona village 108, 111

Domori Island 97, 108, 114

Dopima village 13

dori (headdress) (see also dari (headdress)) xi, 89, 156-157

Doridori (cultural site near Toro Passage) 81

Doropo village (see also U'uwo village) 114-116

Drageli village 100

dry developing chemicals, description of 65

Drysdale, Albert (missionary) 108

Dudi coast 3, 24, 70, 81, 106, 114, 116

Dudu-patu (cultural site near Daru) 80

dugong (Dugong dugon) 25

dugong hunting, methods and means of 45, 79, 81, 82, 84, 86, 93, 95, 98, 140, 144, 145, 174

Dutch New Guinea (see also West Papua) 17, 71

emoa (stone axe or adze) 135

empiricism 7

Erub (see also Darnley Island) 95, 116, 161

ethnographic photography 63-64

ethnography 9

ethnology 9

Evangelical Church of Papua New Guinea (mission) 108

Faifeau Samoa (Samoan pastors) 13, 28

Field Museum of Natural History, Chicago xi, 113

file snake (Acrochordus spp) 158

film substitutes, description of 65

Finlands svenska folkdikting (book title) 174

Finlandssvenskar (Swedish-speaking Finns) 174

Finno–Ugric (Uralic) people 7, 8, 9

Fisheries

    bêche-de-mer fishing 12, 14, 21, 61, 80, 82, 87, 95, 124, 139, 158, 174

    mother-of-pearl 14

    pearling 12, 13, 14, 21, 22, 36, 38, 40, 52, 82, 87, 97, 124, 131, 139, 140,146, 174

    trochus 14, 151

Fly estuary, description of 1-3

Fly River, description of 1, 2, 30, 108, 110

Fly River, exploration of 12, 13, 32, 52, 81, 107

Fly River, missions 13, 31, 61

Folklore 8, 10, 131, 174, 177

Folktro och trolldom (book title) 174

Forbes Islands 135

Frazer, J. G. xii, 132

Frazer-Westermarck school 132

Freshwater, J. B. (trader and planter) 23, 28, 29, 42, 50, 52, 53, 61

Functionalism 11, 175

gabagaba (stone fighting club) 90, 135, 167-168

Gabia (informant) 38

gagare (bamboo bow) 165

Gaima village 32, 35, 52, 57, 69, 108-113, 161

gama (drum) 158

Gamea (culture hero) 80, 81, 101

Gamobolo village 128

gamoda (Piper methysticum: kava) 37, 98, 12

gara oro (bamboo headcarrier) 168

Garran, Andrew 64

gatere (tuberous root basket) (see also Suki Bag) 143

Geadap (Gidap) (culture hero) 74, 76

Gebarubi people 81

genaio or gesa (dogs' teeth necklace) 149

Gename (servant) 44, 50
    wedding scene 55

genealogical tables 39

Gewi (cultural site near Toro Passage) 81

Gidra people 4

Gimioturi (Manowetti Kiwai word for Fly River) 108

Girara (Gogodala word for language) 111

Giringarede village 100

Gizra people 4, 74, 165, 167

Goaribari Island ix, 13, 56

Gogodala houses, description 82

Gogodala people 13, 32, 34, 52, 107-109, 111-113, 173

Goilala people 67

Goodwill (boat) 21, 22 28-31, 53

gope (oblong shield-like boards used in canoes) (see also dogai) 139

Granqvist, Hilma 9

green sea turtles (Chelonia mydas) 25

Gulf District, Papua ix, 17, 43, 56, 57, 173

Gunnar Landtman
    bibliography of works on the Kiwai 179-183

    career after Papua 173-174

    Christmas at Badu, description of 38, 40, 41

    collection of legends and stories ix, 40, 60, 132, 173

    correspondence with W. Beaver 60

    correspondence with J. H. P. Murray 60

    correspondence with G.H. Murray 60

    correspondence with the Walker family 59

    correspondence with E. Zahel 60-61

    family background 19

    food supplies and camp cooking 28, 32, 50, 52, 63

    malaria 23, 38, 39, 41

    material culture collection x, xiii, 69, 133, 171, 173

    meeting with A. C. Haddon ix

    meeting with J. H. P. Murray 58-59

    mosquitoes, description of a plague 43, 44, 46

    recordings of Kiwai songs and dances x, 39, 40, 47, 50, 52

Haddon, Alfred Cort, support and use of research ix, xii, xiii, 4-7, 10-12, 39, 40, 50, 64, 67, 78, 93, 104, 111, 112, 173, 175

Haddon collection 131-133, 135, 136, 139, 140, 143, 144, 146, 147, 150-159, 161, 163, 165-170

hawa (mat) 142

Headhunters, black, white and brown (book title) 6

Hedley, Charles 94, 148

Hely, Bingham (Resident Magistrate) 73, 102, 116, 117, 127

hero cults 135, 174

Hiamo-Hiamo people 82, 93

Hido (culture hero) 76

hoboro (rain hood) 141

Hocart, A. M. 10

Hodel, William (Fred) (trader) 37

homosexuality among the Kiwai 174

Horiomu (ceremony) 93, 94, 181, 183

Huboturi (cultural site near Toro Passage) 81

hunting, descriptions of marine hunting 25, 26, 45, 84-86

hunting, descriptions of terrestrial hunting 43, 44, 50, 100, 177

Iamega village 107

Iasa Ura (see also Kiwai Island) 2

Idealism 7

Iko (culture hero) 76

im Thurn, Everard 64, 65, 67

Imperial Aleksander University, Helsinki 7

infödd, defiition of 23

infödda, definition of 23

inföding, definition of 23

infödingar, definition 23

Informants
    Gabia 38
    Kaku 38
    Namai 46, 47, 51, 85, 91, 115

ini (nose stick) 149

ipegi (comb) 149

Ipidarimo, meaning of 106

Ipisia village 28, 31, 32, 36, 38-40, 42, 49, 54, 56, 127-129

Irupi village 100

Island Industries Board (IIB) 62

Islander Board of Industry and Service (IBIS) 62

Jabi (culture hero) 75, 76

Jibaru village 79

Jibu village 46, 48, 103

Jiear, A. H. (Resident Magistrate) 96, 108

Kabiri (Kabili) (name of a lagoon between Balimo and Dogona villages) 111

Kadawa village vii, 4, 74, 80, 82, 95, 139

Kadawarubi people 81

Kagaro Point 79, 114

Kaku (informant) 38

Kalama Wasewa (Gogodala word for Fly River) 108

Kalevala (book title) 8

karara (turtle shell mask) 161

Karsten, Rafael 8, 9, 19

Katatai village 4, 80-82, 96, 139

Katau village 80

Kattegat Strait off Denmark 59

Kaviapu village 108

Kesave [Kesawe] (Kiwai policeman) 74

Kikori River 54, 57

Kiwai houses, description of 82

Kiwai Island, description of 2, 3, 114-116

Kiwai Papuans of British New Guinea (book title) ix, 1, 10-11

Koabu village 106, 107

koima (cassowary feather plume) 153

Koipomuba 81

kokare (hand rattle) 161

Konakan, site on Yam Island 135

Kowdi, former husband of Makar 74

Kowio (name of drum) 91

Krohn, Julius 8

Krohn, Kaarle 8

Kubira village 115, 116, 170

Kubu village 108, 161

Kudin, name of a longhouse 114, 181

Kuiam (culture hero) 73, 75, 76, 78, 79

kuior (harpoon dart) 84, 144, 168, 169

Kuke (culture hero) 80, 81

Kulalae (Togo) village 167

kumu (butt end of a dugong harpoon) 144

Kunini village 82, 100

Kuru village 80, 81, 101

Kutai, wife of Kesawe 74

kwashiorkor (malnutrition caused by protein deficiency) 113

Kwato Mission 20, 61, 64, 107

Lake Murray 1

land lizard (Varanus spp) 158

Lawes, Rev. W. G. (missionary) 64

Lee-Bryce, W. (Protector of Aboriginals, Thursday Island) 21

Lett, Lewis 11

Lewada village 114

Lewis, Albert B. xi, 113

Lindt, J. W. 64

Lloyd Bay 78, 135

Louisa (boat) 40

London Missionary Society (LMS) (mission) 12, 24, 54, 57, 86

London School of Economics and Political Science 10

Lönnrot, Elias 8

Lord Canning 63

Lovett-Cameron, Captain V. 164

Loyalty Islander (Lifu Islander) pastors 12

Lyons, A. P. (Resident Magistrate) 109, 111

Mabudawan [Mabunardi] 2, 4, 12, 46, 47, 51, 71, 73-75, 77, 78, 80, 82, 101, 114, 135, 140

mabuo (arm shells) (see also wawri [wauri]) 96, 97, 150, 153, 154

MacFarlane, Rev. Samuel (missionary) 12, 13, 81, 158

Macfarlane, Rev. William (missionary) 104

Macgregor, Sir William (Administrator of British New Guinea) 106, 107, 114, 116, 122, 127

Madame village 61, 106, 107

Madiri village and plantation 23, 30, 32, 42, 50, 52, 53, 60, 61, 107, 108

Mai Kussa inlet 52, 73, 95, 167

Maind-amin people (see also Tugeri) 71, 136

Maipani village 95, 108, 113

Maiva, dugong hunter 85

Makar, widow of Kowdi and wife of Kesawe 74

makeso (woven frontlet) 157

malaria, danger of an attack 23, 32, 38, 39, 41, 50, 61

Malinowski, Bronislaw (anthropologist) 66, 68, 69, 132, 175, 181 182

Malo/Bomai cult 151, 158, 164, 168

Mannerheim, Marshal Carl Gustaf 64

Människan som kulturvarelse (Man as a cultural being) 10

Manowetti coast 3, 61, 70, 81, 95, 97, 106-108, 114, 115, 140.

marine geography of Kiwai dugong and turtle hunters 174

Martin, trader killed at Mawatta 71

Marukawa Island 46, 51, 73

Masa'ingle people 100, 101

Masingara village 41, 82, 100, 102, 167

Masingle village site 100, 101

material culture

adigo (forearm bracer) 153

amo (dugong rope) 145

bata or bage (woven belts) 152

bidibidi (breast ornaments) 96, 150, 151

boroboro (drum) 158

boromo kokai (pigs' tusks ornament) 153

buruburu (drum) xi, 91, 92, 158, 159

daguri (headdress made fro cassowary feathers) 154, 155

dari (headdress) 30, 156, 157

darimo (communal men's house) xi, 106

dori (headdress) xi, 30, 156, 157

dibidib (breast ornament: Kala Lagaw Ya) 150, 151

dibidibi (breast ornament: Meriam Mir) 150, 151

dogai (oblong shield-like boards used in canoes) 139

emoa (stone axe or adze) 135

gabagaba (stone fighting club) 90, 135, 167, 168

gagare (bamboo bow) 165

gama (drum) 158

gara oro (bamboo headcarrier) 168

gatere (tuberous root basket) (see also Suki Bag) 143, 144

genaio or gesa (dogs' teeth necklace) 149

gope (oblong shield-like boards used in canoes) 139

hawa (mat) xi, 142

hoboro (rain hood) 141

ini (nose stick) 149

ipegi (comb) 149

karara (turtle shell mask) 161

koima (cassowary feather plume) 153

kokare (hand rattle) 161

kuior (harpoon dart) 84, 144, 168, 169

kumu (butt end of a dugong harpoon) 144

mabuo (arm shells) (see also wawri [wauri]) 96, 97, 150, 153, 154

makeso (woven frontlet) 157

mihere or koumiri (broom) 145

mooa (wooden mask) 161

moto (communal longhouse) xi

motomoto (double outrigger canoe) xi, 52, 54, 96, 98, 140

narato (dugong huting platform) 45, 81, 85, 86

nese (pearl-shell breast ornament) 150

obo-marabo (bamboo water container) 146

otame (man-arrow) 167

paike (harpoon shaft) 144

pe (canoes) 95, 138

puputo (double outrigger canoe with one mast) 140

sito (coconut leaf basket) xi, 143

Suki Bag (see also gatere (tuberous root basket)) 143, 144

susare, tusare or tutae (plaited armlets and leglets) 152

tataku (single outrigger canoe) 124, 139

tene (arrow) 166

Tinny (flour-tin drum) 124

tiro (mat) 124, 141, 142

uere (bamboo headhunting knife) 169

waduru (tobacco pipe) 163

wagi or soke (casowary bone dagger) 165

wap or wapo (dugong harpoon) xi, 25, 86, 144

wapa or eere (fibre skirt) 148

warupa (drum) xi, 91, 100, 158

wawri [wauri] (arm shells) (see also mabuo) 153

wedere (pubic shell) 147

wedere moa (shell hoe) 134

Mauwa, name of a canoe 98

Mawata village (see also Mawatta village) 58, 95, 135, 149, 158

Mawatta village (see also Mawata village) 95-98, 100-103, 115, 135, 140, 142, 144, 159, 161, 164

Mawatto, meaning 81

McCulloch, Alan 94, 148

McDougall, William 4

Meai village 106

Mekeo people, Papua 11, 67

Mer (Murray Island) 5, 94, 95, 116, 143, 146-148, 151, 153, 154, 158, 161, 163, 165, 168, 169

Merauke, West Papua and formerly Dutch New Guinea 71

Merrie England (boat) 58

Meuri (culture hero) 78, 114

Mibu Island 24, 30, 77, 115

Mibu plantation 24, 48, 146

Mida village site 108

mihere or koumiri (broom) 145

Milman, Hugh (Resident Magistrate, Thursday Island) 16

missionaries
    Abel, Charles 19, 64
    Baxter-Riley, Rev. Edward 12, 13, 17, 20, 24, 28
    Berger, Theo 108
    Chalmers, Rev. James 13, 24, 38, 54, 57, 95, 114, 127, 136
    Drysdale, Albert 108
    Lawes, Rev. W. G. 64
    MacFarlane, Rev. Samuel 12, 13, 81, 158
    Macfarlane, Rev. William 104
    Murray, Rev. A. W. 12, 13
    Thompson, Rev. Wardlaw 12, 17, 20, 28
    Tomkins, O. 13, 57
    Twyman, Len 108
    Walker, Charlie 21
    Walker, Rev. F. W. 16, 19, 20, 21, 23, 24, 28, 29, 37, 41, 42, 49, 53, 61
    Walker, Rosalie 21, 22, 41, 53, 61, 63
    Zahel, Ethel 37, 60, 61

Missions
    Asia Pacific Christian Mission 108
    Congregation of the Sacred Heart, Yule Island 12
    Evangelical Church of Papua New Guinea 108
    Kwato Mission 20, 61, 64, 107
    London Missionary Society (LMS) 12, 24, 54, 57, 86
    Papuan Industries Ltd 20, 21, 23-25, 28-30, 32, 37, 41, 45, 46, 49, 53, 61, 103, 107
    Unevangelised Field Mission (UFM) 61, 107, 108

Moa [Mua] 25, 41, 61, 71, 72, 95, 138, 164

Mogeru (ceremony) 93

Mono-Alu people, Shortland Islands 10

Monubi (Monuhi) (mythical human) 136

mooa (wooden mask) 161

Moralens uppkomst och utveckling (book title) 132

Morehead River 71, 91, 92, 165

mosquitoes, description of a plague 43, 44, 46

mother-of-pearl (Pinctada maxima) (fishery) 14

moto (communal longhouse) xi

motomoto (double outrigger canoe with two masts) xi, 52, 54, 96, 98, 140

mouth of the Fly 33, 34, 52, 97, 131, 161, 168

Mugu village 106

Muiam (culture hero) 74, 76, 167

mu-mu (Mother Hubbards) 22

Muralag [Muralug] Island 95, 144, 164, 168

Murray, G. H. (trader and planter) 23, 32, 42, 45-50, 52, 53, 60, 103

Murray, Judge (later Sir) J. P. Hubert 10, 11, 58-60, 111
(Lieutenant Governor of Papua)

Murray, Rev. A. W. (missionary) 12, 13

Murray, C. G. (Resident Magistrate) 108

museology 133

Museum of Cultures, Helsinki (Kulttuurien museo) xiv, 19, 133

Myers, Charles 4

Nagi [Nagir] Island 95, 161-164

Namai (informant) 46, 47, 51, 85, 91, 115

narato (dugong hunting platform) 45, 81, 85, 86

National Archives of Australia, Canberra 68

National Museum of Finland, Helsinki (Suomen Kansallismuseo) vii, ix, x, xi, xiii, 26, 29, 133, 163

Nemau, sacred Malo drum 158

nese (pearl-shell breast ornament) 150

Normandor [Numandorr] (cultural site near Mabudawan) 74

Nya Guinea färden (book title) vii, 21, 60, 173

Nyland (Uusimaa) province, Finland 174

Nylands Nation, Swedish students' association 173

objectivity in photography 66, 68

obo-marabo (bamboo water container) 146

oboro (spirits of the dead) 94

Odogositia village 107

Ok Tedi mine, Western Province, Papua New Guinea 175

Olive Branch (boat) 20

Omati River 13

Omebwale (culture hero) 100, 104

Oriomo Plateau (see also Cape York-Oriomo Ridge) 1, 23, 107

Oriomo River 4, 80, 107, 140, 160

Oromo-rubi oboro (river-people-spirits) 93, 94

Otamabu Reef 114

otame (man-arrow) 167

Oumo (culture hero) 76

Paara village see Sumai [Paara] village

Paho Island 77

Pahoturi River 4, 12, 47, 73, 74, 160, 164, 167

paike (harpoon shaft) 144

Pälsi, Salkari 173

Papuan Industries Ltd 20, 21, 23-25, 28-30, 32, 37, 41, 45, 46, 49, 53, 61, 103, 107

'Papuan Wonderland' 132

Para, war chief 71

Parama Island and village 2, 4, 40, 80-82, 95, 96, 106, 114

Pastors
    Apineru 42, 88
    Baidam 35
    Faifeau Samoa (Samoan pastors) 13, 28
    Loyalty Islander (Lifu Islander) pastors 12
    Rarotongan (Cook Islander) pastors 12
    Tovia 39, 55

pe (canoes) 95, 138

Pearl (boat) 31, 32, 34, 36

pearling (fishery) 12, 13, 14, 21, 22, 36, 38, 40, 52, 82, 87, 97, 124, 131, 139, 140, 146, 174

pearling lugger, description of 14, 25

Percy Sladen Trust Expedition to Melanesia, 1908 10

Picturesque 64, 67

Picturesque Atlas of Australasia (book title) 64

Picturesque New Guinea (book title) 64

Pidgin-English 22-24, 29, 31, 181

Pied or Torresian pigeon (Ducula bicolor) 30

political ecology of the Wartha people (Torassi/Bensbach River area) 175

positivism 7

pre-Christian Swedish people 7

Psychological Institute, Berlin 37, 39, 50

punctum, definition 68

puputo (double outrigger canoe with one mast) 140

Purari Delta 56

Queensland Museum, Brisbane 161, 163, 164

Quoin Island 135, 136

Radcliffe-Brown, A. R. (anthropologist) 175

Rarotongan (Cook Islander) pastors 12

Ray, Sidney 4, 5

Resident Magistrates
  Beaver, Wilfred 43, 60, 74, 83, 107, 108, 109, 111, 113, 114, 180, 181
  Cameron, J. B. 73
  Hely, Bingham 73, 102, 116, 117, 127
  Jiear, A. H. 96, 108
  Lyons, A. P. 109, 111
  Milman, Hugh 161
  Murray, C. G. 108

Rivers, William H. R 4, 5, 6, 10, 39, 67

Romanticism 69, 176

Roth, William (Chief Protector of Aboriginals, Brisbane) 37

Rousseau, Jean-Jacques 176, 182

saga, definition 40

Sagapadi village 78, 114, 116

Sagaru (culture hero) 77, 78

Sagasia village 116

sägen, definition 40

sägner, definition 40

sagor, definition 40

Saguane village 13, 24, 114, 127, 136

Saibai Island 1, 5, 71, 73, 75, 79, 81, 82, 93, 95, 109, 114, 116, 139, 148, 158, 161,164, 168

salvage anthropology 176

Samare [Samari] village 28, 114, 127

Seligman, Charles (Seligmann) 4, 5, 67, 181

Sepe village 106, 107, 114-116

servants
  Apau (Daniel) 31, 40
  Gename 44, 50, 55

Severimabu village 106, 107, 114, 116

Sewota (culture hero) 81

Siblemete (cultural site near Kura Creek) 101

Sido (culture hero) 73, 75, 78, 114, 131, 132

Sigabarduru village 73, 74

Sir Charles Hardy Islands 135

sito (coconut leaf basket) xi, 143

social class 176

social evolutionism 133

social inequality 176

social mapping 175

Soriame (culture hero) 101

Souw (culture hero) 76

Spencer, Herbert 7

Staniforth Smith, Miles (Acting Lieutenant Governor of Papua) 43-44, 60

State Museum of History and Ethnology, Helsinki 9

stone axes, origins on Kiwai Island 175

stone headed clubs, Torassi/Bensbach River area 175

Strickland River 43

Strong, W. Mersh (Government Medical Officer and Government Anthropologist) 11

studium, definition 68

Sui village 106, 114, 115

Suki Bag (see also gatere (tuberous root basket)) 143, 144

sukuba (tobacco) 162, 163

Sumai [Paara] village 24, 50, 51, 53, 96, 114-116, 120-124

Sumogi Island 2, 114

susare, tusare or tutae (plaited armlets and leglets) 152

svarta, definition 23

svartingar, definition 23

Svenska folkpartiet i Finland (Swedish People's Party) 8

Svenska litteraturesällskapat i Finland (Swedish Literature Society) 174

Taera (ceremony) 93

Taibobo (formation dance) 13, 39, 89, 124

Tamate (boat) 54, 56, 57

tataku (single outrigger canoe) 124, 139

Teapopo village 106

tene (arrow) 166

The Federal Hotel, Thursday Island 15, 16

The Origin and Development of Moral Ideas (book title) 132

The Pearler (newspaper) 37

The People of India (book title) 63

The Picturesque Atlas of Australasia (book title) 64

Thompson, Rev. Wardlaw (missionary) 12, 17, 20, 28

Thomson, Donald (anthropologist) 78, 135, 136, 164

Thomson, J. P. 13

Thursday Island, Queensland 14-16, 21, 28, 31, 37, 38, 40, 41

tidal bore, description of 2, 32, 34, 35, 110

Tinny (flour-tin drum) 124

Tirio village 106, 107, 114

tiro (mat) 124, 141, 142

Todas tribes, Nilgiri hills, India 67

Tomkins, O. (missionary) 13, 57

Toro Passage 40, 81, 114

Torres Strait, description 1-2

Toura Toura village (see also Turituri village) 80

Tovia (pastor) 39, 55

trade and exchange, patterns of traditional 92, 95, 98, 107, 116, 138, 146, 148, 157, 161, 162, 163, 175

trade in tobacco 32, 34, 36, 40, 44, 49, 58, 80, 95, 96, 162, 163

traders and planters

Cowling, J. 24, 30, 46, 48, 49, 51

Freshwater, J. B. 23, 28, 29, 42, 50, 52, 53, 61

Hodel, William (Fred) 37

Martin, trader killed at Mawatta 71

Murray, G. H. 23, 32, 42, 45-50, 52, 53, 60, 103

trochus (fishery) 14, 151

Tudu Island (Warrior Island) 14, 100, 104, 153, 157, 164, 169

Tugeri (see also Marind-amin people) 71, 136

Tureturerubi people 81

Turituri village (see also Toura Toura village) 4

Två Papuanska sagor (book title) 60

Twyman, Len (missionary) 108

Tylor, E. B. xii

Ua-ogrere (culture hero) 100

Ubrikubri (culture hero) 71, 72

uere (bamboo headhunting knife) 71, 72

Ugar [Stephens Island] 95

Ui-balee (culture hero) 104

Unevangelised Field Mission (UFM) 107, 108

University of Cambridge see Cambridge University

University of Helsinki 8, 9, 19, 173

University of London 7

University of London, School of Oriental and African Studies 64

University of Papua New Guinea, Port Moresby 64

U'uwo [Doropo] village 76, 78, 115, 116

Veddas (Wanniyala-Aetto) people, Ceylon (Sri Lanka) 67

view camera, description of 65

von Hügel, Baron Anatole 131

Wabuda Island 28, 49, 56, 113, 149, 170

waduru (tobacco pipe) 163

wagi or soke (casowary bone dagger) 165

Waidoro village 167

Walker, Charlie (missionary) 21

Walker, Rev. F. W. (missionary) 16, 19, 20, 21, 23, 24, 28, 29, 37, 41, 42, 49, 53, 61

Walker, Rosalie (missionary) 21, 22, 41, 53, 61, 63

Wamimuba (Wami Point) 116

wap or wapo (dugong harpoon) xi, 25, 86, 144

wapa or eere (fibre skirt) 148

Wapa-Ura village and district on Kiwai Island 114, 116, 130

Warigi village site 108

Wariobodoro village 108

Warraber [Waraber] Island 95

Warrior Reefs 14, 153

warupa (drum) xi, 91, 100, 158

Wasigena, name of a longhouse 81, 114

Wasikor, sacred Malo drum 158

Wassi Kussa inlet 71

Wawa (culture hero) 73, 75, 76, 135

wawri [wauri] (arm shells) (see also mabuo) 153

wedere (pubic shell) 147

wedere moa (shell hoe) 134

Wederehiamo village 106, 107, 114

West Papua (see also Dutch New Guinea) 17, 149

Westermarck, Edvard 7-9, 112, 131, 132, 175, 176

Western District of Papua 24, 43, 60, 107

Western Division of British New Guinea 1, 6, 10, 12, 13, 82

Western Province of Papua New Guinea 1, 4, 83

Wheeler, C. Gerald (anthropologist) 10

White Australia policy 13

white reef heron (Demigetta sacra) 156, 157

Wilkin, Anthony 4, 64, 168

Williams, F. E. (Government Anthropologist) 11, 68

Williamson, R. M. 67

Wiorubi ('sand beach people' also name of district) 54, 114, 116

Yam Island/Yam Islanders 61, 101, 135, 159

Zahel, Ethel (missionary and teacher) 37, 60, 61